# *Beside Still Waters*

THE KADE FAMILY SAGA

VOLUME 4

# *Beside*
# *Still Waters*

LAUREL MOURITSEN

STRATFORD
**BOOKS**

ISBN: 0-929753-21-6
*The Kade Family Saga, Volume 4: Beside Still Waters*

Stratford Books
Eastern States Office
4808 37th Road North
Arlington, VA 22207

Stratford Books
Western States Office
P.O. Box 1371
Provo, UT 84603-1371


*Beside Still Waters*
First printing: November 2006

The acid-free paper used in this book meets the guidelines for
permanence and durability of the committee on Production Guidelines
for Book Longevity of the Council on Library Resources.


Dust jacket painting: *Cliffs at Promontory, Great Salt Lake, Utah*
by Alfred Lambourne
© Intellectual Reserve, Inc.
Courtesy of the Museum of Church History and Art


Printed in the United States of America

*"Now therefore ye are no more
strangers and foreigners,
but fellowcitizens with the saints,
and of the household of God."*

Ephesians 2:19

# PROLOGUE

When Alexander arrived home for supper, Elizabeth immediately noticed his irritable mood. "Sit down here, sweetheart," she said, pulling the chair away from the table for him. She hoped to mitigate his ill humor before he expressed it in James' presence.

"Hello, Alexander," James said in greeting. "How was your day at the mill?"

Alexander slid into his chair. "Well enough. And you? What did you do today?"

Elizabeth took the seat next to her husband. "James went to see some of the old sights in town," she answered for her brother. "We've been talking a bit about the years we spent together growing up in Nauvoo." Elizabeth glanced at her younger brother. She was pleased he'd come back to visit. She hadn't seen him or any of her family since they'd left Nauvoo for the Salt Lake valley four years before. James' looks had changed since then. He was no longer the gangly teenager she remembered. His face was more angular and firm now and his shoulders broader. There was an air of self-assurance about him that hadn't been present before. Perhaps it came with maturity or as a result of his experiences away from home while attending medical college.

"Did you ride down Durphey Street?" Alexander asked. He shook out his linen napkin and laid it across his knee. Elizabeth poured a quantity of claret into his wine glass. The fluid sparkled in the belly-shaped crystal goblet. She caught the quick, disapproving glance James cast at the glass of wine.

"Yes, I saw the brick home where we lived. The grounds look well tended."

Alexander and Elizabeth started on their supper. James hesitated for an instant. Elizabeth knew her brother preferred to say a blessing on the food before partaking of it, but such prayers were never said in her household.

"What else did you see while you were down on the flats?" Alexander asked, cutting the roasted chicken on his plate with a gleaming silver-plated knife and fork.

James picked up his napkin and spread it across his lap. "I stopped outside the Mansion House. Young Joseph Smith was there working in the yard, and I had a nice chat with him."

Alexander forked a piece of meat into his mouth.

"I visited some of the old public buildings on Main

Street—the Cultural Hall and the printing complex where my father worked."

"Ah, yes. The printing office of the *Nauvoo Neighbor,* wasn't it?" Alexander replied.

Elizabeth stiffened. She heard the disdain in her husband's voice. She hoped James hadn't noticed, too.

"That's right. The *Nauvoo Neighbor.* It was a fine newspaper. Until a few over-zealous men forced the closure of the printing house."

A bead of sweat broke out along Elizabeth's brow. James *had* noticed, and he wasn't going to let Alexander's sarcasm pass unchallenged. She hoped to head off what she knew would be her husband's snide reply. "Have some more creamed potatoes, Alexander," she offered quickly, holding the serving bowl out to him.

He brushed the bowl aside witha wave of his hand. "If my memory serves me correctly, James, I believe it was the mayor and the city councilmen who first took matters into their own hands by terminating the printing of the Mormons' rival paper, the *Expositor.*" Alexander took another bite of chicken.

Elizabeth put a hand on her husband's arm. "Please, Alexander," she whispered. She knew James' anger would be kindled if Alexander pursued the topic. The seizure of the printing office and destruction of the *Expositor's* press was the pivotal event leading to the Prophet's martyrdom. Joseph Smith had been not only the Church's spiritual leader, but also mayor of the city. He and members of the city council had carried out the council's order to dismantle the

*Expositor's* printing press because the antagonistic paper was deemed a public nuisance. They were subsequently arrested on a charge of riot, brought against them by the publishers of the newspaper. The Prophet went to appear before a justice of the peace in Carthage, where he was detained and committed to the Carthage jail. A mob with blackened faces stormed the prison, and shots were exchanged. As he tried to escape through the window of the jail, Joseph was shot and killed. James had loved and revered Joseph Smith. Elizabeth knew he would not countenance any derogatory remark from Alexander concerning the Prophet.

James' eyes flicked from Alexander to Elizabeth. "It's all right, Elizabeth. This conversation isn't really about the printing house or the newspapers. Is it, Alexander?"

Elizabeth was confused. Some unspoken communication was passing between Alexander and her brother, and she didn't know what it concerned.

"Did your customer keep his appointment this afternoon?" Elizabeth heard her brother ask Alexander in a cold voice.

Alexander set down his fork. "As a matter of fact, no, he did not. I probably have you to thank for that. I could have finished my business last night if you hadn't meddled in it." Sparks glinted in Alexander's eyes.

"What are you talking about? What business?" Elizabeth asked. Her throat was dry and the palms of her hands itched.

"Go ahead, Alexander. Tell her." James' voice was as sharp as a spike.

"If you wish to spend another moment under my roof, I advise you to keep your mouth shut."

"Alexander!" Elizabeth was shocked by his words and appalled by his behavior toward her brother. Her body began to tremble with emotion.

James glared at his brother-in-law for an instant, then he slowly pushed himself away from the table and stood up.

"Where are you going, James? Sit down and eat your supper," Elizabeth cried.

"I believe I need a breath of fresh air," James answered without expression. He set his napkin on the table, turned, and walked out of the room. Elizabeth heard the front door close behind him.

In anger she turned to confront her husband. "I'm stunned by what I just heard from your lips. How could you speak to my brother in that manner—ordering him from the house! I'm ashamed and embarrassed—"

Alexander's fist slammed down on the table. "Silence! I'm not in the mood for your whimpering. Your brother had it coming. He's been poking his nose where it doesn't belong ever since he arrived."

Elizabeth watched the water in the glasses dance from Alexander's blow to the table. He snatched up his wine goblet and drained it in a single gulp. "What is it you're keeping from me?" Elizabeth demanded.

Alexander replaced his glass on the table and scowled at her. "Last night at the lumber mill, I had your thieving uncle by the scruff of the neck when James interfered."

Elizabeth hid her surprise behind a stoic stare. She was unaware that her father's brother, Benjamin Dawson, had returned to the city. Whatever Alexander had done to threaten or intimidate her uncle, Elizabeth knew that James would have tried to defuse the situation.

"Because of James, your uncle slipped away without paying the debt owed me—the debt he incurred after you persuaded me to loan him money against my better judgment," he said with rancor.

What Alexander had just said was true; she had encouraged him to lend money to her uncle for an investment. She'd done it because she'd been desperate to establish a tie with her father's family. She'd had no contact with them since her father's death when she was a child and her mother's subsequent remarriage. But that incident paled in comparison to what had just transpired at the table. "You shouldn't have spoken so rudely to James. I doubt he'll be back except to collect his trunk. I don't know if I can forgive you for this."

"Forgive me?" Alexander repeated scornfully. "Do you think it concerns me whether you do or not? Come, come, Elizabeth. You forget yourself. Your place is to be agreeable— that is, if you value the comfortable circumstances you presently enjoy."

Tears welled in Elizabeth's eyes. "You're a despicable man, Alexander. You attack people in the areas where you know it will hurt them the most." She wiped away a fallen tear, leaving a smear on her cheek. "I am going upstairs. I can't abide looking at you."

# CHAPTER ONE

Jessica Scott turned away from the window and arched her tired back. Her whole body ached from the hours of sitting on the hard bench and the constant motion of the train. A cool May breeze blew in from the window opened a crack at her side, but the noisy clacking of the wheels on the iron track tempted her to close it. She shifted in her seat, her eyes on her lap. When she raised her gaze a moment later, she noticed the man across the aisle staring at her. He flashed a wide, leering grin when he caught her eye.

Jessica immediately glanced away. The man's stare unnerved her. He'd been boldly eyeing her and trying to strike up a conversation ever since he boarded the train at Denver and had chosen the bench across the aisle from where she sat. Dressed in wrinkled, gray trousers and a worn-out coat, with shaggy hair and stubble on his chin, he looked coarse and unkempt. The brim of his hat concealed his brow, but flinty, dark eyes brooded in his narrow face. And those eyes sent a shiver down Jessica's spine. She clutched the beaded handbag resting in her lap, feeling the contours of the Smith and Wesson revolver secreted inside. The cold, hard feel of the gun restored her confidence. Her father had given her the revolver to carry on her trip west as a means of protection. And he had taught her how to use it. She relaxed, knowing the gun was at her fingertips.

Despite the breeze from the open window, the passenger car was hot and stuffy. Jessica felt perspiration trickling down her back. She slipped a finger between her neck and the high lace collar of her silk dress, trying to release some of the warmth from her body. Her long cotton stockings and high-topped laced shoes trapped the heat against her legs.

"Pardon me, miss, but I couldn't help noticin' the color of your hair, shinin' as it is in the sunlight from that window. It's real purty."

Jessica turned to find the distasteful man in the opposite seat leaning toward her.

"I don't think I ever laid eyes on quite that color of hair before. Copper, like a new penny."

Jessica shrank to the far corner of her seat. She wished she'd kept her bonnet on her head, but she disliked its close-fitting confinement, especially in the stuffy heat of the passenger car. She'd taken it off and set it on the bench beside her. Her auburn hair was caught up into a bun, but some of it had loosened and fallen onto her neck. She resisted the impulse to gather the straying strands back in place and slip on her scoop bonnet. The man's eyes roving over her hair soiled it. She wanted to wash out his gaze. She tossed him a quick, disapproving glance.

"I been sittin' here wonderin' what a young gal like yourself is doin' travelin' all alone," he said.

His words sounded an alarm in Jessica's head. He'd been watching her, and he knew she was traveling without a companion or a chaperone. For the first time since starting the trip, she wished she hadn't been so stubborn about making the journey by herself. A family friend who was going west for a visit had been planning to accompany her on the train, but he'd taken sick a day or two before their scheduled departure and was unable to travel. Jessica had insisted on going forward with the trip as planned, despite her parents' objections. She turned her back to the man, hoping he'd leave her alone if she ignored him.

"I'm from the territory of Colorado. On my way to Californy." He paused, as if expecting some response from her. When she gave none, he asked, "Where might you be from, miss?"

She pretended she hadn't heard him.

"Miss?" He leaned closer to her.

If she didn't answer, she feared he would slide even closer. "Illinois," she said tersely. "A town called Nauvoo."

"Illinois, huh? Ain't ever been there myself." He retreated to the center of the bench. "You headed for Californy?"

She darted a glance at him. "Yes. Sacramento."

"What you gonna do in Sacramento?"

"I'm taking a teaching position there," she answered curtly.

The answer was only partially true. She did want to teach school, but she didn't have a position secured yet. She'd learned that teachers were needed in California, and several opportunities were open to her, but she'd avoided making any definite commitment. She intended to find a post when she reached Sacramento. In fact, that was one of the things that had so disturbed her parents, especially her mother. Her mother thought it imprudent to set out for a new destination without having a place and position established beforehand, and to travel unchaperoned. In truth, her mother disapproved of her going out west at all. She and her mother had had numerous disagreements over Jessica's desire to leave home and embark on a trip across the continent.

Jessica thought her mother's attitude on the matter was out of character. After all, it was her mother who had instilled in Jessica her own progressive ideals and values. For as long as Jessica could remember, her mother had been a champion of social reform and an advocate for women's rights—all of which had antagonized Jessica's father and provoked rancorous feelings at home. Given her mother's feelings on a woman's right to be independent, Jessica thought it peculiar that her mother was so against her idea of going west. She supported Jessica's ambition to become a teacher, but not her desire to locate on the frontier, an environment far removed from the social and cultural mores of Illinois.

But the vast, rugged regions of the West held a fascination for Jessica. Ever since reading an account about the West in a newspaper article, complete with descriptions of painted Indians, cowpunchers, spacious vistas with grand mountains, crystal streams and lush green valleys, she had been captivated by the whole idea of it. The pictures planted in her mind by the descriptions in the article had stayed vivid over the months since then. Now that she was eighteen, old enough to decide her own future, she intended to follow her dream of visiting the wide open spaces of the West and see for herself the wonders it held. In the end, it was her father who gave his consent. He silenced her mother's protests, purchased the Smith and Wesson for her, and gave her a liberal sum of money to get started in her new life. Most of the money was secreted in the bottom of her traveling bag, which she kept constantly with her.

"You a school marm, then?" The stranger's voice intruded into her thoughts. "I would have pegged you for somethin' more exhileratin' than school teachin'.

His remark annoyed Jessica. "Schoolkeeping is a fine occupation for a woman. She can improve society through the education of its children." Her words carried more passion that she actually felt. Although Jessica liked the idea of teaching, she was more intrigued with the adventure of striking out on her own. And it was a good opportunity to get away from the tension that existed at home. She squared her shoulders and stared out the train window.

Mercifully, the man said nothing more. The clicking, clacking sound of the train wheels on the track filled her ears. The rows of benches in the passenger compartment were nearly all filled; most of the passengers sat silently reading or gazing out the windows. The noise of the rails, and the hissing and belching of the steam-driven locomotive, limited conversation.

The large bell perched atop the engine suddenly began to clang, and then came a shrill blow of the whistle. The signal meant the train would be stopping shortly to take on more fuel to feed the engine or to let passengers board or exit. Jessica reached into the traveling bag sitting at her feet on the floor of the Pullman car, and rummaged inside for the small, gray book she'd put there. Locating it, she withdrew the book and glanced at its cover. *Crofutt's Trans-Continental Tourist's Guide—1872*, the printing on the cover read. Jessica thumbed through the pages until she found what she was searching for, the description of towns and cities through which the Union Pacific would pass on its journey from the East to the West coast. She had followed the schedule assiduously throughout her trip.

Even having the opportunity to ride the new transcontinental railroad was a dream come true for her. East and West had been united by rail only three short years before, in 1869. Traveling at a speed of forty miles per hour, in a mechanized carriage, over the breadth of the continent was nothing short of a miracle. And Jessica was awed by it. Six days ago she had boarded a riverboat at Nauvoo, steamed down the Mississippi to St. Louis, and then climbed aboard the Missouri Pacific Railroad, which took her from St. Louis to Kansas City. From there, she took the

Kansas Pacific across the prairie lands of Kansas—where she witnessed a terrifying prairie fire that raced over acres of land belching flames and smoke into the sky—to the base of the Rocky Mountains near Denver. She'd been captivated by the magnificence of the Rockies with their rugged slopes and lofty, snow-capped peaks. She had never seen anything more breathtaking.

At Denver, she changed to a nine-car Union Pacific train. The ride through upper Colorado and across Wyoming was stunningly beautiful as the train twisted and turned through narrow canyon passes and crossed sparkling streams. Jessica kept track of every town they passed through, matching what she read on the pages of *Crofutt's Guide* to what she saw outside the train window. The ride into Utah Territory had been highlighted by glimpses of a vast lake shimmering like silver in the sun. As the train approached the town of Ogden, Utah, Jessica got her first clear look at the lake. *Crofutt's* gave a name to the huge body of water, The Great Salt Lake, and an explanation about its high salt content. The tracks wound for miles beside the shining, still waters of the lake.

They had passed Ogden about thirty-five minutes ago, with the jagged mountain peaks of the Rockies continually outside her window to the east. Jessica ran a finger down the column of place names in her copy of the transcontinental guide book. The next town was called Corinne. It should be coming into sight any moment. Jessica pressed her nose against the window pane as the train crossed a wooden bridge spanning a river and then a simple sign beside the tracks sporting the word "Corinne" came into view. The train's whistle sounded again, and the wheels ground slowly to a halt.

Jessica slipped on her bonnet and tied the ribbon strings beneath her chin as several of the passengers left their seats and started toward the door of the Pullman car. The train carried about 130 passengers, and at each stop some of them detrained while others boarded. Grasping her traveling bag in one hand and slipping her wrist through the strings of her handbag with the other, Jessica prepared to step from the train for a breath of fresh air and a stroll around the depot to stretch her legs. From the corner of her eye, she noticed the man who sat across the aisle rise from his seat, also. She ignored him as she made her way off the train.

A small town that appeared hastily thrown together met her gaze as Jessica stepped from the train. A hodgepodge of squat buildings and tents constructed of canvas and board seemed to make up the town. The dirt road before her was teeming with sound and motion—wagons carrying freight rumbled past, mule teams stirred up clouds of dust, riders on horseback galloped by, dogs yapped, and children darted across the road dodging carriages and animals. The scene was raucous and confusing compared to the quiet, gentle air that graced her little home town of Nauvoo. Jessica felt a sudden pang of homesickness. She hadn't experienced any melancholia since leaving Illinois because of her enthusiasm for the trip ahead. But now she wished her parents weren't so far away.

Thrusting such thoughts aside, she stepped off the platform of the station and into the street. A refreshing breeze blew from the east, cooling her brow. She stood for a moment on the rutted road enjoying the feel of the breeze on her face, then she walked a few paces down the street and stopped beside a store front. She set her heavy traveling bag down at her feet, watching people hurrying about their business. Shading her eyes against the glare of the afternoon sun, she gazed overhead at the string of telegraph wires running from pole to pole parallel with the railroad tracks. The poles stretched in either direction as far as her eye could see. The telegraph system had marched mile after mile across the country, linking the nation together as profoundly as the railroad that followed on its heels. Jessica marveled at the ingenuity of the invention. Messages carried along its wires could be sent and received in a matter of moments. The telegraph had revolutionized communication. She didn't understand the science of how it worked, but she was impressed by the telegraph's capabilities.

A freight wagon came careening around the corner of the street, its driver cracking his whip and swearing at the mules pulling their heavy load. Jessica was forced to jump backward against the wall of the building to keep from being struck. The wagon's rear wheel splashed through a puddle of rain water, flinging the muddy water onto the skirt of Jessica's black silk traveling dress. An unladylike exclamation passed her lips as she shook off the mud and water splattered on her dress.

Then suddenly, from the corner of her eye, she caught a glimpse of the unsavory man from the train swoop toward the traveling bag she'd set down beside the road. He snatched up the bag, bolted away with it, and vanished into the press of people all in a single breath. It took an instant for Jessica to comprehend what had happened. As she stood rooted to the spot, her mouth gaping, the consequences of his action came thundering down on her. "Stop!" she cried. "Stop that man! He's a thief. Oh! My bag! My money!"

A few people on the street paused to stare at her, and one elderly man came to her side. "What seems to be the problem, miss?"

"That man stole my bag! Please stop him," she shouted. When the old man only stood staring blankly down the road in the direction the thief had gone, Jessica hitched up her skirt and dashed off herself in pursuit of the culprit. Even as she began the chase, she knew the effort was pointless; the man who had robbed her was nowhere in sight. After a few moments she stopped, panting and out of breath.

As she stood in the road, her outrage began to seep away and was replaced by desperation. The traveling bag held nearly all of the money her father had given her for the trip west and many of her personal belongings, as well. She felt sick at heart as she thought of the irreplaceable framed portrait packed in the bottom of the satchel.

A rider on horseback came galloping down the road, swerving out of her path only an instant before striking her. "Get out of the street, woman!" the horseman yelled as he twisted in his saddle to shake a fist at her. The near miss set

Jessica's heart pounding. With stumbling steps, she made her way back to the roadside.

She stood there trembling, not knowing what action to take, then started back for the train. Climbing aboard the passenger car, she began searching for one of the railroad attendants traveling with the train. She walked through the nearly empty car and into the adjoining one before locating a uniformed trainman. "My traveling bag has just been stolen by a passenger who is riding this train," she blurted out to him.

The attendant looked startled. "Where is this passenger?" he asked.

"Gone! He's disappeared with my money and my belongings." She recounted in jumbled sentences what had happened.

"Since the robbery did not occur aboard the train, there's little I can do to assist you. I'm sorry, miss," the attendant said in response to her explanation. "Perhaps you should check with the sheriff here in Corinne."

Jessica left the train, feeling more desolate than before. If she stayed in Corinne to talk to the sheriff, he might be able to recover her traveling bag; but her passage was paid all the way to the coast, and the thief might even get back on the train. He'd told her he was going to California, hadn't he? Her head ached with the weight of the decision being thrust upon her. Perhaps it was best to speak with the sheriff, she reasoned. If she had to return home to Illinois because of her loss, it might be better to start back from here, rather than hundreds of miles further on.

As she stood beside the depot, the train whistle sounded. Its bellowing hurt her ears. She covered them with her hands as the whistle sounded a second time, long and loud. Knowing the whistle was signaling passengers to return to the train for departure, Jessica paced beside the locomotive, torn by indecision. The whistle sounded a third time. Its piercing voice drove her away from the train and onto the street. People passed by on either side, none of them giving her a second glance.

She started up the road, and spying a chair placed outside the door of a building, went to it and sat down. Loosening the strings of her handbag, she rummaged through the collection of odds and ends she carried within, searching for her coin purse. She had put a few bills in the purse for easy access in case she needed money while traveling aboard the train. She located the money and counted it out in her lap—five, six, seven dollars, and a few coins. She had exactly seven dollars and thirty-four cents; barely enough to buy two or three days' worth of meals and lodging, she thought in despair. She stuffed the money back into her handbag and drew the drawstring taut.

The train whistle sounded a final time. It seemed low and distant, even though she was only a block from the tracks. She heard the head of steam building, and then the chug-chug-chug of the engine as it slowly began to move along the tracks. At that instant, a terrible thought struck— her trunk with all her clothing packed inside was stored in the baggage car of the train! Now it was gone, too. Jessica's stomach started churning.

The train was picking up speed now. She turned to watch it glide down the tracks. Her head hurt, and she felt sick to her stomach. She sat motionless, watching the cars disappear around a bend down the tracks. When the train was out of sight, Jessica burst into tears.

"I can assure you, Miss Scott, that my deputies will make every effort to apprehend this thief," the sheriff of Corinne was saying. "But you should realize this is a freight town, a junction for the rich mines of the territories. All kinds of lawless characters pass through here."

"The man told me he was from Colorado and on his way to California, if that's any help to you," Jessica responded, her mind and body as tense as a strung bow.

The sheriff leaned back in his chair and laced his fingers. He was a stern-looking man, with harsh eyes and a bristly beard, and a face as ruddy and hard as an apple. "All right, Miss Scott, I believe that's all for now. Have you a place to stay? If not, I can recommend a hotel for you."

"I would appreciate that," Jessica answered wearily. The interview with the sheriff had been long and taxing. Jessica's nerves were frayed, and she felt suddenly exhausted.

"The Hastings House is a reputable establishment. It's located about three blocks to the north of here."

"Thank you." Jessica clutched her handbag and started to rise from her chair.

"It could take some time to catch this criminal. And there's the possibility that he may not be found at all. Do you have friends or relatives nearby whom you can contact if necessary?"

Jessica sat back down on the chair. "No. No one." She frowned, thinking about the matter. "Actually, I believe my mother has a brother living in Salt Lake City. I have no idea where in the city, however."

"Salt Lake City." The sheriff ran a thumb over his whiskered chin. "That's about seventy-five miles from here. Do you know your uncle's name? Perhaps you could telegraph him."

"His name is James Kade. I know he's a doctor, but I've never met him or had any contact with him. No, I wouldn't want to notify my uncle."

"Then I believe you'll find the Hastings House to your satisfaction. I'll call on you there as soon as I have any word to report."

Jessica got to her feet. "Thank you for your help, sheriff."

He nodded, then walked with her to the door. "I'm sorry your introduction to our town has been so unfavorable. Perhaps your fortunes will take a turn for the better."

"Yes, perhaps so," Jessica replied, but her voice didn't hold much hope.


Jessica found the hotel Hastings House without difficulty, though the town seemed to be laid out in a haphazard fashion. It consisted primarily of a main street and four or five connecting roads. Jessica saw little to commend the town to her; it was a barren place, set in the middle of a bleak landscape, with no flowers or cultivated fields to beautify it. Corinne's main resource appeared to be its many saloons. Every third or fourth building she passed housed a saloon or gambling establishment. The hotel was a two-story, white frame building, weather-beaten and in need of a new coat of paint, but Jessica found the inside to be comfortable enough. She paid a dollar-and-a-half for the room, and fifty cents for a light supper in the hotel's dining hall, then climbed the stairs to her quarters. Casting a glance over her shoulder, she let herself in the door and slid the bolt into place to lock it behind her. She set her handbag on top of the bureau that squatted beside the door and removed her bonnet. The room was small and spare, with only the bed and bureau to dress it, and a single window facing onto the street. She went to the window and looked out, thinking again about the events that had befallen her that afternoon. She chided herself for letting go of the traveling bag, and for not paying closer attention to the stranger who followed her off the train.

She closed her eyes and leaned against the window pane. How was she going to explain all of this to her parents? Her father would be furious with her for losing the money, and her mother would point her finger and say, "I told you not to go." No, she couldn't tell her parents about the theft. She'd have to find a way out of this situation by herself.

From the street, Jessica could hear the rattle of wagons and the pounding of hoofbeats on the dirt road. Raucous shouts, conversation, and laughter played accompaniment to the clatter of hoof and wheel. Jessica felt very vulnerable; she was worried about not having enough money to see her through until her traveling bag could be recovered—if, indeed, it was recovered—and apprehensive about being all alone in a wild and unfamiliar place so far from home.

She sighed and turned away from the window. Pouring a bit of water from the pitcher into the washbasin resting on top of the bureau, she rinsed her face and hands. Then she sponged the mud spatters from off her dress as best she could. When she finished, she went downstairs to the dining room to eat, though she was too upset to have much of an appetite.

It was dusk by the time she returned to her room. She slipped off her dress and climbed under the covers of the bed. Glancing at the door to be sure it was securely locked, she turned out the oil lamp. She lay in the darkness thinking about her loss. Losing the money her father had given her was a serious offense, but even more significant than the money was the pencil-drawn portrait her mother had entrusted to her care just before Jessica left Nauvoo. The portrait was her mother's most cherished possession, a treasured keepsake. Jessica had tucked it safely into the bottom of her traveling bag. And now the drawing was gone. Surely her mother would never forgive her for losing it.

Jessica shivered. She wiggled deeper into the bed, pulling the thin quilt up over her shoulders. It occurred to her to offer a prayer for help. But even if she believed God would condescend to assist her out of this predicament, she had no idea how to approach Him in prayer. She discarded the prompting to pray and instead turned over onto her side, tucked her legs up against her body, and tried to sleep.

Two days had passed since Jessica's bag had been stolen, and as she counted out the change left in her coin purse she began to tremble. She stared at the money resting in the palm of her hand. There was not even enough to pay another night's lodging at the hotel. She regretted not staying with the train all the way to California. Her ticket had been paid for in advance, and all she'd needed to do was get to Sacramento and secure a teaching position. She wished she'd pursued that course. Had her father known, he would have scolded her for making such a foolish decision. One mistake had been compounded by another, she thought bitterly.

Well, she knew what must be done now. She'd been thinking about it ever since the sheriff first mentioned the idea. She had no choice but to contact her uncle in Salt Lake City and hope he would be kind enough, and compassionate enough, to assist her in her plight. The man was her mother's only brother, but her mother had seldom spoken of him. Jessica knew little about her uncle, only that he was a doctor who lived in the Salt Lake valley. And that he was a Mormon.

Jessica had heard about the Mormons who'd been driven out of her home town of Nauvoo years earlier, before she was even born. Her mother, and especially her father, had only derogatory things to say about the Mormons and their peculiar brand of religion. And that was part of the reason why she'd been reluctant to contact her uncle. That, and the fact that she had no idea what sort of man he was. This time she would be on her guard. Her recent experience had taught her a hard lesson—to be wary of strangers and distrustful of their motives.

Jessica eyed the money lying in her palm. She was sure there was not enough to secure passage on the train to Salt Lake. She pondered the problem a few moments longer, then thrust the coins back into her handbag. Her fingers nudged the Smith and Wesson revolver lodged there. The gun, at least, provided some measure of safety for her. She drew the strings of the handbag, looped them around her wrist, and left her quarters in the hotel.

Hurrying downstairs, she went straight to the desk where the proprietor of the hotel stood working and asked him for directions to the telegraph office. Then she left the hotel. The day was overcast; gray clouds hid the sky and rain threatened. Jessica wished she had her blue velvet cape to wear, but it was gone along with the rest of her clothing packed in the traveling bag. When she'd spoken again with the sheriff yesterday, he'd told her they had no leads on the man who had stolen her bag, but advised her not to give up hope yet. His deputies were still looking. Jessica guessed they would never find the thief; he was probably miles away from Corinne by now—with her money in his pocket.

That thought made her angry and she quickened her pace. She ignored the spattering of rain that began to fall. Her dress was soiled already, and she had no other clothing to change into. She found the telegraph office, went inside, and waited behind a fellow who was in the midst of dictating a message to the operator. She rehearsed in her mind the words she was about to telegraph to her uncle in the city. The message would be short and to the point.

# CHAPTER TWO

"Mother, I'm home." Ethan removed his felt hat and slapped it against his thigh to beat off the dust, then stepped through the open door into the front hall of his parent's two-story adobe house. "Mother?"

Inger Kade appeared at the top of the staircase, her face brightening with pleasure on spying him. "Welcome home, son," she smiled, hurrying down the stairs to embrace him.

A curly, yellow strand of her hair brushed against his cheek, and he smelled the hint of rosewater cologne that she always wore. "It's good to be home," Ethan replied. "How is everything here?"

"Fine. Your father is away tending to a patient, and Birgithe should be back shortly from school. Did your brother come with you?" Inger tucked into place the wisp of hair that had escaped the braided bun she wore at the nape of her neck.

"No," Ethan answered. "Samuel's planning to stay at the ranch until after branding, but he sends his love."

"I'm disappointed he didn't come too, but I'm happy you're here, Ethan. Are you hungry? Go wash up, and I'll heat some supper for you."

"Thanks, I'd like that." Ethan climbed the stairs to the room he and Samuel shared. He found everything in its usual place—his bed was neatly made and covered with the colorful patchwork quilt his mother had sewn, his collection of miniature wood carvings rested on the bedside table, and the watercolor landscape painted by his uncle hung on the wall.

He rinsed the dust off his hands and face in the basin sitting on the washstand and dried himself with the towel. He was glad to be home. The night he'd just spent in a bedroll on the ground had put a cramp in his back. He stretched his arms and shoulders, working the creak out of his tired back.

The sound of hoofbeats and rumbling carriage wheels coming up the dirt road toward the house brought his attention to the window. He walked over to the wide-silled window and pushed the curtains aside. Through the paned glass, he watched his father rein in his horse and climb down from the buggy, his black physician's bag in his hand. Ethan raised the window and leaned over the broad, pine sill. "Evening, Pa," he called down into the yard.

James Kade glanced to the upper window. "Hello, son. It's nice to see you. I've a matter to discuss with you." His father walked to the porch and let himself in the door.

Ethan finished drying his hands and replaced the towel on the rack of the washstand. He combed his fingers through his hair, briefly inspecting his appearance in the framed mirror fastened to the washstand, then he left the room and trotted downstairs.

Ethan met his father in the hallway, where James was greeting his wife with a kiss. "How are you, son?" he asked on spotting Ethan. "How is your work at the ranch?" The three of them walked together down the hall and into the large, square kitchen.

"We're keeping busy," Ethan answered in reply to his father's question. Each of them took a seat at the table. "I wanted to come home for a few days before spring chores begin in earnest."

"Your brother didn't come too?" asked his father.

Ethan shook his head. "He decided to stay and work."

"Is Samuel well? Have you boys been eating enough?" his mother questioned, resting a hand on Ethan's arm.

Ethan patted her hand. "Yes, Mother, we're fine. Though both Samuel and I miss your cooking. He asked me to bring back some of your sourdough biscuits."

A smile illuminated Inger's face. Ethan liked the way her smile reached all the way to her eyes, making them sparkle and dance. His mother's cheerful nature was one of the things he loved best about her. Samuel was most like her, he thought; Samuel possessed the same ready smile and sunny disposition. Ethan resembled his father in temperament, though he was not as serious-minded. He might be found whiling away a summer afternoon fishing or lounging in the sun whittling a piece of wood, activities his father seldom had the time or inclination to pursue.

"You haven't had more trouble with the neighboring rancher, have you?" his father inquired.

Ethan frowned. "Samuel and I were out mending fences yesterday morning."

"Oh?" His father's face took on a look of concern.

"Mr. Travers, who owns the adjacent ranch, is still angry with Brother Bartlett for fencing in the range. Some sort of dispute over water rights for their cattle. I think it will all sort itself out in time."

Ethan decided to say nothing else about the circumstances at Bartlett's ranch, where he was employed; he didn't want to worry his parents with the genuine alarm he was feeling. The cowhands who worked for Travers' Double Seven Ranch were becoming bolder about destroying Bartlett's newly strung barbed wire fence. Charles Travers had moved his large herd of steers into the South Willow Creek area of the valley only six months earlier. His outfit was bigger than Bartlett's ranch, and Travers employed twice as many drovers to tend his 3,000 head of cattle.

As Travers' cattle mingled with Brother Bartlett's stock on the open grazing range, it wasn't long before Ethan and the other hands noticed Travers' "Double Seven" brand burned into the hides of cattle already wearing the "Running W" brand. Hot words had been exchanged between Travers' men and Brother Bartlett's hands over the alleged rustling. Rather than risk an escalation of bad feelings, Bartlett decided to fence in his range. Travers became irate over the fencing of what had been a common grazing ground, and accused Brother Bartlett of stealing more than his share of good grazing land and water rights. The situation at the moment was explosive, much more so than Ethan was willing to admit to his parents.

"You said you had a matter to discuss with me?" Ethan asked, referring to his father's greeting outside the house.

"Yes, both you and your mother." Inger's eyes widened with curiosity as James reached into his vest pocket and withdrew a folded slip of paper. He opened it and set it on the table. Ethan glanced inquisitively at the paper.

"What is it?" Inger asked.

"A telegram from Western Union. A messenger was on his way to the house with it when he spied me on the road." James smoothed out the sheet of paper displaying the message.

"What's it say, Pa?" asked Ethan.

"I'll read it aloud." James cleared his throat and took the paper in hand.

DR. JAMES KADE. AM IN NEED OF ASSIS-
TANCE. HAVE SUFFERED THE LOSS OF
MY BAGGAGE AND ALL MY PERSONAL
BELONGINGS. ANY AID YOU CAN RENDER
WOULD BE APPRECIATED. YOUR NIECE,
JESSICA SCOTT.

"Jessica?" Inger exclaimed. "Elizabeth's daughter?"
James nodded.

"Who's Jessica?" Ethan wanted to know.

"Jessica is your cousin. My sister's daughter," his father explained.

"Oh my, James, we haven't had any contact with Elizabeth or her family in years. Where is Jessica? We must help her at once." Inger's blue eyes filled with concern.

Ethan knew almost nothing about his Aunt Elizabeth's family. He'd never met any of them, and though his parents had spoken of them on occasion, he'd paid little attention.

"The message was telegraphed from Corinne. That's a railroad town. Jessica must have been traveling through by train," James said.

"How could she lose her belongings on the train?" Ethan asked.

James shrugged. "I don't know. You can ask her that question yourself when you meet her. I've already sent a telegram to her in reply arranging for her passage on the line from Corinne to Ogden, and from there on the Utah Central Railroad into Salt Lake. She'll be arriving at the train station tomorrow afternoon. I'm hoping you'll ride to the depot to get her and bring her home."

"Sure, Pa, I can do that." Ethan felt a stab of disappointment. He'd planned to visit the Quill and Ink book shop tomorrow, and now he wouldn't be able to do so.

Instead, he'd be sharing his time with a cousin who was a complete stranger to him.

"I'd go myself, Ethan, if I could. But I've a surgery scheduled for tomorrow that can't be postponed."

"I'm happy to do it, Pa." He said the words, but truthfully he didn't feel happy about the task assigned him for it would necessitate delaying his visit to the Quill and Ink.

As he considered that thought, a young woman's face took shape in his mind. Her complexion was like ivory; and raven black hair framed her emerald eyes, slender nose, and dimpled smile. The image brought him a shiver of pleasure. Though he didn't know her name, he'd been smitten with her the first moment he'd seen her, working behind the counter of her father's book shop and bindery.

But he intended to make himself acquainted with her— that was one of the reasons why he'd come home for a few days. He'd planned to visit the Quill and Ink under the guise of wishing to purchase a book, ask her opinion regarding the merits of the volume, then introduce himself and thoroughly charm and impress her. He had it all thought out; had so, in fact, for weeks. The pretty, dark-haired proprietress of the book shop had seldom left his thoughts over the last few months while he'd been working at the ranch.

"That doesn't give me much time to prepare for Jessica's arrival. She can share Birgithe's room; I'll make up the bed for her there. And Birgithe can lend her some clothing if she's in need of them."

Ethan smiled grudgingly. His mother was already laying plans for his cousin's stay. In spite of his disappointment about not being able to visit the booksellers as he'd intended, Ethan felt a stirring of curiosity over meeting this cousin who lived in the East.

"I hope Jessica will stay with us for a time. It will be such a treat for us to get to know her," Inger continued.

A sudden thought occurred to Ethan. "Pa, how old is Jessica?"

"Well, let's see. She's the middle daughter of Elizabeth's three girls. She must be eighteen or nineteen. About the same age as yourself, Ethan. In that case, you should enjoy her visit."

"Yes, you and Jessica will be good company for one another," Inger added.

Ethan put on a smile he didn't feel. His parents would expect him to entertain Jessica; spend some time showing her the town. He could see his visit to the booksellers slipping further and further away.

Ethan's fourteen-year-old sister, Birgithe, arrived home from school a short time later and the family sat down together to eat supper. Inger had made beef stew, full of vegetables and spices, and Ethan ate three bowlfuls before feeling satisfied. Afterward, the family retired to the parlor. Ethan relaxed on a cozy chair and dozed off to sleep.

"Ethan, I'm talking to you!"

He heard his sister's raised voice through a fog of fuzzy dreams. "I heard you," he mumbled, straightening up in the chair.

"What is your answer then?" she demanded. Her brown eyes were fastened on his, and her mouth was set in a petulant frown.

"To which question?" he hedged.

"See. You weren't listening to me," Birgithe accused. "I asked if you'd help me with my composition for school."

"Your composition? You know I'm no good at writing, Birgithe. Why don't you ask Mother to help you with it?" Ethan was fully awake now, and feeling irritated because of it.

"No, Ethan. I don't need help *writing* my English composition," she returned in an exasperated tone. "I need assistance with the subject matter. I'm writing an essay about cowboys."

"Oh. Why didn't you say so?"

"I *did* say so."

"All right. All right. What do you want to know?" Ethan shifted in his chair, trying to find a more comfortable angle to rest his body.

Birgithe picked up a score of papers from her lap and tapped them with her fingers until they fell uniformly together. Then she wet the point of her pencil with her tongue. "First of all, what kind of clothing does a cowboy wear?" she asked with a professional air.

From the corner of his eye, Ethan saw his mother smile. She sat in an old hickory rocking chair, sewing strips of fabric together to make a rag rug. "You know how a cowhand dresses, Birgithe," Ethan complained. "Why are you asking me that?"

Birgithe wound a finger through one of the long chestnut curls draping her shoulders. "Because this is supposed to be a composition where we gather facts. So I have to ask someone for the facts."

"But you already know the answer," Ethan protested.

"Ethan."

Ethan's eyes darted to his mother. She sent him a meaningful look.

"Oh, all right," he conceded moodily. "A cowboy wears leather pants over his trousers, called chaps, to protect his legs from brush and thorns, and the horns of the cattle."

Birgithe scribbled down the information.

"And he wears a hat to keep the sun off his face and rain off his head."

Birgithe nodded as she wrote.

"Cowboys wear neckerchiefs, too, when they're riding the range or looking after the stock." Ethan could see his sister's lips form the letters as she penciled them onto her page. "And he carries a lariat."

"How do you spell 'lariat'?" Birgithe asked.

"Oh, for goodness sakes, Birgithe," replied Ethan, rolling his eyes.

"Just tell me and don't be rude," Birgithe said indignantly.

Ethan glowered at his sister. "L-A-R-I-E-T."

"A-T," his mother corrected from her place in the rocking chair. "Lariat is spelled with an A-T on the end, Ethan."

Ethan's father chuckled. He moved aside a corner of the newspaper he was reading and gave Ethan a sympathetic wink.

"A-T, Birgithe. L-A-R-I-A-T," he spelled emphatically.

Birgithe shot him a dark scowl.

Ethan twisted in his chair to scratch an itching spot on the back of his shoulder. "What else?" he asked his sister.

"Well, let me think a minute." Birgithe's dark brows gathered together in concentrated thought. "What kind of chores does a cowboy do at the ranch?"

"You already know the answer to that question, too," he replied.

Birgithe heaved a sigh. "I told you, Ethan. I have to ask for the facts."

Ethan's gaze roamed the ceiling as he recited a cowhand's chores. "After the spring roundup the cowpuncher has to count the cattle, gather up strays, brand newborn calves, sort out the four- and five-year-olds to take to market . . ."

"Wait a minute. You're talking too fast," Birgithe complained.

". . . dig post holes, string barbed wire, help with the crops on the ranch, break wild horses," he went on more slowly.

Birgithe wrote as fast as she could, her tongue pinned to one corner of her mouth.

"Is that enough?" Ethan asked.

Birgithe studied the page she'd been writing on. "Yes, I believe it is." She laid aside her papers, walked over to her older brother, and put her arms around his neck. "Thanks, Ethan. I knew I could count on you to help me."

Ethan grinned at her. "Just make sure you earn a good grade on this paper, or I won't be so quick to help you again."

Ethan heard his father chuckle from behind the newspaper.

# CHAPTER THREE

Jessica nervously fingered the strings of her handbag. The train was slowing as it approached the Salt Lake City depot. In a matter of moments, she would be dependent upon the charity of an uncle she had never met. Perspiration gathered along her brow. She loosened the ties of her bonnet and retied them snugly under her chin, making sure every hair was tucked in place underneath the wide-brimmed hat. With her heart pounding, she waited for the train to stop. What kind of man was her uncle? Would he be annoyed for burdening him with her troubles? The thief she'd encountered on the train had embodied the worst qualities of a Westerner—crude, brash, callous. She fully expected her uncle to be the same. Perhaps he might not come for her at all! She forced that thought out of her mind. He'd sent a telegram in answer to her plea for assistance, hadn't he?

The bell on the engine began to clang, apprising the passengers of the train's impending stop in Salt Lake City. The ride from Corinne to the city of Salt Lake had taken about two hours. Jessica had been relieved to leave the freight town of Corinne behind, with its canvas tents and crude buildings set in an endless plain of sagebrush. Outside of Corinne, the tracks hugged the base of the mountains the rest of the way into the valley. The transcontinental railroad had bypassed Salt Lake City in favor of a northerly route around the Great Salt Lake, and Jessica had had to change trains at Ogden for the last leg of the trip. The mountains near Ogden were humped and rounded, but the closer they came to Salt Lake City, the more defined and majestic the mountains grew.

Jessica clutched her handbag and stared out the window as the train approached the fringe of a large and bustling town. She spotted mercantiles, banking institutions, bakeries, and a saddler shop; the various establishments seemed to be housed in tidy, well-tended structures made mostly of wood or adobe.

When the train rumbled to a stop amid a cloud of smoke and steam, Jessica stepped off, pausing on the wooden platform of the depot. The station was crowded with people, a few hugging one another in welcome, but she didn't see anyone coming forward to greet her. Her uncle wasn't here! With sinking heart, Jessica started toward the ticket office.

"Uh, Miss Scott?"

Jessica turned at the sound of someone calling her name. A young man of about her own age came walking toward her. "Yes, I'm Jessica Scott," she said guardedly.

"Welcome to Salt Lake City, Miss Scott. I'm Ethan Kade. Your cousin."

The young man stood awkwardly before her, his hands plunged in the pockets of his trousers. He looked uncomfortable, as if he wasn't used to wearing the smartly tailored trousers and frock coat he was clothed in. His head was bare, revealing disheveled, yellow hair that came to the bottom of his ears. His eyes were blue, his nose sharp, and his mouth expressive.

"Oh. I was expecting my uncle . . ."

"My father had to attend to a surgery, so he asked me to come instead." Ethan took his hands out of his pockets and thrust his blonde hair behind his ears. "Have you any baggage I can carry for you?"

Jessica shook her head. Her cousin looked suddenly sheepish, as if he felt foolish for asking the question. Her Uncle James had undoubtedly informed him of her loss.

"The buggy is this way," Ethan said, motioning to a spot just beyond the depot.

Jessica grasped a tighter hold on her handbag and followed him to a shiny, black buggy, harnessed to a bay horse. He offered his hand to help her into the carriage. "Thank you," she said stiffly, seating herself inside.

Ethan stepped to the other side of the buggy, grabbed a hat that had been resting on the seat, and clamped it on his head. Then he swung up into the carriage beside her. He shook the reins, and the horse started forward in a trot. "We don't live far from here. Just about seven blocks," he said, darting a glance at her.

Jessica didn't reply, instead she tried to calm her fears by studying the buildings as they drove along the street. She saw a sign outside one establishment that read, "Deseret National Bank." They passed the Wells, Fargo and Company building, and a handsome structure of red sandstone and adobe.

"Is this your first trip out west?" Ethan asked her.

"Yes," she nodded. She hoped her uncle would help her make new connections to the West coast as speedily as possible. She didn't want to rely on his charity any longer than necessary.

"Where were you headed? I mean, before your luggage was stolen?"

Jessica felt her cousin shift nervously in his seat. He probably felt as ill at ease as she did. "Sacramento," she replied without offering any details.

"Oh? My father was in Sacramento once a few years ago for a medical convention."

Jessica glanced at him without speaking.

"My father is a physician," he added.

"Yes, I know." She felt his eyes flicker toward her, but she didn't return his gaze.

Neither of them said anything more, and they drove along the dirt road in uncomfortable silence. The places of business gave way to homes, gardens, orchards, and cultivated fields. Rimming the valley were towering, purple mountains. In the afternoon light, shadows filled the crevices of the craggy peaks.

"It's not much farther," Ethan offered at last. "My mother has a room at the house all prepared for you."

His comment heightened Jessica's curiosity about her relatives. She wondered if her aunt and uncle had other children in addition to Ethan. She almost asked him about it, but then decided to wait and see for herself.

Finally, Ethan reined the horse into a yard bordered by a white, picket fence. An adobe home, painted pale pink, rested in the middle of the yard, shaded by tall trees and framed by colorful flowers. A covered porch ran along the front of the house and down both sides. Ethan guided the horse to a hitching post, pulled on the reins, then jumped down from the buggy and secured the bay horse to the post.

As he helped Jessica from the carriage, the front door of the house flew open and a teenaged girl with long, dark hair stepped out onto the porch. She was joined by a slender, blonde-haired woman whose face shone with a smile when she spotted Jessica.

"Here we are," Ethan said to his cousin. "And that is my mother and my sister."

He'd barely gotten the words out of his mouth when the pair started hurrying toward them. "Jessica, welcome to our home," Inger said, giving Jessica a kiss on the cheek. "This is your cousin, Birgithe," she added, indicating the girl standing beside her. Birgithe stepped forward and smiled shyly. "Come inside, Jessica, and rest. You must be tired from the long train ride," Inger invited, taking her by the hand.

Jessica walked beside her aunt up the stone-edged path toward the house. As they drew nearer, Jessica's eyes wandered over the handsome structure. With a chimney at each end, and a door in the center, the two-story home looked cozy and inviting. She mounted the porch steps, noticing that both porch and steps were painted the same pink color as the house.

"Did Ethan have any difficulty finding you at the train station?" her aunt asked.

Jessica shook her head. Accompanying her aunt into the house, Jessica found herself in a wide hall with a side table leaning against one wall and a stairway leading to the floor above. A room opened on each side of the hallway. To her left lay the parlor, carpeted in a pink and green floral print, with walls painted a soft pink. On the right was another room of about the same size, but containing a bed, chairs, table, and a medicine cabinet. This was evidently her uncle's medical office, where he treated patients. She caught a glimpse of a watercolor hanging on one wall, featuring leafy trees and a golden stream, as her aunt led her down the hallway, past the parlor and doctor's office, and into a large kitchen.

"Sit down, dear," Inger invited. "Can I get you something to eat? Perhaps a slice of pumpkin cake? Birgithe made a nice pumpkin cake this afternoon."

Jessica seated herself at the table, then removed her bonnet and set it in her lap. "No, thank you," she answered. "I'm not hungry." Truthfully, she would have enjoyed a slice of cake—pumpkin was her favorite—but she felt too nervous to eat anything just yet.

"A glass of lemonade, then?" her aunt offered.

Jessica shook her head.

"I'll have a glass of lemonade and a piece of pumpkin cake," Ethan volunteered.

Birgithe took a seat next to Jessica. "Was the train exciting to ride?" the girl asked timidly.

Jessica turned to face her cousin. She looked to be fourteen or fifteen—about the same age as Jessica's younger sister, Clarissa. She was taller than Clarissa, though, and prettier, with eyes the shade of brown sugar. Her dark hair was pulled away from her face with tortoise shell combs, and she wore a brown muslin dress that matched the color of her eyes. Jessica glanced at her own soiled traveling dress and winced with embarrassment. She thought about the stylish dresses packed in her trunk, which was now wending its way to California without her. "Yes, it was. I liked it," she answered.

Birgithe stared eagerly at her, waiting for more information about the excursion.

"It went very fast—forty miles an hour," Jessica said to appease her.

Birgithe's eyes widened.

"And there was a place to eat and to sleep on the train."

"I should like to see that!" Birgithe exclaimed.

"Have you ever been on the train?"

Birgithe shook her head. "No. Father promised to take us on a train ride, but we haven't been able to go yet."

Jessica's aunt set a plate of pumpkin cake in front of Ethan, who had taken a chair across from Jessica at the table. Jessica smelled the spicy goodness of the cake and wished she hadn't been so quick to decline a piece for herself.

"How is your family, Jessica?" Inger asked. "Are your mother and father well?"

"Yes. Fine," she answered without elaborating.

"Is your father still employed in the lumber business?"

Jessica nodded. An image of her father flashed into Jessica's mind—his gray, hard eyes, the haughty curl of his mouth. She envisioned him arguing heatedly with her mother. She blinked, and the picture faded.

"Your older sister is married, isn't she?" Inger inquired, giving Jessica her full attention.

Jessica searched her aunt's clear, blue eyes for an indication of her character. There was no guile in those eyes, only kindness and gentleness. "Yes. Emmaline is married to a man named John Wylie. They've been married about a year now."

"Your mother wrote Millicent about it," Inger explained. "Oh, Millicent will be so thrilled to meet you. And Roxana, too."

"Those are Father's two sisters," Ethan said, forking another piece of pumpkin cake into his mouth.

Jessica had heard her mother mention the names of her younger sisters, Millicent and Roxana, but she was reluctant to make their acquaintance. She already felt overwhelmed by her situation. "You know, Aunt Inger, what I'd really like to do is rest for a bit."

Inger immediately got to her feet. "Here we've been pestering you with questions when you're weary from your long trip. Come with me; you can share Birgithe's room."

Jessica stood up to follow her aunt out of the kitchen. Birgithe, too, promptly left her chair and accompanied Jessica up the stairs to the second floor. Ethan remained at the table, finishing his cake.

Inger led her down the hallway, passing one bedroom and then another before entering a third. The cozy room was dominated by a bed covered with a quilted spread and a handsome chest of drawers. Jessica spied a smaller bed stored underneath the adult-sized one.

"The first thing we need to do is get you some clothing," Inger said. "We were distressed to hear about the theft of your belongings; perhaps after you've had a chance to rest, you can tell us what happened. I'm sure your Uncle James will be able to do something to help recover your lost articles." Inger bustled about the room as she spoke, adjusting the window shade, smoothing the quilt on the bed. "For now, you can borrow some of Birgithe's things—I think her clothing will fit you—and then, tomorrow, we can go to the mercantile and purchase what you need."

Jessica stood at the foot of the bed, watching her aunt make the room comfortable and inviting for her.

Birgithe went to a small closet and selected two dresses, a green and white checkered gingham and a blue feather-patterned calico. She held both dresses up for Jessica's inspection. "I'll bet these will fit you," she said to Jessica. She laid the dresses on a chair beside the bed.

"All right, Birgithe. Let's go now and let Jessica rest. There's fresh water in the pitcher, dear, and a clean towel for you. Make yourself comfortable. The bed is yours," Inger added, gesturing to the bed with the brightly-colored quilt. "Birgithe can use the trundle. After you've rested and freshened up, we'll have supper."

Her aunt and cousin left the room, closing the bedroom door behind them. Jessica sat down on the bed and studied her surroundings. The walls of the bedroom were painted a pastel blue and the rag rug covering the wooden floor was woven in colors of blue, yellow, and pink. She noticed a pile of schoolbooks stacked on top of the chest of drawers, and a beautiful china doll sat on a little corner table. Sunlight streamed from a single, large window over the bed. The feather tick felt comfortable, and the quilt smelled clean and fresh. She glanced at the two dresses Birgithe had set out on the chair. They weren't as attractive as Jessica's own frocks, but she had the feeling that Birgithe had chosen her very best dresses to loan.

The opening and closing of a door downstairs, and then footsteps in the hallway, brought Jessica to her feet. She went to the bedroom door and listened. She heard a man's voice, and then her aunt's reply—her uncle was home. Jessica walked to the chair and picked up the green and white gingham Birgithe had chosen for her. It was trimmed with a ruffled collar, and puffy sleeves ended in a cuff at the wrist. She glanced at the second dress. The feather pattern was pretty, and the cloth was dyed an attractive shade of blue.

Jessica quickly unbuttoned the soiled black silk dress she wore and replaced it with the blue feathered calico, then stood before the mirror attached to Birgithe's chest of drawers and studied her reflection. The sleeves were a bit too short, but other than that, Jessica thought the dress fit well. She turned away from the mirror and went to the closet where Birgithe had removed the two dresses. Quietly, she peeked inside. Two more frocks hung from pegs inside the closet, and a little pile of underclothing lay folded neatly on a shelf. A pair of high-topped shoes sat on another shelf. On a third shelf was nestled a couple of bonnets, their ribbon ties rolled smoothly into neat coils.

A tap sounded at the bedroom door, startling Jessica. "Just a moment," she called. She hastily shut the closet, took a quick glance at herself in the mirror, then hurried to the door and opened it.

Ethan stood in the doorway. "My father's home. He wants to know if it's convenient for you to come downstairs and speak with him."

"Yes," Jessica replied. "Please tell him I'll be right there."

Ethan nodded and started to walk away. After a step or two, he paused and turned back around. "You look real pretty in that frock," he said. His face flooded with color.

Jessica couldn't keep from smiling as she watched him barrel down the stairs. Although he seemed awkward and self-conscious, Jessica suspected she might like him, if she got to know him better. But, of course, that wasn't going to happen. She wouldn't be staying with the Kades long enough to get to know any of them better.

Drawing a nervous breath, she stepped out into the hallway. She descended the stairs and peeked around the corner into the parlor. Her aunt was seated by the window, and a tall, dark-haired man stood beside her. His back was turned toward Jessica when she entered the room.

"Oh, here she is, James. Come in and sit down, dear," Inger said on spying her in the doorway.

The tall man turned to face her. Jessica expected him to resemble her mother, but her first glimpse of him didn't bear that out. His eyes were dark brown, and his hair was the same color.

"Jessica, I'm so pleased to meet you." He extended a hand in greeting.

The kindness in his voice and the warmth of his handshake revealed a cordiality Jessica wasn't expecting. "Thank you. And thank you for the telegram and for your assistance. I hope I won't be troubling you long. As soon as my things are recovered, I'll be on my way." The words tumbled out sounding much harsher than Jessica intended. Her tone obviously disconcerted her uncle, for he glanced from her to his wife with a bewildered expression.

"You're welcome to stay with us as long as you like. I hope you can spend several days with us, at least," her uncle replied, "so we can get to know one another."

"Sit down, Jessica, dear," Inger invited, indicating a chair next to hers.

Jessica took the seat offered her. "I spoke with the sheriff in Corinne about the theft of my belongings," she began hastily. "He assured me that he'd put every effort into searching for the thief. But I had no means with me to stay any longer in that place, and that is the reason why I contacted you."

"And I'm glad you did," her uncle returned. "Was your baggage stolen from off the train, if I may inquire?"

"Not exactly." She briefly described what had occurred. Her voice began to tremble with the telling of the tale. She paused, not wanting her uncle and aunt to know how upset she was by the thievery.

James leaned forward in his chair. "And your money and your personal belongings were in that bag, is that correct?"

Jessica nodded glumly.

"I imagine that it was a difficult decision whether to get back on the train without your satchel or to remain in Corinne and contact the sheriff."

She glanced up quickly at him. Her uncle was the first person to express an understanding for her predicament at the train station. He'd seen directly to the heart of the situation.

"And the rest of your luggage?" he asked, stroking a thumb across his chin.

"I had a trunk on the train. It's now somewhere between here and Sacramento."

James straightened in his seat. "At least we can solve that problem easily enough. I'll telegraph the depot in Sacramento and ask them to put your trunk on the next train coming east to Salt Lake." He gave Jessica a sudden, warm smile. "Then we can hope the sheriff does his job. Perhaps a wire to the sheriff might be in order as well, just to encourage him in his endeavors."

Jessica's aunt smiled at that last remark.

"I'm sure everything will work out, Jessica. Try not to worry too much. In the meanwhile, we're delighted to have you here with us," James said.

Jessica wanted to tell her uncle about the theft of the pencil drawing entrusted to her care. She yearned to hear the same kind of reassurance concerning the return of the portrait. But she decided not to mention it; the loss was too personal.

"Notwithstanding your misfortune, I suspect your trip across the country by train was extraordinary. You traveled through some spectacular scenery. How long was the ride from Nauvoo to the valley?" James inquired.

"I boarded the train at St. Louis. It took five days to travel from there."

James issued a low whistle. "Five days. Imagine that, Inger," he said, turning to his wife. "It took our families three-and-a-half months to make that trek by wagon."

"It's hard to conceive of that trip taking such a short amount of time," Inger replied, shaking her head.

"And Nauvoo? Is the city unchanged?" James asked. "I haven't been back there in years."

"I suppose it's much the same as the last time you saw it. At least Mother says it hasn't changed much."

A melancholy look crept into James' eyes. "The city was bustling with activity in the old days. It was one of the largest and busiest towns in Illinois. Nauvoo was a wonderful place when I was a boy."

Watching her uncle, it was hard for Jessica to imagine him being a boy who once lived in Nauvoo. The picture he described seemed out of proportion. She knew Nauvoo to be a small, quiet village where nothing much out of the ordinary happened, and where people kept to themselves and minded their own business.

"Your Aunt Inger's family lived across the river in Montrose," James added.

Jessica stole a look at her aunt. Her face, too, wore a nostalgic expression. Jessica had been to the town of Montrose on an occasion or two. It was sparsely populated, and most of the older buildings had fallen into disrepair.

"Well," James said, returning his focus to the present, "let me tell you again, Jessica, how pleased we are to have you here. I hope you'll enjoy your stay with us."

"I'll be continuing on to California as soon as possible," she responded. She swallowed noisily, fearing she'd made an unfavorable impression on her uncle and aunt. Though she'd thought that wouldn't matter to her, somehow it did.

# CHAPTER FOUR

Ethan glanced at his cousin as Jessica walked beside him down the plank sidewalk fronting the shops along Main Street. Since leaving the house earlier that afternoon to travel the few blocks into town, he'd tried unsuccessfully to engage her in conversation.

He dug a small, brown paper sack from his pocket and held it open toward her. "Care for a piece of candy?" he asked.

She shook her head. "No, thank you."

"Okay." Reaching inside the sack, he withdrew a marble-sized lemon drop and popped it into his mouth. His lips puckered with its initial sour taste. He rolled the hard piece of candy with his tongue, sucking on it until the sour taste dissipated and was replaced by the morsel's sweet flavor.

"You sure?" Ethan tried offering the candy again. The lemon drops, which he'd purchased from the mercantile that afternoon, were his favorite treat. Whenever he had the good fortune to replenish his stock of them, he carried a pocketful.

Jessica gave the sack a distasteful glance. "I'm sure I wouldn't care for one."

Ethan sucked the candy noisily as he folded the sack and stuffed it back into his pocket. The two of them continued along the sidewalk, gazing into storefront windows while waiting for Ethan's mother and sister to finish their business at the post office. Ethan had driven them in the buckboard to the commercial district of town to purchase some clothing and other items for Jessica.

Ethan wished his mother and sister would hurry. He was impatiently waiting for an opportunity to visit the Quill and Ink while in town—without Jessica at his elbow. He shot a glance down the street. The booksellers was situated on the next block; from where he stood, he could see the shop's hanging sign swinging lazily in the slight breeze. His heart quickened just looking at the sign.

"What building is that?" asked Jessica abruptly.

Ethan started. "What?"

"The large building over there," she said, pointing across the street.

"That's the Council House. It's sometimes used for church meetings, and the territorial legislature meets there." Ethan studied for a moment the exterior of the handsome, square building. The ground floor was built of red sandstone, and the upper story was constructed of adobe, giving the edifice a striking appearance. He saw Jessica gaze at the two-story building as they walked past it. "And that's Zion's Savings Bank and Trust Company down the block," Ethan told her.

The hours spent in town had been a good opportunity to acquaint Jessica with the city and the Church. Ethan's mother had pointed out the granite temple under construction, as well as the Endowment House and Tabernacle, and explained to Jessica the reasons why the Saints were raising such structures. She told Jessica a bit about the history of the Church since Brigham Young and the Saints had come west.

Then Birgithe mentioned the Book of Mormon. Jessica was only slightly familiar with the book, which seemed strange to Ethan. Living in Nauvoo as she had, where The Church of Jesus Christ of Latter-day Saints had once prospered, it was surprising how little she knew about the book of scripture Joseph Smith had translated through the gift and power of God. Ethan wondered how much his cousin understood of Church history in Illinois, and if his Aunt Elizabeth and Uncle Alexander had ever discussed the gospel with her.

Since arriving at the Kades' home the day before, Jessica had revealed little about herself. She was guarded in her conversation and mostly kept to herself. At first, Ethan assumed she simply felt uncomfortable around the family because they were strangers to her, but he was beginning to think Jessica was both selfish and unfeeling. She seemed unappreciative of all his parents had done to make her feel welcome and aid her in her plight. He hadn't heard Jessica offer a sincere word of thanks to his parents, including this afternoon when his mother purchased a pretty, new dress for her to wear. Jessica's ingratitude irritated him.

The disturbing thoughts concerning his cousin disappeared as they drew abreast of a two-story, brick building on Main Street. Painted on a wooden sign outside the building was a depiction of a quill pen and ink bottle, with the words "Quill and Ink" printed in large, fancy letters.

Ethan's heart started pounding. He might not get another chance to go inside once his mother and sister returned from the post office. "Just a minute, Jessica," he said. "Let's stop here."

Jessica's eyes swept to the swinging sign hanging from the store front. "A bookstore?"

Ethan nodded. Now that he was at the shop, he felt a sudden attack of anxiety. Every clever phrase he'd practiced to say to the raven-haired, young woman fled his memory. He wished Jessica wasn't tagging along at his side; having her in tow was going to make his introduction to the proprietress of the book shop more difficult. He cleared his throat and wiped his sweaty palms on his trouser legs. The day was cool and breezy and the sky overcast, but Ethan felt as though the scorching rays of the summer sun were beating upon him.

When he entered the shop, a bell above the door tinkled, signaling his presence. His eyes flicked to the counter where a slender, dark-haired, young woman stood, wrapping a book in brown paper and string for a customer. Alerted by the bell over the door, her gaze slid to his face. Ethan felt the blood rush to his cheeks.

"I want to purchase a book," he mumbled to Jessica, who followed him inside the booksellers. He knew his face was flaming, and he could feel the blood pulsing through his veins. "I think it's on the shelf over there." He hurried to one of the tall bookcases holding a number of volumes.

"What book are you looking for?" asked Jessica as she trailed him to the shelf.

"Uh . . . a book of poetry." It was an absurd answer—he knew that as soon as he uttered the words. Although he'd planned out in detail the conversation he intended to hold with the proprietress, he'd completely overlooked *which* title he was under the pretense of searching for.

"Poetry?" Jessica's brows lifted. "I wouldn't have guessed you enjoy reading poetry."

"Well, it's growing on me," Ethan hissed in a whisper. He ignored Jessica and began thumbing through the books lined neatly on the shelf. More bookcases crowded the room, and a couple of chairs and a small table occupied one corner. As his fingers walked over the spines of the books, he stole a surreptitious glance at the girl behind the counter. She was handing the wrapped book to the customer. Ethan watched him tuck the book under his arm and leave the shop.

Ethan drew a shaky breath and started toward the young woman standing behind the counter. He nearly choked when she lifted her head and fastened her emerald eyes on him.

"Can I help you with something?" she asked, gazing evenly at him.

"I, uh . . ." His voice evaporated in his throat.

"Yes?" the young woman repeated. An impatient frown flickered across her brow.

"He's looking for a book of poetry," declared Jessica.

Ethan glanced at his cousin. A slight smile warmed Jessica's eyes.

"Yes, that's right. A book of poetry," Ethan said, trying to recover from his awkwardness.

"By which poet?" the young woman at the counter asked. She gazed steadily at him out of two glistening emeralds set in an oval face, lustrous as a pearl. A green, velvet ribbon wound through her hair, and her frock was of matching shade. Ethan noted how the full-skirted dress hugged her tiny waist. He could have encircled her waist with his two hands. That thought made him feel almost dizzy.

"Umm, Wordsworth." It was the first name that came to mind. He desperately hoped Wordsworth was a poet and not a painter or sculptor or some other kind of artist. Though his education was liberal, Ethan had little head for remembering notable names in the arts.

"William Wordsworth. A good choice."

Ethan breathed easier. The name matched with the occupation, and she was pleased with his choice of subject matter.

"The books of poetry are in this direction. If you'd like to follow me, I'll show you where you can find a volume of Wordsworth." The young woman in the tight-waisted, green dress led Ethan and Jessica to a bookcase located near the rear of the shop. Ethan couldn't keep his eyes off the way her skirt swayed with each step she took.

"Here you are." She pulled a book from the shelf and held it out to Ethan. "This is Wordsworth's best work. It contains many of his nature poems and his most well-known sonnets."

Ethan looked at the title of the book. *Lyrical Ballads.* He knew nothing about poetry. "Thank you. This is exactly what I wanted."

He felt Jessica peeking over his shoulder at the volume, and so he held it out to her. She took the book, opened it, and flipped slowly through the pages. "This volume also contains poetry written by Coleridge," Jessica observed, turning to the proprietress.

"Yes, it does. Coleridge and Wordsworth collaborated in the writing of this book of poetry. I think the first volume was printed about 1798. It has remained a very popular book over the years."

Jessica examined a few pages more of the book. "I like Coleridge's poetry, especially the 'Rime of the Ancient Mariner,'" she said.

"I'm sure that particular poem is included," the proprietress replied, nodding at the book. "As well as Coleridge's other fine poems."

Ethan listened to the young woman with rapt attention, enthralled by every word she spoke. Her voice was light and melodious and fell like music on his ears.

"Coleridge and Wordsworth were close friends. The two of them spent some time together in Germany, and when they returned to England they lived near one another," the young woman explained to Jessica.

"They must have had a great influence upon one another's work, although their poetry has distinct differences," Jessica responded.

"You're right. Coleridge had an extraordinary gift for imagination and melody in his writing. I think Wordsworth's poetry is more simplistic, though equally as romantic."

Ethan shifted from one foot to the other. The conversation was not going in the direction he'd planned. The attractive girl at his side seemed more interested in conversing with Jessica than with him.

"Wordsworth received many accolades for his writing. I believe Queen Victoria appointed him poet laureate," the proprietress said, glancing from Jessica to Ethan.

"Really?" Jessica replied with interest. "I didn't know that."

Ethan felt compelled to make a comment, if for no other reason than to garner the young woman's attention. "That must have been quite an honor for an American poet," he offered.

The proprietress gave him a cool stare. "Wordsworth, of course, was British," she said.

Color leaped to Ethan's cheeks. He lashed himself for making such a blunder. He'd been foolish to comment on something that was unfamiliar and parade his ignorance. "Thank you for your help," he blurted. "We'll take this book. How much is it?"

The proprietress told him the amount, then he and Jessica followed her to the counter. Ethan dug in his pocket for the coins to pay for the book. He was determined to redeem himself by leaving her with a good impression. He handed the money to her and accompanied it with what he supposed was a charming grin. The smile he gained in return was a wan one.

Ethan tried again. "This is a fine book shop," he said as the young woman began to wrap his purchase in brown paper. "Is it a family business?"

She looked up at him. Ethan found himself drowning in the brilliant green sea of her eyes. He would have given his right arm for an attentive glance from those liquid eyes. "Yes. My father owns and operates the Quill and Ink," she replied without smiling. Ethan received the distinct impression that she considered his question to be inappropriate. He winced with embarrassment.

He could think of nothing more to say. Every clever shred of conversation he had prepared now seemed silly and trite. The young woman's apparent disinterest in him caused his self-confidence to shrivel.

She completed wrapping the book and handed it to Jessica. "I don't think I've ever seen you in our book shop before," she said to Jessica. "And I know most of our customers. Are you new in town?"

Ethan looked from the proprietress to Jessica, baffled as to how the whole conversation had veered off the course he'd set for it.

"Yes. I'm from Illinois and am only passing through Salt Lake City on my way to California, where I'll be taking a teaching position. My name is Jessica Scott."

"It's nice to make your acquaintance. I'm Susannah Hamilton."

*Susannah Hamilton.* The name rang in Ethan's ears. He thought it was the loveliest name he'd ever heard.

Jessica gestured toward him. "This is my cousin, Ethan Kade. I'm staying with his family for a few days."

Ethan latched onto the opportunity Jessica provided for him. "How do you do, Miss Hamilton? I'm happy to meet you."

"And you," Susannah replied. Her eyes rested on Ethan for only a moment, then she addressed Jessica. "Please let me know how you like the poetry. If you enjoy it, we have other poets' works as well."

How *she* enjoys the poetry? Ethan thought with annoyance. He was the one who came into the shop to purchase a book. Somehow, Jessica had managed to strike up a rapport with Susannah Hamilton where he had not. And why had his cousin become so talkative all of a sudden? he grumbled. This was one time and place where he would have preferred her to maintain her customary silence and leave the talking to him.

Jessica handed the wrapped book to Ethan as they left the store. "There's your book. It should make good reading, Ethan."

"Thank you," Ethan answered in a sour tone. He tucked the book under his arm and stared straight ahead.

The two of them walked in silence as they retraced their steps up the street. "Miss Hamilton seems like a nice person," Jessica commented after a few moments. "Pretty, too." She looked at Ethan and he saw a twinkle spring into her gray eyes. "Didn't you think so?"

Ethan's scowl deepened. "I guess," he mumbled.

He heard Jessica chuckle softly, but he didn't turn to look at her. Instead, he quickened his pace.


After Ethan unharnessed the horses from the buckboard and put the animals into a stall with a handful of oats, he went to his room. He tossed the wrapped volume he'd purchased at the Quill and Ink onto his bed and stood staring at it. Susannah Hamilton hadn't shown the least bit of interest in him; and after this afternoon's visit, he was more smitten than before with her. He grudgingly admired his cousin's ease in friendshipping Susannah and was surprised by Jessica's amiability. She hadn't spoken a dozen words to Ethan or his family since her arrival, yet she was quite capable of striking up an acquaintance when she chose to. He knew that Jessica had sensed his attraction for Susannah Hamilton—and she, no doubt, had found his bumbling behavior amusing.

That thought embarrassed Ethan. He disliked appearing foolish in front of anyone, but particularly in the company of females. He picked up the package and unwrapped it, intending to put the book away. He had no interest in poetry; the flowery phrases and flowing lines of rhyming verse made little sense to his objective, logical mind. He decided to give the book to Jessica before she departed for California.

Idly, he opened the book to the first page, then rifled through several more pages; but the title of a short poem appearing on one page caught his attention. "She Was a Phantom of Delight," he read silently. His eyes moved over the first few lines.

> She was a phantom of delight
> When first she gleamed upon my sight;
> A lovely apparition, sent
> To be a moment's ornament.
> Her eyes as stars of twilight fair;
> Like twilight's, too, her dusky hair;

A picture began to form in Ethan's mind. Susannah Hamilton's dusky hair and gleaming eyes shimmered in his memory. He held his breath as he read on.

> But all things else about her drawn
> From May-time and the cheerful dawn;
> A dancing shape, an image gay,
> To haunt, to startle, and waylay.

Ethan felt infused with a sudden, sweet understanding. This poem spoke to him. His mind painted the words in images of shifting hue, and his heart felt the gentle brushstroke of each sentimental phrase. The effect was remarkable—like nothing he'd ever experienced before. He eagerly read on. The remaining two stanzas of the poem lodged in his consciousness, becoming the very embodiment of Susannah Hamilton, the most exquisite woman he'd ever encountered.

His musing was cut short by his mother's call to supper. He stumbled down the stairs, Susannah's form and voice saturating his thoughts. During the blessing that his father offered upon the food, Ethan had to consciously ban Susannah from his mind. His father's prayer was comprehensive. He thanked God for their food, their home and health; he asked for a blessing upon each member of the family and upon Jessica, too. He prayed for the recovery of Jessica's belongings and expressed his appreciation for Jessica's safe arrival and her presence in the Kade home. Every head around the table remained bent in prayer and every eye closed until the "Amen" was pronounced.

Conversation at the supper table revolved around the trip into town, the family's activities scheduled for the morrow, and Ethan's work at the cattle ranch; but Ethan's attention was consumed with the vision in his head of Susannah Hamilton. After supper Ethan's father left the house to visit a patient, and his mother and sister retired to the parlor. Ethan assumed Jessica would join the women in the sitting room, but she remained at the table while Ethan took his turn washing the supper dishes.

"So when you get to California, you want to teach school?" Ethan asked in a congenial tone. His question was designed merely to make conversation; he didn't expect Jessica to answer in any depth.

Jessica rested her elbows on the table. "Yes. I want to be a school teacher."

"Why in Sacramento? Is there something special about California?"

Jessica was silent for a moment before responding. "I read an article in a newspaper about California, and it captured my interest. And I wanted to come out west to see the country."

Ethan nodded. He scrubbed the residue of gravy off a soapy dish in the sink.

"I gathered from the discussion at the supper table that you work at a ranch," Jessica remarked.

"Yes. A cattle ranch located in the south end of the valley. It's owned by a fellow named John Bartlett. Both Samuel and I work at the ranch."

"Samuel is your brother?"

"That's right. My younger brother. You should meet him; you'd like Samuel."

Jessica didn't reply to that, instead she asked, "What sort of things do you and Samuel do at the ranch?"

Ethan dried the dish with a towel. "Well, we tend cattle mostly. Get them ready for market."

"How many cattle does Mr. Bartlett own?" she asked.

"About 1,500 head. Many Mormon cattlemen join the co-op cattle companies, but Bartlett's ranch operates independently. He has a good-sized herd for an independent rancher." Ethan picked up another dish and began toweling it dry.

"What kind of cattle do you raise on the ranch? Texas Longhorns?"

Ethan shook his head. "No. Not so much anymore. My father said that when he was a young man here in the valley in the early 1850s, most of the cattle brought in by the Saints were shorthorn breeds, mainly Devons and Durhams. But they were soon producing calves sired by the Mexican longhorn cattle introduced to Utah during the Spanish era."

Ethan put away his dish and towel and sat down at the table across from his cousin. "This was during the gold rush days, and California was experiencing a big influx of people. Pa said that cattle cost little to buy in Utah, but were bringing $60 to $150 a head in California. Later on, when gold and silver were discovered in our mountains, Utah had its own Gold Rush and cattlemen weren't able to keep up with the demand for beef. So they imported Texas longhorns. But cattle were also being purchased from Oregon trail herds."

Jessica seemed to be listening attentively, so Ethan went on. "The Oregon herds were Durham cattle, which for the most part had not interbred with the Texas longhorns and therefore maintained purer bloodlines. Brother Bartlett is trying to upgrade his cattle by introducing purebred Durhams into his herd."

"And so cattle ranching in the Utah Territory is thriving?"

"That's right. Now we export more cattle than we import." Ethan gave his cousin a quick grin. "I didn't know you were so interested in the cattle business."

A smile settled on Jessica's face. "I'm not. But I like learning about the West."

"And I thought you mainly liked poetry," Ethan teased.

Jessica dropped her gaze. "I hope you weren't annoyed with me today at the booksellers."

"Why would I be annoyed with you?" Ethan asked.

"I'm afraid I may have embarrassed you in front of Miss Hamilton. I didn't mean to—I was only trying to help you get acquainted with her, because you seemed to be feeling a little backward about it."

"A little backward, huh? I guess you could say that."

A sparkle crept into Jessica's eye. "Are you sweet on Miss Hamilton?"

"Like you said, I've only just become acquainted with her," he hedged.

"But you'd like to become better acquainted, wouldn't you?"

Ethan laughed. "Even if I did, I wouldn't admit it. I already have one too many books of poetry as it is."

"May I borrow your book of Wordsworth's poems when you're through reading it?" Jessica asked in a more serious tone.

"You can have it. I intended to give it to you, anyway."

"Really? You don't want the book?"

"Let's just say I'm not in the habit of reading poetry in the saddle while I'm tending steers."

Jessica laughed, and the sound of it was pleasing to Ethan's ears. He gazed at his cousin—she looked attractive in the new frock his mother had purchased for her that day, with her auburn hair pulled into a loose bun at the nape of her neck and a touch of warmth lighting her gray eyes. Perhaps his initial impression of her had been wrong. Perhaps she wasn't as disagreeable as he'd first thought. In a few days more she'd be back on the train traveling toward California, and he'd likely never see her again. That thought carried with it a hint of disappointment. He would have liked getting to know his cousin better.

# CHAPTER FIVE

While Jessica was outside in the back yard with Birgithe, her aunt came out of the house carrying a letter in her hand.

"This just arrived for you," Inger said, giving her the note. Her aunt's face wore a smile, and her eyes sparkled with expectation. "Along with your traveling bag."

"What?" Jessica exclaimed. "My bag is here?"

Her aunt nodded.

Jessica opened the letter and quickly read it. The note was from the sheriff in Corinne, stating that he'd recovered her satchel and put it on the train. A hotel owner in town had found the piece of luggage left in one of the rooms after the occupant left, and when no one came to claim it, he brought it to the sheriff's office. The man renting the room had apparently left town, but the sheriff felt sure he was the thief who had stolen Jessica's bag.

Jessica breathed out a sigh of relief. With her heart pounding, she followed her aunt into the house and saw her satchel resting in the hallway. She carried it upstairs to the room she shared with Birgithe and set it on the bed; holding her breath, she unfastened the clasp and thrust her hand inside. She found a few articles of clothing lying crumpled in the bottom of the bag, but all of her money was missing. With trembling hands, she pushed the clothing aside. There, resting in one corner of the bag, was the framed portrait her mother had given her.

Tears nearly started in her eyes as she removed the drawing from the bag and sat down to look at it. The pencil sketch, mounted in a simple, wooden frame, was a portrait of her grandmother, Lydia Kade, drawn when Lydia was a young woman. Her husband had sketched the drawing before they were married. Lydia had wed Christian Kade after the death of her first husband, who was Elizabeth and James' natural father. The portrait was precious to Elizabeth because it was the only likeness she had of her mother. Lydia had given it to her as a remembrance when the family moved west; and Elizabeth had, in turn, given it to Jessica when she left home.

Jessica ran her finger over the smooth glass protecting the sketch, studying the features of her grandmother's face. The young woman pictured on the page had wide, lovely eyes, a petite nose, and a serene smile. Her hair was drawn flowing and loose to her shoulders. Jessica's mother had once remarked on Jessica's strong resemblance to her grandmother. They had the same thick, red hair, similar shaped eyes, and fair complexion, her mother had told her.

She tilted the drawing toward the window to catch more sunlight. She'd never met her grandparents. She knew only they'd met and married in Missouri, lived for a few years in Nauvoo, Illinois, and then come out west with the Mormons to Utah Territory. Jessica had not been much interested in their history until now.

She carefully replaced the drawing inside her traveling bag, then tucked the satchel safely inside the closet of Birgithe's room. She left the bedroom and started downstairs, intending to go back outside to join Birgithe in the yard.

As she reached the bottom step, the door to her uncle's office opened and he stepped out of the room, accompanied by a youth who bore a clean, white, cloth bandage wrapped around his left forearm. Her uncle paused to smile at her. "Hello, Jessica," he said. The boy glanced at her, too. "Billy, this is my niece, Jessica Scott. She's staying with us for the time being," her uncle said to the youth at his side. "Jessica, meet Billy Fenton, a young patient and friend of mine."

The boy gave Jessica a lop-sided grin. "Nice to meet ya," he said.

"And you," she nodded.

"Billy's family live just on the next block. I've known his father for years." James patted the boy's shoulder. "Billy is a fine young man, like his father."

The boy brushed a lock of unruly, brown hair out of his eyes. "Dr. Kade has been looking after this sore arm of mine," he said to Jessica, indicating the cloth bandage on his forearm. "I cut it on a piece of Pa's farming machinery, and it wasn't healing up too well until your uncle started tending it."

Jessica murmured a reply. The boy appeared to be no older than fifteen or sixteen, but his shoulders were broad and he was tall and sturdy-looking. Jessica guessed he was well acquainted with the back-breaking work of farming.

The youth started toward the door leading to the outside. "Come back the day after tomorrow, Billy, and I'll change that dressing for you," James told him.

"Thanks, doc," the boy replied.

James opened the front door for him, and Jessica caught a glimpse of Birgithe sitting on the porch. She saw Billy pause to talk with her and heard Birgithe's shy giggle. Jessica's uncle returned to her side. "Billy's father is an old friend of mine," he said. "He's been living here in the valley for about as long as I have."

Jessica nodded without commenting.

"The boy has developed an ulcer on his forearm, which we're having a difficult time treating. I'm fearful the ulcer is growing larger, rather than shrinking. And it continues to weep fluid and blood." A frown creased James' brow. "I need more medical supplies on hand, but it's often difficult to get them sent out west to me."

Jessica looked at her uncle, wondering why he was bothering to tell her all of this.

"Inger brought your traveling bag to you?" James asked.

"Yes, she did."

"Were any of your personal belongings still inside?"

"A few things. Not much." She thought of the framed portrait and nearly mentioned it to her uncle, but decided against it. "All of my money is gone, however."

"I can help you with that if you'll allow me to."

Jessica swallowed the impulse to accept her uncle's offer. "No, thank you. My father will be sending money to me shortly." She gulped, hoping the words proved to be truthful. She'd sent her father a telegram and written him a letter the day after arriving at the Kades' home, explaining about the theft of her bag and the consequent loss of most of her money. She hoped that he'd send her additional funds so she could continue on to Sacramento.

"If your situation should change, my invitation is always open," James replied.

"I'll keep that in mind."

"Can you step into my office for a moment? I've something I'd like to show you."

Curious about what her uncle wished to share with her, Jessica followed him into his medical office.

"You can take a seat there, if you'd like to," James said, gesturing to a pair of slat-backed, wooden chairs.

Jessica went to one of the chairs and sat down. Her eyes roved over the office. A bed rested against one wall, and beside it was a washstand with a bowl and pitcher. In the corner sat a glass-fronted cabinet filled with books and medical journals. Within a closet off to one side, Jessica glimpsed shelves filled with medicine bottles, bandages, and medical instruments. She tucked her feet under the chair and gazed at a large, framed picture hanging on the wall done in watercolors. The painting depicted a serene, shimmering stream of burnished gold, shaded by graceful trees. The peaceful scene drew her in, creating a feeling of calm.

James stepped to the book cabinet and reached to the bottom shelf. "I've been wanting to show these drawings to you ever since you arrived, and I just haven't had a moment to do so until now." He removed a bulky envelope from the shelf and sat down with it on the chair next to hers.

Jessica glanced at the envelope, waiting to see what was inside.

"You must have been intrigued, as I was, by the journey west," James said. "What interested you the most about the trip? Was it the train ride itself, or the country you passed through?" He bent forward, focused on her reply.

Jessica thought about his question. "Well, at first it was the novelty of traveling by rail."

James nodded.

"But after we left the Eastern cities and moved out onto the prairie, I was struck by the beauty of the land."

"Yes. I agree. I remember how the prairie lands stretched in every direction as far as the eye could see. The tall prairie grass came up to the hubs of our wagon wheels."

Jessica imagined traveling the prairie by wagon, instead of by swift-running train. It would have been a long and arduous trip. She was grateful for the modern steam engine that ate up forty miles of track an hour. Jessica was eager now to share her impressions. "The ride from Omaha to Cheyenne was full of novel sights. We passed across the Elkhorn River and stopped briefly at stations in Fremont, Grand Island, Kearney, and Plum Creek. One of the train officials told me that Plum Creek was the site of an Indian massacre."

"We saw a few Indians ourselves when we made the journey west in 1848—some Pawnee and Sioux." James' face broke into a sudden, unexpected grin. "I wouldn't have admitted it then, but they scared the dickens out of me."

"I saw a group of Indians at the train station when we stopped in Cheyenne. They looked fierce, dressed in their leather leggings and their necklaces of beads and feathers," Jessica related. "I couldn't take my eyes off them."

James chuckled aloud at this last remark. "And then you caught your first glimpse of the Rockies," he offered.

"Yes. In Wyoming Territory. The mountains are even more spectacular than I'd imagined them to be. Such rugged, jagged slopes. Green valleys and lofty, snow-capped peaks." Jessica stopped abruptly. She hadn't intended to be so open with her feelings or allow herself to connect emotionally with her uncle. She swallowed, and dropped her gaze.

"You're right—the mountains surrounding this valley are magnificent. I never tire of looking at them."

Jessica glanced up at her uncle.

"My favorite time of day is just before dusk when the sun is ready to slip behind the western peaks. Its fading rays cast a reddish glow on the mountainsides to the east.

I often stand on the east porch of the house at that time of evening to watch the color wash over the mountain."

Jessica was captivated by the picture her uncle painted.

"The mountains are the crown, and the royal robes of this country spread majestically in every direction. You saw that for yourself as you traveled the breadth of this continent."

Jessica knew exactly what her uncle was referring to—the fields of colorful wildflowers, the crystalline streams, the peculiar rock formations carved by thousands of years of wind and water. Her thoughts returned to the moment as she watched her uncle open the envelope he held on his lap. He withdrew a bundle of loose papers, all of uniform size. He lifted the first sheet from the pile and turned it toward her. On the page was a drawing of something she recognized instantly. "Why, that's Chimney Rock, isn't it? I saw it at a distance from the window of the train!" she exclaimed.

"Yes, that's what it is. And here's a rendering of Devil's Gap and another of Ancient Ruins Bluff."

James showed her the drawings one by one. Some images she recognized from her journey west, others she was unfamiliar with. "These were drawn as you traveled west by wagon, weren't they?" she asked her uncle.

He nodded. "Did you ever see anything like this?" he asked, holding up another sketch for her inspection.

"I surely did. Only once, though, out on the plains." She smiled as she studied the herd of shaggy, hump-shouldered buffalo racing across the page of paper.

There were drawings not only of buffalo and prairie dogs, and wizened-looking lizards; but also depicted were delicate flowers, barren sagebrush, and curiously-shaped rocks.

"Did you make these drawings, Uncle James?" she asked, glancing from one sketch to another. The sketches were not perfect in form or detail, but they conveyed an accurate pictorial account of the journey west.

"Me? No. Absolutely not," James answered with a chuckle. "I can't draw a straight line. These sketches were made by my father as we traveled west."

"Do you mean Christian Kade?" Her mind flew to the pencil drawing tucked inside Birgithe's closet.

James nodded. "Father wasn't the best artist, but he enjoyed sketching things that captured his interest. Someday these drawings will pass to his grandchildren." He gave her a smile, and it was filled with all the warmth of a summer sun shining on the grassy prairie.

Jessica felt a lump form in her throat. She lowered her gaze, pretending to examine the drawings more closely. The very thing she had wanted to avoid had happened—an emotional tie was growing, binding her ever tighter to her uncle and his family.

The following morning after breakfast, Jessica slipped outdoors to help Birgithe clear weeds from the flower garden around the front porch. Spring flowers—crocus, daffodil, and iris—lent a colorful accent to the pink, painted porch. It was a warm, sunny morning with the smell of moist earth strong in the air. Jessica breathed in the heady fragrance of earth and grass and blossoming trees. A trio of sea gulls wheeled overhead, soaring and diving through the air like silver-tipped arrows loosed from a bow. Jessica stood with her hands on her waist, watching the sea gulls wing through the sky.

"They're graceful, aren't they?" Birgithe remarked as she spaded a patch of rich, brown soil.

"Yes," Jessica replied. "But what are they doing out here in the desert? I thought sea gulls made their homes near the oceans."

"It's the Great Salt Lake that attracts them. There're thousands of birds nesting along its shores."

"Is the lake really a salt sea?" asked Jessica. She remembered reading a brief description of the lake in her *Crofutt's Trans-Continental Tourist's Guide.*

"Oh, yes. Anciently, it was a very great sea, much larger than it is today. My Uncle Lars knows all about its history. He once joined Captain Stansbury on an exploration of the lake for a government survey. He's the one who told us about the age of the lake."

"Uncle Lars?" Jessica repeated with a puzzled look.

"Uh huh," Birgithe nodded. "Uncle Lars is Mother's younger brother. You'd like him so much if you met him, but he's away right now exploring. He's probably perched on the ridge of a high cliff to get just the right view of some rare bird, or such."

"Why would he be doing that?" Jessica asked.

"Because Uncle Lars is a wildlife and landscape artist. He travels all over the Territory doing watercolors for a number of magazines to which he sells his work."

"Oh."

"We have some of his watercolors framed and hanging in the house. You've probably seen the one in the parlor, and Father has a landscape scene on the wall of his office. Ethan has one, too, in his room."

Jessica remembered the tranquil painting of brook and trees she'd noticed in her uncle's office. She'd admired the watercolor, and her appreciation for it was enhanced now, knowing the artist's background and his connection to the family.

Birgithe went back to working the soil with her spade.

The sea gulls circling overhead were calling out in their raucous, high-pitched voices. Jessica shaded her eyes and peered up at them again. "These birds are noisy, aren't they? I'd find them bothersome after a time," she remarked, frowning.

Birgithe glanced up at the sea gulls. "The gulls are never a nuisance to us. We like having them around. Just the year before my father came to this valley, the sea gulls saved the people's crops in a miraculous way."

"Really? How did they do that?" The skepticism in Jessica's voice was apparent.

Birgithe sat back on her heels. "Father has told us the story often. It happened the summer before he arrived, but he heard about the incident from those here at the time. The Saints planted crops the first year when they came to the valley. Just before the crops were ready to be harvested, a horde of big, black crickets moved into the fields, devouring all that had been planted. The people came armed with anything they could use—brooms, blankets, shovels—to kill the thousands of crickets who were infesting their fields and eating their crops. But it was useless; there were too many crickets to kill them all. Then, suddenly, a large flock of sea gulls flew in. At first, the people thought the sea gulls, too, were going to eat their crops, but then they realized the sea gulls were eating the crickets!"

Jessica listened to the account without commenting.

"The sea gulls ate as many crickets as they could hold, then they flew out to the lake and regurgitated them. Then they came back to the fields and ate more. They repeated this same thing until the crickets were gone from the fields. It was a miracle, and all the people realized it. That's why the sea gulls are never considered a nuisance to the Saints."

Jessica was doubtful about the truthfulness of this story. She wanted to ask Birgithe for more details because the tale seemed so implausible. But she kept silent.

Birgithe returned to her gardening, humming a cheerful tune as she worked. Jessica gripped a second spade and started digging around a stubborn, prickly weed. She worked in silence, listening to her cousin's lilting melody and thinking about the story Birgithe had just related.

Before long, Birgithe turned to her and asked, "Did you happen to see the boy my father was treating yesterday afternoon? His arm was bandaged."

Jessica looked up from her weeding. "Yes, your father introduced him to me outside his office. I don't remember his name, though."

A soft look crept into Birgithe's eyes. "It's Billy Fenton. Did you think he was handsome?"

Jessica recalled the youth's unkempt hair and coarse farm clothing. "I suppose so," she answered.

"Oh, I think he's very handsome. And so nice, too, and smart." Birgithe ducked her face, but not before Jessica spied the blush growing on her cheeks.

Jessica set down her spade, smiling. "I see. And how long have you had feelings for Billy?"

Birgithe giggled. "Ever so long. In a few more years, when I'm old enough, I'm going to marry him."

"Does Billy know this?"

"Not yet. But I think he likes me, too. He sat beside me at our school picnic."

"That's a sure sign of his affection," Jessica replied.

"Uh huh. I think so, too."

As the two of them set to work again in the flower garden, Jessica's thoughts wandered back to the story of the sea gulls and the crickets. She wondered if her cousin was mistaken about the incident or had embellished it to make the story sound more impressive. But one question kept nagging at her mind. She finally voiced her thoughts. "Birgithe, when the sea gulls came to the fields that time and devoured the crickets, had the people been praying for a miracle to save their crops?"

"Yes, I'm sure they prayed. Perhaps they didn't pray for a miracle, but they would have prayed for help to protect their crops from the insects." Birgithe studied her cousin's face. "Why do you ask?"

Jessica hesitated before answering. "Yesterday, when my traveling bag arrived at the house, you said something about it being an answer to prayer. What did you mean by that?"

"We've been asking Heavenly Father in our family prayers to please help you find your bag," Birgithe replied slowly.

"Yes."

"He answered that prayer, and even though your money was gone and some of your belongings, the thing that was most important to you was still in the satchel. Wasn't it?"

The drawing of her grandmother flashed into Jessica's mind. She had shown Birgithe the portrait and told her how she'd found it in the bottom of the bag, undisturbed. "Yes," she said quietly.

"You see. Heavenly Father answered your prayer. He always answers prayers."

Jessica considered her cousin's words. "But *I* never prayed about the bag being found. It wasn't *my* prayer he heard."

"That's all right. We were praying for you—in your behalf," Birgithe answered simply.

Jessica mulled over this last comment. Then she asked, "How often do you pray, Birgithe?"

"How often?" Birgithe repeated. "Oh, I don't know. Every day, of course, in the mornings when I wake up and in the evenings before I go to sleep. But I pray more than just at those times. I pray whenever I need something or want to thank Heavenly Father for my blessings." She blinked and then asked, "How often do you pray?"

"Me? Never. Well, I haven't for many years, anyway. I've forgotten how to offer a prayer."

"Oh." Birgithe's eyes widened in surprise.

Jessica felt compelled to follow the train of conversation. "When you pray, Birgithe, how long do you do it?"

"Do you mean how much time does a prayer take to say?"

Jessica nodded.

"That depends on what you're praying for. Enos prayed one whole day when he wanted to obtain forgiveness from his sins."

"Who's Enos? A friend of yours?" asked Jessica.

Birgithe's mouth twitched with a smile. "No. Enos was a Book of Mormon prophet."

Jessica stared at her cousin, unsure of the younger girl's meaning.

"Here, let me show you." Birgithe stood up and brushed the dirt off her apron, then motioned for Jessica to follow her into the house.

They went in through the front door and walked down the short hallway into the parlor. Birgithe removed a brown, hard-bound book from the mantle above the fireplace and began thumbing purposefully through the pages. "Here it is. You can read it for yourself." She held the book out to Jessica, her finger marking the appropriate place.

Jessica took the book and stared at the title printed on its spine—The Book of Mormon. She'd heard about the gold Bible that a man named Joseph Smith had supposedly dug out of the ground, but she'd never seen a copy of the book until now.

"The verses about Enos aren't very many," Birgithe said. "It won't take much time to read." She gave Jessica a smile. "Just keep the book as long as you like. When you're through with it, you can put it back on the mantle."

With those words, Birgithe left the parlor to return to her work in the flower garden. Jessica stood eyeing the book with suspicion. In the short amount of time she'd been in the Kades' home, she'd learned that they were devoted to their religion. She'd always been told by her parents and others that the Mormons were a fanatical, egotistical lot, whose beliefs bordered on blasphemy. Yet she hadn't seen any such behavior among the Kades. Despite the tales that filled her head, Jessica was curious about this book that had given rise to such ridicule and persecution against the Latter-day Saints and their church.

# CHAPTER SIX

Ethan poked his head inside the parlor. "Do you know where Jessica is?" he asked his sister. Birgithe, who was seated in the room mending a tear in her white, cotton apron, looked up from her sewing.

"Outside on the porch, I think. That's where she said she was going."

"Thanks." Ethan went out the front door and started across the porch, his boots echoing on the plank floor with each step. The roofed veranda continued along all four sides of the house, and chairs placed at intervals along the long porch gave it an inviting air. Ethan found his cousin seated on the east side of the house. "You're sitting on the wrong porch."

Jessica glanced up at him with a start. "What?"

Ethan chuckled. "If you want to watch the sunset, you're sitting on the wrong side of the house. You should be on the west porch."

"Oh," Jessica said, smiling. "Actually, I wanted to see the glow on the mountains as the sun sets."

Ethan glanced at the mountains' rearing shoulders. A pink light tinted the mountainside giving it the appearance of coral. "Do you mind if I join you?"

In answer, Jessica nodded toward the empty chair next to hers.

Ethan eased into the chair, folded his arms against his chest, and stared out at the mountains. They rose in a jagged block of solid rock, red in the dying sunlight.

"I've never seen anything so beautiful," Jessica said.

Ethan eyed the towering range. "If you think this is beautiful, you should see the mountains in winter all dressed in snow. That's beauty enough to steal your breath away."

Jessica folded her hands in her lap, but didn't reply.

They fell into a comfortable silence, focusing on the glow lighting the mountain peaks. When shadows began to creep across the slopes, Ethan turned to his cousin and said, "You seem to like the mountain scenery and the peacefulness of the valley—have you given any thought to staying here to teach school instead of going on to Sacramento?"

Jessica looked at him in surprise.

"I know my family would like to see you stay longer. Why don't you consider it?"

"No, Ethan. My plans are to go on to California."

"Change your plans," Ethan urged, giving her his best grin. "We're not so bad, are we, as far as relatives go?"

Jessica averted her gaze. "I can't. As soon as my trunk gets here, I'll be leaving."

The grin faded from Ethan's face. "Sounds like your mind is set."

"Yes."

Ethan hunched over in the chair, staring at his hands. "I'm heading back to the ranch in a couple of days. I promised Brother Bartlett I'd be back in time to help round up the cattle for branding. He wants to start sorting and branding the steers by the first of next week."

"Oh. Will you be staying at the ranch for a while before coming home again?"

"Yes. Once we get started with the roundup, our spring chores begin in earnest. Neither Samuel nor I will be back to the city for a couple of months."

Jessica didn't offer a reply.

Ethan glanced at his cousin from the corner of his eye. He would be sorry to say goodbye to her. If given the time and opportunity, he and Jessica might have established a closer tie. He gazed out at the mountains. The rosy glow on the mountainside was fading to gray as the sun slipped behind the western peaks.

Suddenly, an idea occurred to him. "While you're waiting for your trunk, why don't you come out to the ranch with me for a few days? I think you'd like it there. You could stay a day or two, or however long you want, and then Samuel or I could see you back home."

Jessica's eyes widened. "My trunk ought to arrive any day now. I should stay here making preparations to catch the train to Sacramento."

"When your trunk does come, Father can send someone to the ranch to let us know. There are plenty of boys in town who wouldn't mind riding out to give us the message. Then you can come back to the city and be on your way. How does that sound to you?"

"I don't know. I'd have to think about it."

"Oh, come on," Ethan grinned, giving his cousin a nudge with his elbow. "It'd be fun. I could teach you how to rope a steer."

Jessica flung him a sideways glance. "Just what I've always wanted to do."

"Honestly, you'd find the ranch interesting. If you want to see what the West is all about, cattle ranching is the best example there is." Ethan could see her hesitate. Her brow worked, and she chewed her bottom lip. "You want to meet Samuel, don't you? He'd be disappointed if you left without meeting him," Ethan persisted.

Jessica's gray eyes were hidden in shadow. "I'll think about it," she repeated, but this time her tone sounded more amenable to the idea.

"Good. That's good." Ethan turned away, smiling to himself. He felt hopeful that he'd gained a few extra days with her.

The next morning Ethan arose early because he wanted to work for awhile in the field for his father, then ride into town. This time he planned to go into the city alone, without female companions. He intended to visit the Quill and Ink again and try to mend the ill impression of himself he'd left with Susannah Hamilton. He gulped a glass of cold milk, then hurried outside.

Taking the harrow from the shed, Ethan headed for the unplanted field behind the house. The field was not large, just a few acres. Ethan's father did not own a farm outside the city limits like many of the Saints; most of the family's income derived from his father's medical practice. His father wasn't always paid in cash—much of the time payment was made in the form of potatoes, onions, beans, apples, watermelon, or pears. This supplemented the fresh produce the family raised themselves in the field behind the house. That, in addition to the few chickens, pigs, and cows they kept in the yard.

His father had already plowed, and all that remained before planting was to harrow the ground. Ethan pushed the harrow through the thick, rich soil, breaking up the clods left from plowing. Before planting seed, the clods of earth needed to be broken into smaller pieces in order for tender, growing shoots to surface. The implement Ethan wielded consisted of a wooden frame with handles and a row of iron teeth set at the foot. It was smaller than the steel plow his father used to turn the soil.

Ethan worked for more than an hour, his thoughts centered on his task. He'd harrowed a good section of ground by the time breakfast was ready and on the table. After breakfast there were additional chores to do before he could think about going into town. He worked quickly, saying little to Birgithe or Jessica, for he didn't want the girls questioning him about his plans for the afternoon.

At last, when the sun peaked in the sky, Ethan changed out of his work clothes into a fresh shirt and pair of cotton trousers, and carefully combed his hair into place. His mother, sister, and cousin were preparing to visit relatives, which provided a perfect opportunity for Ethan to slip away undisturbed.

Ethan saddled his horse and urged the gelding into a canter. He was excited, though apprehensive, about seeing Susannah again. The palms of his hands itched with perspiration as he reined the horse. The afternoon sun was warm on his shoulders as he rode the few blocks into the center of town.

Before long he reached the vicinity of Second South and Main Street, where the Quill and Ink establishment was located, sandwiched between a mercantile on one side and a tailoring shop on the other. Ethan dismounted and tied his horse to the hitching post outside the booksellers. He removed his hat and ran a hand over his hair to smooth it, drew a deep breath, and pushed open the door. The small bell above the door tinkled invitingly.

He deliberately avoided looking toward the counter and instead headed for a shelf along the wall, pretending to be studying the book titles. He hadn't paid much attention to his surroundings before, because he'd been focused on meeting

Susannah. But this afternoon he took an opportunity to look around. The room was cramped and crowded with bookcases. Two windows let in the sunlight. A set of stairs in a back corner climbed upward to the second floor of the building, where the bindery was located.

After what he guessed was a suitable amount of time spent in browsing, he made a quick, surreptitious glance to the counter at the head of the shop. He nearly choked with disappointment when instead of Susannah's slender form, he sighted a middle-aged, buxom woman behind the counter.

Where was Susannah? Had she left the shop for the day? Was she away on some errand? He stared at the plump woman, his shoulders sagging.

While he stood considering what action to take, a door behind the counter connecting the book shop with the family's living quarters opened, and Susannah entered into the room. Ethan stared at her, unable to draw his eyes away. He noticed at once the way her raven hair was swept up into a loose knot, revealing the soft curve of her chin. He stood, mesmerized, by the slimness of her figure as she moved to the older woman's side and began speaking with her. His eyes reveled in the vivid blueness of her skirt, and the ivory lace collar dressing her delicate throat. Ethan noted every detail about her, from the top of her glistening, dark head to the tips of her high-buttoned shoes peeking from beneath her skirt. He stood motionless, holding his breath in wonder.

As he waited beside the tall bookshelf, partially hidden from the view of the two women at the counter, he heard the older woman's harsh voice. "Your father is very angry with you, Susannah. He told you in specific terms to stay away from that rascal, Edward Grayson."

Ethan shrank back against the bookshelf. The conversation reaching his ears was undoubtedly a private one, yet he couldn't help hoping to overhear a word or two more of it.

"I needed to hear an explanation from his own lips, Mama. That's all I was doing," Susannah replied.

"You're not to see him again, Susannah."

Ethan heard a murmured response. He saw the older woman give Susannah a sharp look, then the woman untied her apron and hung it on a peg beside the counter. She and Susannah exchanged a few words more, then the plump woman exited the book shop through the door leading into the family's private residence. Ethan caught a glimpse of Susannah's frown as she watched the door close behind her mother.

Ethan turned away, feeling guilty for eavesdropping on the women's conversation. He walked to an adjacent bookcase that held a number of thick volumes, pulled one of them from the shelf, and looked at the title. *The Elements of Science.* He opened the book and let his eyes wander over the printed page, but his mind was not on what he read. Who was Edward Grayson, he wondered? And why was Susannah forbidden to see him? The mystery intrigued him only because every aspect about Susannah Hamilton intrigued him. He darted a glance past the bookcase. Susannah was standing behind the counter, deep in thought. Her pink mouth was drawn into a tight little pout, and a line creased her marble brow.

Ethan replaced the book on the shelf and picked up another. The title of this one read *The American Practice of Medicine*. The title captured his attention, and he thumbed through the first few pages of the book. Several illustrations enhanced the text. One of the drawings depicted a physician in the process of lancing a boil. The picture intrigued him because he'd seen his father perform the same kind of procedure.

"Have you an interest in medicine, as well as poetry?"

The silky, female voice startled him, causing the book to nearly tumble from his hand. He fumbled with it, trying to keep it in his grasp. Turning, he found Susannah at his side, regarding him with one lifted brow.

"Uh, no. That is, yes. I mean, I am interested in medicine," he stuttered. He was unprepared for her sudden appearance and her direct question. Beads of sweat broke out on his forehead.

Now both of Susannah's dark brows rose in silent question.

"That is to say, my father is interested in medicine," he continued in a halting voice. "He's a physician," Ethan concluded lamely. He felt humiliated, for he hadn't gotten through one word without stammering. He replaced the book on the shelf, feeling foolish.

"I see. You came in a few days ago, didn't you? I don't recall your name . . ." She let the sentence dangle to encourage his reply.

Ethan cringed—she hadn't even remembered his name. "Kade. Ethan Kade," he muttered.

"So your father is Dr. Kade?"

"Yes. Have you heard of him?" Perhaps here, at last, was some common ground. He stood up straighter, hopeful.

Susannah shook her dark head. "No, I haven't."

"Oh."

"Are you looking for a particular book on medicine for your father?"

"No, not really. I was just browsing."

"Have you enjoyed your Wordsworth?" she asked after an awkward silence.

"I haven't had time to do much reading in it yet," he answered, glancing at her. Her emerald eyes were two glittering gems. She looked like a goddess sculpted from flawless marble. Ethan sucked in his breath. "I appreciate your help in picking out the book, though."

"That's what I'm here for," she replied.

Ethan nodded, breathless.

"Let me know if I can be of further service." She turned, ready to walk away.

"Wait," Ethan blurted. He wanted to still talk with her, look at her, get to know her better.

She paused. "Yes?"

"I, uh, there is something more you could help me with."

She waited for his explanation.

"My cousin . . . I'd like to get a book for my cousin. The one you met the other day—she came in here with me that day." He was babbling on and had to make a conscious effort to stop himself.

"Yes, I remember. She's planning to teach school, isn't she?"

"That's right. I'd like to surprise her with a book she could use in her schoolroom."

Susannah gave him a small smile. To Ethan, that smile was the most wondrous sight he'd ever beheld. He smiled broadly in response to it.

"Well, let me think," Susannah mused, tapping a finger on her chin. Ethan noticed how small and delicate her hands were. His heart beat faster thinking how marvelous it would feel to have her hand rest in his, if only for a moment.

"Let's look over here," she suggested at last, moving toward the opposite side of the room.

Ethan followed her, his eyes fastened on the swaying of her full skirt.

She paused at a bookcase, stood on tiptoe, and reached to an upper shelf, where her fingers traveled over the spines of several books before stopping to pull one from the lot. "This is one she might enjoy having. It's called *Lectures on Schoolkeeping*, written by Mr. Samuel Hall." She held the book out to Ethan. "Is this what you had in mind?"

Ethan took the book from her hand and as he did so their fingers brushed slightly, sending a tingle down his spine. He opened the cover and glanced at a page or two. "Yes, I think she'd like it."

Susannah was already studying the titles of several more books on the shelf. She removed another from the uppermost shelf. "This is a study on schoolkeeping authored by Mr. David Page, entitled *Theory and Practice of Teaching.*" She handed this one, also, to Ethan.

Ethan juggled both books in his hand.

"Or this one," Susannah continued, drawing a third book from the shelf.

Ethan grinned as she held out the volume for his inspection. "You certainly have a number of books to choose from. I had no idea this decision would be so complex."

Susannah's face softened with a smile. "Any of these volumes would be appropriate for your cousin, I'm sure."

Ethan took hold of the third book. He smiled at her, then read the title aloud. "*The Teacher.* That sounds simple enough."

"First impressions can often be misleading," Susannah responded. Her expression was sober, but Ethan thought he detected a gleam of playfulness in her eye.

Ethan's gaze held hers for a brief moment. He felt a pang of disappointment when she turned away. How blissful it would be to spend an eternity gazing into those emerald eyes.

"Perhaps your cousin might like instead a textbook from which to teach her pupils. The texts are over here." Susannah led him to a bookcase near the center of the room and selected a slim volume from among the books arranged on the shelf in a tidy row.

Ethan stood nearby, his arms burdened with the three volumes she had given him already.

"Here's one. *Advanced Lectures on Arithmetic.*" She placed the book on the heap in Ethan's arms and continued to search for other titles. "We also have grammars, readers, and geographies. Here's a copy of McGuffey's *First Eclectic Reader.*" She glanced up at Ethan.

Ethan was busy admiring her head of gleaming dark hair, rather than paying heed to the various books she'd been suggesting. "Uh, the *Reader* might be good," he answered hastily.

She bent closer to the books lining the shelf. "Here's McGuffey's *Sixth Reader,* but we also have his newer 'speakers.'" She raised up until she was eye-level with the shelf above. "Or if you prefer Henry Days' *Elements of the Art of Rhetoric,* it's a very good text from which to teach rhetorics and elocution." She stood and looked him in the eye. "Are any of these to your liking?"

Ethan set the books he'd been holding onto a nearby table. "I don't know," he smiled. "What would be your recommendation?"

"That all depends on what you're looking for. If none of these books appeal to you, we can take a look at the geographies, natural histories, or biological sciences. They're shelved over here." Susannah started toward a different set of bookshelves.

"No, wait," Ethan said quickly. "I already have more books to choose from than I can handle." He picked up the arithmetic book and looked at its cover. "You certainly know your trade," he said, smiling at her. "I could never remember which books contained what, or even where they were shelved."

Susannah eyed him with an even expression. "You could if you spent as much time working at it as I do."

Ethan seized the open door Susannah provided for him. "Do you work here every day?" he inquired in what he hoped was a casual tone.

"I tend the counter Monday through Saturday," she told him. "I usually take the afternoon shift, and my mother is here in the mornings."

"Do you like the work?" Ethan asked with genuine interest. He'd forgotten all about the books on the table.

"Yes. I like meeting people and talking with them."

An image of Edward Grayson—or what he imagined Edward Grayson to look like—darted through his mind. He wondered if Susannah had met Grayson here in the book shop and engaged in clever conversation with him. Ethan felt the sting of jealousy. He tried harder to impress Susannah with his charms. "I like meeting new people, too, but I don't often see a lot of folks where I work." He hoped she'd follow along the trail of conversation he'd blazed for them.

"Oh? Where do you work?" She tilted her head and gazed steadily at him.

Ethan smiled with satisfaction. "I'm a ranch hand. I work on a cattle ranch in South Willow Creek. I hope to have my own cattle ranch some day."

"Is that so?" Susannah replied.

Ethan displayed what he considered to be his most engaging smile. "Yes. Ranching can be a prosperous enterprise if one works hard and manages his resources carefully." He wanted her to know he was a hard working fellow.

"I'm sure. I'm afraid I don't know much about cattle ranching, however."

He grinned at her. "You could if you spent as much time working at it as I do."

A smile surfaced on Susannah's face, and it set his heart racing. "Have you decided on a book yet, Mr. Kade?" she asked, revealing the dimples in her cheeks.

Ethan drove his eyes away from her face and peered down at the title of the book he was holding. *"Advanced Lectures on Arithmetic.* That sounds threatening."

Susannah chuckled softly. Her laughter reminded Ethan of a gently falling spring rain. "It's probably not as ominous as it seems if you have a head for figures," she said.

Ethan pretended to be studying a page from the book. "I'll bet facts and figures have no trouble staying put in that pretty head of yours." Glancing up, he was dismayed to see a hardness settle over her face.

"Do you wish to see any other books?" she asked with an unmistakable chill in her voice.

Ethan shuddered. *Oh, no,* he thought in despair. He'd said the wrong thing. His glib compliment had not impressed her as he'd hoped, but instead given offense. His stomach began to churn. "No, these are fine. I'll take one of these books. Thank you," he said meekly.

"You may bring it to the counter when you're ready, Mr. Kade." Her voice was as frosty as a winter morning. She turned and walked away from him.

Ethan's heart sank. He didn't know how to recover the slight advantage he'd gained with her. He was certain that she suspected he'd made up the entire story about wanting to purchase a book for Jessica as a flimsy excuse to flirt with her. And he had, to begin with. But getting a book for his cousin was a good idea—one he wanted to pursue— though Susannah would probably never believe that now. He gripped the textbook on arithmetic and walked to the counter with it. Susannah was helping another customer, and Ethan had to wait his turn. The waiting was torturous. He'd so wanted to make a favorable impression on her. And he'd totally bungled it. Again.

The customer took his newly purchased book, wrapped in brown paper and string, and left the store. Ethan stepped up to the counter. "Thank you for your help. I'm sure my cousin will find this book useful." He handed the volume to Susannah to wrap for him.

"I'm sure she will," Susannah replied without looking at him. "The price of the book is one dollar and seventy-five cents."

Ethan handed her the money. He watched glumly as she wrapped his purchase in paper and string. She was nearly finished with the packaging when her mother stepped through the door from the adjoining room. "I'll finish that, Susannah. Your father is home and wishes to speak with you," Mrs. Hamilton said.

Ethan saw an apprehensive look flicker across Susannah's face. "All right," she replied to her mother. She smoothed the skirt of her dress and gave Ethan a furtive glance before crossing the doorway and into the family residence.

"I hope you enjoy the book, young man," Susannah's mother said to him as she tied the last bit of string into a tight bow.

"It's not for me. The book's a gift for my cousin," he mumbled. His eyes were fastened on the door closing behind Susannah. He wished he could accompany Susannah into the next room, support her in the reprimand from her father, which he guessed was forthcoming in connection with the Grayson fellow. He felt a strange, fierce desire to shield her, protect her. He consciously shrugged off the feeling. What right did he have to think he could protect her from anything? She didn't like him—hadn't even remembered his name from when he came into the book shop four days before.

"Here's your package. I hope your cousin is pleased with the book," Mrs. Hamilton said to him.

Ethan took the parcel from her hand. For an instant he studied the woman's face, hoping to find a trace of her character etched on it. But the older woman's expression was inscrutable. "Thanks," he murmured. He turned and walked out of the book shop.

# CHAPTER SEVEN

Jessica took another bite of her apple cobbler. The soft, flaky crust melted in her mouth. Its rich apple flavor, enhanced with a hint of cinnamon, was a perfect conclusion to the meal her Aunt Inger had prepared for the family that evening. Jessica sat outside on the porch with her aunt, uncle, and cousins, enjoying her dessert and the family conversation.

"And then Johanna showed us her flower garden," Inger was saying. "You know how much she adores that garden. She'd rather work in her garden than do almost anything else. And there wasn't a weed in sight, was there, Jessica?"

Jessica looked up from her plate. Her aunt was smiling at her, gently prodding her to join the conversation taking place on the porch. Inger's flaxen hair was drawn up into a tidy bun, and her blue eyes sparkled with good humor. She had on the same sunny yellow gingham she'd worn earlier that day when she, Jessica, and Birgithe went to visit Inger's sister, Johanna. Although Inger's outward appearance was ordinary, Jessica recognized the beauty that radiated from within. As Jessica had become acquainted with her aunt over the course of the last week, she'd grown to value Inger's kindness, warmth, and cheerful disposition. "Not a single weed," Jessica responded to her aunt's comment. "The garden was in perfect order."

"That's because she marshals her flowers in the same way she does her children," James remarked with a twinkle gleaming in his eye.

Birgithe giggled at her father's comment.

"Now, James, you know Johanna likes her surroundings to be orderly," Inger protested, a smile tugging at the corners of her mouth. "There's nothing wrong with that."

Jessica guessed the context behind her uncle and aunt's remarks. From the hour she'd spent in Johanna's home, she witnessed how the woman ran her house with a strict regimen, and her children like a contingent of soldiers. Jessica noticed she was quite without humor, and her no-nonsense manner permeated her surroundings. Johanna was plain-faced and stout, and wore her graying hair in a tight braid wound around the crown of her head. Her disposition seemed as severe and harsh as her hair style, different in every aspect from her younger sister, Inger.

"Who's ready for more dessert?" Inger asked, smiling.

"I am!" cried Birgithe.

"What about you, Ethan?" his mother inquired.

Ethan shook his head. "I've already eaten more than my stomach can hold."

Jessica glanced at her cousin. He was seated comfortably on a veranda chair with his legs stretched out in front of him.

"Well, I'm going to have a second helping," Birgithe declared.

"May I get you some more cobbler, Jessica?" Inger asked.

"No, thank you, Aunt Inger. I'm still not finished with what I have." The apple cinnamon cobbler was the best Jessica had ever tasted. She made a mental note to ask her aunt for the recipe. "Supper was delicious, Aunt Inger. You're a marvelous cook."

"Your Aunt Inger makes the best apple cobbler in the whole Territory," James said with a grin. Jessica saw the look he exchanged with his wife, filled with pride and genuine affection. It was easy to feel the love existing between this husband and wife, and between parent and child.

Inger laughed. "If that's true, it comes from many years of experience." She stood up from her chair and turning to Birgithe said, "Come inside, Birgithe. When you've had your fill of cobbler, you can help me with the dishes."

"I'll help, too," James offered, rising to his feet. "You two relax and enjoy the sunset," he said to Ethan and Jessica. He followed Inger and Birgithe into the house.

Ethan yawned and stretched his arms over his head. "I believe my little sister is capable of eating more cobbler than I am," he said, smiling at Jessica.

The sun was sinking in the west, turning the sky the shade of ripe apricots. Jessica rested her hands in her lap, watching the sky change color. "Did you know that your sister is sweet on Billy Fenton?" she idly remarked.

"No. Is she?" Ethan responded, his brows arching in surprise.

Jessica spooned another bite of dessert into her mouth. "She told me so yesterday. I met him when he came to the house to have his arm attended to by your father."

"Billy is a nice fellow. His family owns a farm near here. His father served in the Union army during the War Between the States and was injured in battle, so it's hard for him to work the land. Billy carries a man's load."

"What kind of injury did he suffer?" Jessica asked.

"An artillery shell exploded a few feet away from him, nearly killing him. His leg had to be amputated."

Jessica gasped. "Oh, that's awful."

"Yeah, the whole war was awful."

Jessica thought back to her girlhood years. She had been only seven years old when the Civil War broke out, but she remembered seeing the soldiers in their blue uniforms. Illinois had sent its share of Union soldiers into the bloody conflict. Even the small town of Nauvoo had not escaped the horror of the war; many of its sons were lost in battle or returned home maimed or crippled.

Before the fighting began, Illinois had basked in the glory of its most famous citizen; Abraham Lincoln had served four terms in the Illinois legislature, and then was elected on the Whig ticket to the United States House of Representatives. By the time Lincoln took his seat in Congress in 1857, the United States had won the war with Mexico and was on the cusp of expanding its territory by nearly one-third. During his tenure in Congress, Lincoln made no secret of his opposition to slavery. He threw his support behind the proposed Wilmot Proviso, which called for banning slavery in any territory acquired from Mexico.

After Lincoln's term ended, he returned to Springfield, Illinois, and resumed his law practice. Later, Lincoln joined the newly formed, antislavery Republican party. Lincoln's debates with Democratic senator, Stephen A. Douglas, made Lincoln a prominent figure in national politics.

Although she was young, Jessica remembered the parades, speeches, and fireworks display accompanying Lincoln's election to the presidency in 1860. But by the time of his inauguration, seven Southern states had seceded from the Union, and a month later the first shots rang out at Fort Sumter. More than 600,000 Americans died during the four-year conflict.

Jessica stared out at the rocky peaks silhouetted against an orange sky, remembering her feelings of fear and confusion as a young girl during the war. "Do you recall much about the war?" she asked Ethan.

"Some. I was eight when the conflict began, but we didn't feel the brunt of its effects here in the valley.

I remember hearing Brigham Young say that had we as Latter-day Saints not been persecuted and driven, we would be involved in the midst of the war and bloodshed desolating the nation. But instead, we were safely located in the peaceful mountains and valleys."

Jessica felt envious of Ethan's comfortable circumstance during the war years, when she had suffered such distress. "But some of the men must have gone off to fight. You said Billy Fenton's father did."

Ethan changed position in his chair. "I guess some men did feel the need to enlist; I know the Saints as a whole were loyal to the Union. When President Lincoln asked for a company of soldiers to guard the transcontinental telegraph lines and transportation routes, our men willingly agreed. But I think that was the only organized military unit of Latter-day Saints to serve in the Civil War."

The sun was slipping behind the mountains now, and the sky was a flaming red and orange. Jessica sat gazing at the fiery horizon as she listened to Ethan's explanation.

"It was during the war that Utah made an attempt—its third—to gain statehood. When one of our representatives went to Washington, D.C., to talk with President Lincoln about his intentions concerning the Mormons and the possibility of statehood, the President responded with a fitting anecdote."

"What was it?" she asked.

"Let me see if I can remember the exact words. Father is fond of reciting it to us," he added. Ethan rubbed a hand across his chin. "It went something like this: 'When I was a boy on the farm in Illinois, there was a great deal of timber on the farms which we had to clear away. Occasionally, we would come to a log which had fallen down. It was too hard to split, too wet to burn, and too heavy to move, so we plowed around it. That's what I intend to do with the Mormons. You go back and tell Brigham Young that if he will let me alone, I will let him alone.'" When Ethan had finished reciting the story, Jessica heard him chuckle in the soft dusk gathering around them. "President Lincoln's tolerant attitude earned him the respect of the Saints," Ethan concluded.

"He must have been a wise and honorable man," Jessica said in a subdued tone. "He's buried in Springfield, Illinois, about a hundred miles from Nauvoo, where my family lives."

"You've never said much about your family. Do your parents favor the Republicans or the Democrats?"

"The Democrats, without question. When Andrew Johnson took over the presidency after Lincoln's assassination, I remember my parents complaining that if he continued with Lincoln's plan of reconstruction, the nation was apt to burst apart at its mended seams. Although President Johnson was a Democrat, he embraced Republican policies so thoroughly that Father used to say Johnson was a Republican masquerading as a Democrat."

Ethan chuckled at that remark.

"Perhaps that stand contributed to his party's decision not to nominate him for a second term. I think he would have lost to Grant anyway."

"Ulysses S. Grant was a great military leader, but I think he's been a weak president," Ethan commented. "From what I've read in the newspapers, his administration has been riddled with scandals and political corruption. I'll be surprised if he's re-elected this year."

"My parents have said the same thing."

"Do you agree with your parents' political sympathies?"

"I don't agree with much of anything that my parents do or say," Jessica replied, thinking about the contention that characterized her home life. She felt Ethan staring at her.

"Don't you get along with your parents?" he asked.

Jessica smiled grimly. "About as well as two dogs sharing a bone."

"That's too bad. I can't imagine having serious disagreements with my family."

Even though Jessica knew her cousin was speaking honestly, his comment rankled her. "That's not the impression I got this evening. Your father sounds like he's not too fond of your mother's sister, Johanna."

The sound of Ethan's chuckle filled the still, night air. "He was only teasing my mother. Although Aunt Johanna can sometimes be trying, both Father and Mother would do anything for her."

Jessica glanced at her cousin. His features were growing indistinct in the fading light. Dusk was settling in the trees and spreading across the yard. She finished the last of her dessert and set the empty plate on the porch. "I'd never met any of my mother's family until I came here," she said with a sigh.

"But now you're acquainted with Aunt Millie and Aunt Roxy."

Jessica smiled as she recalled her visit that afternoon to her mother's two younger half-sisters. "Yes. Aunt Millicent is as lively as a kite in a March wind. And Aunt Roxana is so pretty with her dark hair and eyes."

"Our parents had a younger brother, too, who died when he was seven or eight years old," Ethan added.

"They did? Mother has never said anything about that to me." Jessica's brows rushed together. Why hadn't her mother ever spoken about this brother? "What was his name?"

"Zachary, I believe."

"Zachary," she repeated softly. She sat silently in her chair, digesting this new information.

"Doesn't your mother talk much about her family?" Ethan asked.

Jessica shook her head. "I've heard only a few stories about them. She's mentioned a few things about her mother, but seldom speaks of her stepfather."

"Grandfather Kade was very kind and patient. Intelligent, too. He worked in the newspaper business when he was younger."

Jessica listened closely to what Ethan was telling her.

"And Grandmother Kade was a nice lady. Before they died, they lived here in town not too far from us and visited often."

Jessica tried to conjure a mental picture of her grandparents. The only image to come to mind was the pencil-drawn portrait of Lydia that her mother had given her.

"Your father showed me some of the sketches Grandfather made. My older sister, Emmaline, has a talent for drawing, too."

"She does?"

"Yes, she enjoys painting and sketching, and is quite skilled at it."

Ethan gave his full attention. "What sort of things does she like to paint?"

"Still lifes mostly. She paints flowers and trees, or objects in the house that strike her fancy."

"What about your younger sister? Does she draw, too?"

"Clarissa? No, not really. But Clarissa has a beautiful singing voice. She can sing like a nightingale. I envy her that talent."

"What about you? What's your talent?"

"I don't have a talent. Not a single one, I'm afraid."

Ethan folded his arms across his chest. "Perhaps you'll uncover a hidden talent. God gives each of us individual talents and abilities."

Jessica wasn't surprised by the context of his remark. She'd already noticed that her Utah relatives often included in their conversation some reference to God or their religion. In her home, religious references were never part of the daily conversation. The Kade family had attended church meetings together the Sunday before, and each night they knelt in prayer together before retiring to their beds. The family prayed each morning, too, she'd observed, and at every meal. Her uncle invited her to join them in prayer, but Jessica had always refused.

She thought about her own experiences with prayer. Jessica's mother had taught her as a small child to say her prayers by her bedside at night, but as she'd grown older Jessica had let the convention slide, and her mother had not encouraged her in it. Her mother occasionally attended the Presbyterian church on Mulholland Street in Nauvoo and used to take her young daughters with her; but those instances, too, dwindled as the girls grew older. Emmaline still went to church once in awhile on her own, but Clarissa seldom did. Jessica's father had never set foot inside the church door, as far as she knew.

Ethan stirred restlessly in his seat. Jessica cast him a sidewise glance, wondering what her cousin's position was on the subject of religion and if he'd read the book of scripture Birgithe had loaned her the day before. Out of curiosity, she'd read all of the verses in "The book of Enos," and to her surprise had been touched by Enos' mighty prayer and great faith. But she hadn't understood everything she read. There was mention of a group of people Enos called the Nephites and another group referred to as Lamanites. Jessica knew only that the two groups were bitter enemies. This, she'd gathered from her reading.

She had shivered at the description Enos drew of the Lamanite people, characterizing them as wild, ferocious, and blood-thirsty; living in tents and wandering about in the wilderness wearing only a short skin girdle to cover their loins, and their heads shaven. He wrote of their fierce skill with the bow and the ax. That depiction bore an uncanny resemblance to accounts of the wild and savage tribes of Indians she'd read about in magazines and newspapers. The similarity had raised questions she was unable to answer.

"I think I'll go inside," Ethan said, getting to his feet. "Are you coming?"

"No, not yet. I'll sit outside a little while longer."

"Okay." Ethan started toward the door of the house, then paused. "I hope you'll change your mind about coming out to the ranch. It might be the only chance you'll have to see a cattle ranch in operation."

Jessica stared up at him from her place on the porch. She could see his figure outlined against the light coming from the coal oil lamp burning in the window. "Thanks for the invitation, Ethan, but I don't think so."

"You're sure?"

"Uh-huh."

"All right. Goodnight, then."

"Goodnight."

After Ethan had gone inside, Jessica tucked her skirt around her legs. A cold breeze had sprung up, and the thin cotton dress she wore, borrowed from Birgithe's closet, provided little protection against the night's chill. Her conversation with Ethan had left her feeling unsettled. She couldn't help comparing his family to her own. Her parents' relationship with one another was beset with contention. Jessica and her two sisters had been reared in an atmosphere of disharmony, where bickering, backbiting, and unkindnesses were commonplace. Her older sister, Emmaline, had traditionally played the role of peacekeeper; she was the one to smooth things over when disagreements arose. Jessica's younger sister, Clarissa, tended to be sullen and surly. As for Jessica, she characterized herself as the rebellious one. For as long as she could remember, she'd pressed the boundaries her parents had established for her, wanting to experience life on her own terms—as exemplified by her decision to come west. But now she wasn't so sure she'd made the right decision, for things hadn't turned out like she'd planned.

Jessica shuddered as she thought of her father reading the letter she'd sent him. He would be angry with her and think her careless and foolish. Even if he enclosed money in his return letter to enable her to go on to California, she knew his reply would include a scathing tirade concerning her irresponsibility and ineptness in protecting her possessions. And she also knew her mother would blame her father for Jessica's predicament, as she blamed him for nearly everything that went awry in their lives. A rancorous argument would ensue between the two of them, followed by a period of days or weeks, or possibly even months, when they wouldn't speak to one another except when absolutely necessary.

Jessica hugged her knees, shivering in the cool, night air. Her situation was the reverse of what she'd witnessed in the Kades' home. Here existed peace and kindness and unconditional love. She wondered what attribute inspired such harmony and contentment, and was found so lacking in her own family. She realized something significant was missing from her life, but she didn't know what it was or where to turn to find it.

# CHAPTER EIGHT

Ethan climbed out of bed and ran a hand over his face, feeling the prickly stubble on his chin. He squinted against the blaze of sunlight coming through his curtained window. It was early—he could hear robins singing in the sycamore tree outside in the yard. He yawned and stretched his arms above his head, then padded over to the washstand where a basin and towel awaited him. Dashing cold water onto his face, he reached for the towel. The oval mirror fixed to the washstand reflected a young man whose eyes were blurry from sleep and whose straw-colored hair was rumpled and in disarray. Ethan dipped a hand into the bowl of clear, cold water, then ran his dripping fingers through his hair, hoping to tame it.

He changed into his work clothes, reviewing in his mind the chores for the day. He wanted to finish harrowing the field, then clean out the barn. Hurrying down the staircase, he found his mother in the kitchen stirring a batch of griddlecakes. "Morning, Mother."

"Good morning," she returned. "Getting an early start?"

Ethan nodded. He snatched a piece of freshly fried sausage cooling on a plate and popped it into his mouth. "Umm," he mumbled. "That's good."

"Wait for your breakfast," Inger said, smiling.

"I miss your cooking. Sister Bartlett's fare is a poor substitute," he replied, giving her a kiss on the cheek. "I'll be in the field until breakfast is ready."

Whistling a tune, he started toward the shed where he'd replaced the harrow after using it the day before; he felt rested and refreshed now that he was out in the brisk, sweet-smelling morning air. He noticed the trees in the yard growing bright, new leaves; and his mother's spring flowers planted beside the doorstep added a splash of color to the brown earth.

His mother had created a pathway leading from the back doorstep to the herb garden beyond, by clearing a narrow swath of ground and lining it on both sides with stones to form a border. Ethan followed the rock-lined path to the garden, pausing to eye his mother's tidy patch of herbs and plants. Though Inger cultivated the plants for the seasonings and garnishes they provided for her cooking pot, her primary purpose in growing them was for use in her husband's medical practice. James employed an arsenal of medicinal drugs to treat his patients, which included compounds derived from seeds, blossoms, and roots as remedies. Inger, too, was knowledgeable about the health benefits these plants provided, frequently dosing her children with such natural remedies as spearmint to cure an upset stomach, boiled parsley to ease a fever, and raspberry or strawberry leaves to treat an attack of the influenza.

Each day throughout the spring and summer, except on the Sabbath, Inger weeded her herbal garden directly after breakfast. Now, as Ethan surveyed the patch, he noticed a few weeds and thistles poking their heads above the soil. He bent down and tugged at the weeds near his feet, pulling them from the soft earth. Then ranging through the garden, he removed all the small weeds that had popped up since his mother last weeded. With a smile resting on his face as he plucked the noxious plants, he thought how pleased his mother would be when she came to the patch with her hoe to find not a single weed in sight.

Ethan spent a few minutes working in the herb garden, then took the harrow from the shed and strode out to the field. The furrows he had tilled with the harrow yesterday morning stood ready for planting. In a few days' time potatoes, cabbage, lettuce, and carrots would be silently growing beneath the moist earth; and tomatoes, corn, and squash would soon be thrusting their heads toward the sun.

Spring was Ethan's favorite season of the year, when everything was new and growing. He liked to walk through a plowed field in his bare feet, feeling the soil between his toes. The earth seemed alive and thriving at this time of year, anxious to embrace the seeds that it would nourish throughout the summer, then yield its bounty at harvest time.

For an instant he envisioned Susannah Hamilton at his side, her arm linked through his, strolling the fertile field together. The picture brought a smile to his lips and a warmth into his heart. But the image crumbled almost as soon as it began. The reality of Susannah's dislike for him was as real as the soil beneath his feet.

He'd just begun to drag the harrow through the soil when he heard a commotion coming from the street—fevered voices and the frantic whinnying of horses. He left the harrow and jogged toward the road, and to his horror, spotted a wagon overturned in the street. The two horses harnessed to it were rearing and bucking in their traces. Boxes of goods lay strewn in the road, some split open and spilling their contents from their fall off the wagon. Ethan glimpsed a molasses barrel on its side, its lid cracked and the dark, gooey molasses oozing onto the ground.

Ethan took in the whole scene in an instant—the wagon tipped on its side, the frenzied horses, the driver shouting for help. Though Ethan's mind felt dazed gazing at the shambles, his legs propelled him toward the scene. He reached the plunging horses in a few seconds' time and grasped the bridle of one of the animals. The horse's tossing head nearly lifted him off his feet as he clung to his handhold on the strap. His heart was racing in his chest, and perspiration collected along his brow. Ethan glanced at the overturned wagon; he could see only the undercarriage of the vehicle and one wheel still spinning slowly in the air.

The driver, a bearded man in a plaid shirt, limped towards him, a cut above his eye oozing blood. He grabbed hold of the other horse by its harness. By this time, a few more people began rushing forward to offer assistance. Ethan caught sight of the front door of his home burst open, and his father dash down the porch steps toward the street. "The wagon, Pa!" Ethan cried to him.

Although Ethan's eyes were locked onto the pair of frightened horses, his ears captured the grunting and straining of the men gathered around the wagon struggling to right it. Ethan's father joined the cluster of men, and in another moment they succeeded in getting the vehicle upright.

By now, the horses had calmed. Ethan left them in the care of the driver and hurried toward his father, who was hunched over what looked like a heap of crumpled clothing lying in the street on the far side of the wagon. Ethan gasped when his eyes made sense of the scene—a young man, barely past boyhood, lie limp and motionless on the dusty ground. A gash on the youth's head was bleeding badly, and blood seeped from his nose and mouth. The boy's arms were bent at an unnatural angle, and his legs lay askew. A spreading patch of scarlet stained the coarse homespun shirt he wore.

Ethan halted, repulsed and frightened by the sight. He stared as his father lifted the unconscious boy and carried him toward the house. His father's eyes met his, and the grim expression in them nearly made Ethan's heart fail. "Ethan, run ahead and make sure the door to my office is open so I can bring the boy inside," his father directed.

Ethan galloped to the house. He had seen injury and death before in connection with his father's work, but the immediateness of this grisly scene shocked all his senses. His sister and cousin were standing on the front porch, white-lipped and shaken. Ethan hurtled past them through the open doorway. He made a wild glance inside his father's office to make certain it was clear of obstructions.

His father entered the room carrying the injured boy in his arms, and carefully laid him on the bed. Ethan stood in the hall beyond the doorway, watching. He deliberately avoided looking at the youth's face, focusing instead on the boy's right forearm, which was bandaged. The trim-fitting, cloth bandage covering his lower arm was dirt-stained and smudged with blood.

"Ethan?"

He jumped at the sound of his sister's voice.

"It's Billy, isn't it?" Birgithe's face was ashen, and her eyes flooding with tears.

Ethan swallowed hard; he knew it was the Fenton boy lying unconscious in his father's office, but he hadn't wanted to admit that truth to himself. He put an arm around Birgithe's shoulders and pulled her in close, feeling her body shuddering with sobs. His eyes traveled to Jessica's stricken face. His cousin stood beside the stairway, one hand clutching the railing.

He heard someone on the porch volunteer to fetch the boy's father and shivered at the thought of the horrific news about to be delivered. Ethan closed his eyes, trying to shut out the reality of the event and the pain piercing through him. Suddenly, he was conscious of his mother in the midst of them; hugging Birgithe, patting Jessica's hand, caressing Ethan's cheek with a gentle touch. She was an angel of mercy, Ethan thought, gliding through the thick of sorrow and gloom.

Ethan felt helpless in the face of this tragedy and anxious to leave the somber stillness lowering in the hallway outside his father's office door. He didn't want to be present when Billy's parents arrived and witness their grief. He started for the kitchen, intending to go out the back door and return to the field, but as he entered the room, he noticed the brackish odor of burnt bread. At first he was confused by the smell; then he spied half a dozen hotcakes, black and smoking, on the griddle. He hastily removed the pan from the hot stove top. The griddlecakes, left unattended when the accident occurred, were inedible now. Ethan was glad breakfast would be delayed. Only minutes before, he'd been eagerly anticipating his mother's ample meal; but now his stomach felt as if he'd swallowed a field full of rocks.

He strode out the door, past the herb garden, and across the stretch of orchard into the field beyond. Grasping the harrow, he began pushing it through the plowed furrows. The harrow bumped and jerked through the soil, but Ethan's steady pressure on it did not lessen. He forced himself to think about the earth underfoot and not the gravely injured boy inside his father's office. Keeping his mind and hands occupied was the best way for him to cope with the tragedy he'd witnessed.

Ethan worked the harrow for the better part of an hour. When he paused to wipe the sweat from his brow, he spotted Jessica coming toward him from the house. He mopped his face with his handkerchief, then stuffed the cloth back into his trouser pocket and waited for Jessica to reach him.

"Ethan, your mother asked me to tell you that breakfast is ready," she said in a subdued tone.

Ethan glanced toward the house. The morning's grim events had eradicated every pang of hunger. "Will you tell her I'm not hungry right now? I'll come in later to eat, when I'm through here." He took hold of the harrow, ready to start his work again.

"Wait, Ethan."

He looked up into his cousin's face.

"Did you see it happen?"

Ethan knew instantly what she meant. "No. I didn't. I was out here working when I heard the noise. By the time I got to the street, people were already starting to gather, offering help." He drew a breath. "He's dead, isn't he?"

"Yes," Jessica whispered.

"I thought so." He heaved an audible sigh. "Billy must have been at the side of the road and was struck by the wagon when it tipped over."

"Yes, that's what happened. Your father spoke to the driver of the wagon. The horses bolted, dragging the runaway rig behind them. The driver tried to stop the team, but the wagon careened out of control when it rounded the corner of the street."

"I imagine my father is upset. He sometimes blames himself when he's unable to save a patient." The words came out sounding cold and hollow, but if Ethan had injected the emotion he felt, tears would have started in his eyes.

"Not only your father, but Birgithe, too. You know she had feelings for that boy." Jessica's voice quavered. "She's inside the house, weeping."

Ethan stared at the ground, not trusting himself to speak.

"Ethan, do you believe there is a heaven? Do you believe it's a real place?" Jessica asked in a hushed voice.

"Yes, of course I do. Don't you?"

Jessica nudged the ground with the toe of her shoe. "I don't know. I'm not sure that I do. I can't imagine what heaven would be like."

Ethan remained silent, not knowing how to answer her.

"When I saw the face of that dying boy as your father carried him into the house, I thought about Zachary."

"Zachary?" Ethan frowned, puzzled by her reference.

"Zachary, our uncle—the one who died while Grandfather and Grandmother Kade were traveling across the plains by wagon to Utah."

"Oh." Ethan searched his memory for details of the story his father had told him about Zachary's death on the prairie.

"Of course it wasn't Zachary who died this morning, but I imagined for a moment that it was him, lying pale and still on the bed."

Ethan flinched. Jessica's words opened a wound inside him.

"I guess Zachary and Billy are in heaven, aren't they? After what's happened today, I want to believe that heaven exists." Jessica lowered her gaze and looked away.

Ethan swallowed. He didn't want to talk anymore about Billy Fenton's death. The shock of seeing the mortally wounded boy had shaken him to the core. "I have to get back to work," he muttered to Jessica. He grasped hold of the harrow and forced its iron teeth to bite into the soil.

He heard Jessica walk away but didn't turn to look at her. The sweet-smelling morning air that had lifted his spirits earlier, now seemed oppressive; and the sun on his shoulders no longer felt warm and cozy, but relentless in its heat. He stayed outside tilling the ground until his back and shoulders ached, then cleaned out the barn, and after that the chicken coop. Stopping only briefly to eat, he labored until the sun set, all the while laying plans for his return to the ranch in South Willow Creek.

The next morning, word came that Jessica's trunk was at the station, having arrived by train from Sacramento. Ethan volunteered to pick it up from the depot. Hitching the horses to the buckboard, he set out on the rutted dirt road that led into the heart of the city. His shirtsleeves were rolled up to his elbows, for the day was warm; the old, felt, floppy hat he wore shaded his eyes from the sun's rays. As he neared the center of town, he deliberately avoided the area of Main Street where the Quill and Ink was located, for he was still smarting from the rejection he'd suffered at the hands of Susannah Hamilton. Soon the tracks came into sight, and Ethan reined in the horses beside the adobe building that housed the station.

He tied the reins to the hitching post and strode inside the building. A few people were milling about the room, and some sat on benches, waiting for the next train to arrive. Ethan went directly to the clerk who stood behind a tall counter.

"I'm here to collect a trunk being held for us. The owner's name is Miss Jessica Scott. I'm her cousin, Ethan Kade."

The clerk was of slight build, with spectacles resting on the end of his nose. He squinted at Ethan behind the spectacles, then reached for a pile of loose papers. "Scott . . . Scott . . ." he mumbled as he searched through the pages. "Oh, yes. Here it is. Miss Jessica Scott, is that correct?"

"Yes."

"And her trunk is arriving from . . . let me see here," the clerk said, consulting the paper in his hand. The small man's voice was high-pitched and shrill. It grated on Ethan's nerves.

"Sacramento," Ethan supplied for him. "The trunk was on its way to Sacramento when we sent a wire asking to have it sent here."

"Ah, yes, Sacramento. I see it written down."

"Good," Ethan replied with a hint of impatience in his voice.

"I'll need to get the trunk for you. It's stored in the back room." The clerk adjusted the spectacles on his nose, then stepped away from the counter.

While he waited, Ethan idly watched the people in the depot. Most of the men were dressed in top hats and frock coats; the ladies wore bonnets and fringed shawls. A woman with a small boy beside her sat on the bench looking anxiously out the window toward the tracks.

Ethan drummed his fingers on the countertop. The clerk seemed to be taking his time in retrieving the trunk. Ethan grew impatient with standing in one spot, so he wandered outside onto the platform. Several people were waiting here, too, to meet the next train. Ethan shoved his hands into his pockets and stood staring down the tracks. They went some distance past the station in a straight line before curving around a bend and out of sight.

A raucous laugh drew Ethan's attention to two men standing near the tracks. Both men were grinning as they conversed, and one of them carried an opened bottle in his hand. Ethan could see the bottle's label easily from where he stood—"Red Jacket Whiskey," it read.

Ethan wrinkled his nose and turned away, but the men's boisterous talk and harsh laughter made it impossible for him to ignore them. He was repelled by their sordid comments and crude remarks.

"Hey, take a look over there," one of the men said, pointing to the door of the station house. Ethan's gaze slid to the door as well. The woman and child he'd noticed sitting inside on the bench were exiting the building. She had her child by the hand, urging him along. The little boy's lip was turned down in a pouting frown.

"Ain't she a tasty little morsel," the man with the whiskey bottle remarked loudly. Ethan's gaze swung toward the man just in time to see him take a deep swig from his bottle.

"I'll bet she's a fiery one. Look at the tilt of her chin," the other commented in a coarse tone.

Ethan saw the woman glance at the two men; it was obvious that she'd heard their comments. Just then, a train's whistle sounded in the distance. Ethan turned toward the tracks; when he looked back, he was surprised to see the pair approaching the woman.

"You wouldn't happen to know the time, would you, ma'am?" the man carrying the whiskey bottle asked her.

"No, I don't. I'm sorry," the woman replied, flushing under the man's bold stare.

"You see, I'm expectin' a friend comin' in on the train, and I was hopin' the whistle we just heard was gonna be his train." The man with the bottle in his hand took a step toward her.

The woman drew her young son to her side. Ethan watched the exchange from the corner of his eye. Now that he could hear the men's voices more distinctly, Ethan recognized their thick, Texas drawl. The men were dressed in rumpled cotton trousers, flannel shirts, and vests. They wore their hats cocked to the back of their heads and their six-shooters on their hips. Silver spurs with jingle bobs were fastened to the heels of their tall, leather boots. Texas drovers, Ethan guessed, probably in town to do cattle business. He watched the one man take another drink from his whiskey bottle.

"You got a cute little feller there," the other Texan remarked. Ethan saw him bend down and pinch the boy's cheek. The child snuggled closer to his mother and hid his face in her skirts.

"If you'll excuse me . . ." the woman said, starting to move away. Her eyes darted between the two men, and the look reminded Ethan of a cornered deer.

"Excuse you?" the man harboring the whiskey bottle said with sarcasm. "I ain't yet had the pleasure of makin' your acquaintance, ma'am. My name's Peyton, and this here is Mr. Quaid."

The Texan referred to as Quaid swept off his hat and offered an insolent bow. "Pleased to meet you, little lady." He grinned broadly, revealing crooked, yellow teeth.

"Perhaps me and you could get to know one another a little better," the man named Peyton suggested. He took another step toward her and reached for her arm.

"No, please. I have to go." Ethan witnessed her trying to pull away from the Texan. The man leered into her face, then jerked her roughly toward him. Her young son clung to her skirts, whimpering.

Ethan's blood ran hot in his veins. Before he even realized what he was doing, he strode over to the two Texas drovers. "I believe the lady wishes to be left alone," he said.

The man who had introduced himself as Peyton turned bleary eyes onto Ethan. "This ain't none of your concern, boy. You best back off."

Ethan moved closer to the woman. "Take your hands off her, mister," he replied with an unflinchingly stare. "Right now."

Peyton released his grip on the woman's arm, focusing his attention onto Ethan. "Why, you young upstart. Didn't your mama learn you nothin' about manners?" The man's eyes glowed with angry heat.

Ethan realized he'd put himself in danger; his body tensed, making every nerve tingle and every muscle taut. Peyton glared at him; then without warning the Texan slammed his whiskey bottle against the side of the building, shattering the lower half of the bottle. The upper portion, which he held by the neck, remained intact with sharp, jagged edges. He lunged toward Ethan with the razor-sharp, splintered bottle, thrusting it at his face. Ethan jumped backward, surprised by the man's vicious attack.

Peyton came at him again, shouting profanities and directing wild passes at him with the broken glass. Dodging the dangerous weapon, Ethan strained to stay out of the man's reach. He heard the woman's startled cry and the sobbing of her young son.

"You sniveling son of a ..." Peyton's sentence erupted into vile obscenities as he charged at Ethan with the shattered whiskey bottle. The sheared edges of glass flashed in the sunlight.

Peyton made a sudden, quick jab. This time Ethan wasn't fast enough—the jagged edge of the bottle caught him on the cheek. Pain seared through his flesh. He staggered backward, stumbling. As he tried to regain his balance, the other man, Quaid, grabbed Ethan from behind and pinned his arms. Ethan struggled to free himself, but the blow to his cheek had stunned him, leaving him unable to break away.

The whistle from the oncoming train blared again, nearer this time and louder, its sound shrill in Ethan's ears. The noise roused Ethan to a spurt of strength. He gave a quick, hard tug and wrenched one arm free from Quaid's grasp. He was about to smash an elbow into Quaid's face, when Peyton rammed a fist into his belly. Ethan doubled over, the breath driven out of him.

The whistle signaled a final time, two short blasts followed by a longer one, and then a clacking of wheels sounding on the track as the train slowed and pulled into the station. Steam belched from the smokestack atop the engine; Ethan felt its hot breath against his cheek.

Peyton bent down and his face swam before Ethan's blurry eyes. "Next time, boy, you mind your manners. Don't go pokin' your nose into somethin' that don't concern you." Dazed, Ethan watched as the Texan drew back his fist and plunged it a second time into his midsection. Ethan grunted in pain and crumpled onto the platform. Quaid gave him a shove, sending Ethan sprawling face down onto the plank flooring. His nose ground into the hard, splintery wood.

He heard the two men walk away, their boots clicking on the wooden floor of the platform. He groaned and tried to get up, but his stomach felt sick and his head buzzed. He sank back down, dizzy and weak.

Then he felt a gentle touch on his shoulder. "Are you all right? Let me help you to your feet."

Ethan shook his head, trying to clear the cobwebs from his eyes. He focused on the attentive face of the young woman Peyton and Quaid had been molesting.

"I'm so sorry," the woman apologized, her voice quivering with emotion. "But, thank you. You were very brave to stand up to those two men."

Ethan slowly climbed to his feet. The woman, with her young son's hand clasped in hers, peered anxiously into his face.

"I'm fine," Ethan assured her. His tongue felt thick in his mouth.

People were exiting the train now, and the platform was filling with travelers. Through the crowd, Ethan caught sight of the two Texas drovers greeting a third man dressed in similar garb, who was stepping off one of the cars.

"My husband is arriving on this train," the young woman explained. "I'm here to meet him. I know he will be very appreciative of what you did for me."

"It wasn't much," Ethan replied with a smile.

"Oh, yes, it was. You protected my son and me from those awful men, and I thank you from the bottom of my heart." The young woman clutched his hand and gave it a squeeze.

Ethan was warmed by her genuine show of gratitude.

"Oh, there's my husband now." The woman's face flooded with relief as she spotted her husband getting off the train. "Thank you again," she said to Ethan, then gripping her son's hand she hurried away.

Ethan started for the station house. His steps were slow, for his stomach ached and his cheek hurt; and his pride was bruised, too, from being bested in the scuffle with the two Texans. As he walked, he took his handkerchief from his pocket and dabbed at the blood drying on his cheek where the ragged edge of the whiskey bottle had cut him. He flinched with pain at each application of the handkerchief. Inside the building, a line of people stood waiting to buy tickets for the next train. He took his place in line, conscious of the stares he was getting from those around him.

When his turn came at the counter, the bespectacled clerk stared at him, blinked, and then cleared his throat.

"Is the trunk ready for me to take?" Ethan asked irritably.

"Yes, it's right here," the clerk replied, pointing at a large, leather-bound trunk resting beside the counter. "Just sign this paper indicating you've taken possession of the luggage."

The clerk thrust out the paper and a lead pencil for Ethan's signature. As he signed his name, Ethan felt the small man's eyes probing the cut on his face.

"There," Ethan said, handing the paper and pencil back to the clerk. "Thanks for your help."

Ethan hoisted the traveling trunk onto his shoulder and walked out to the buckboard with it. The trunk was big and heavy; he hefted it into the bed of the wagon, then climbed into the wagon seat and gave the reins a shake. The horses lurched forward. As he left the depot, Ethan cast a look behind him to make sure the two, rough Texans he'd encountered weren't following him. He had no intention of tangling with them again.

# CHAPTER NINE

$A$ melancholy gloom had fallen on the household with Billy Fenton's death. Jessica felt it hanging heavy over all the members of the Kade family, but especially so with Birgithe. She wanted to do something to help ease her cousin's grief, so she'd invited Birgithe to help unpack her traveling trunk. The task seemed to brighten Birgithe's spirits.

"That gown is so beautiful," said Birgithe.

Jessica smoothed the wrinkles out of the plum and gray striped silk dress she'd removed from the traveling trunk. "My mother had this gown made for me for my eighteenth birthday. It is pretty, isn't it?" She stroked the smooth, shiny fabric.

"It's just about the prettiest dress I've ever seen," Birgithe responded.

Jessica reached into the trunk again and this time withdrew a maroon frock with rosettes and ribbons decorating the skirt. The sleeves ended in a frilly, ruffled cuff.

"Oh, that one is lovely, too!" Birgithe exclaimed.

Jessica laid the maroon dress on the bed between the striped silk and a blue gown with a lace collar, then removed the rest of her clothing from the trunk until she had all her frocks resting in a row on the bed along with an assortment of underclothing, stockings, and stylish shoes.

Birgithe stood ogling her cousin's apparel. The full, hooped skirts of the Civil War period had gone out of fashion, and Jessica's clothes reflected the newer style—dresses worn over a bustle and trimmed with frills and flounces.

Jessica considered whether she should put the clothes away in the bureau drawer her Aunt Inger had cleared for her or repack them in the trunk in preparation for taking the train to Sacramento. She was only awaiting now a reply from her father. She pictured the glare in his stone gray eyes as he read her letter. She hoped, after his anger had cooled, that he'd send her additional money so she could continue on to California. She stood with her hands on her hips, mulling over the decision.

"Jessie?"

"Umm?"

"Would it be all right if . . . I mean, would you allow me to . . ." Birgithe paused, and color sprang to her cheeks.

"What is it, Birgithe?"

"Would you mind if I tried on one of your frocks? Just for a moment?"

Jessica smiled at the younger girl. "Of course you may. Which one would you like to put on? You may choose any one of them you like, Birgithe. I certainly don't mind."

Birgithe's eyes moved from one attractive gown lying on the bed to the next. "That one," she said at last, pointing to the plum and gray silk.

"All right." Jessica picked up the dress and held it out to Birgithe. "I think it will fit you nicely."

Birgithe quickly removed her own cotton gingham and with Jessica's assistance slipped into the soft, smooth frock. She stood in front of the mirror above the dresser to see her reflection.

"You look very pretty in that gown," Jessica told her as she straightened a section of pleats on the skirt and adjusted the satin bow at the collar.

"It's so lovely!"

"The color complements your dark hair and eyes," Jessica replied with a smile.

Birgithe turned away from the mirror to look at her cousin. "Did you wear this frock on your last birthday?" she asked.

"Yes, I did."

"What did you do on your birthday?"

"Well, let's see. It was my eighteenth birthday, and I was already planning the trip to come out west. So my father gave me money for the journey and a lovely pendant necklace to wear, and my mother presented me with this gown. Then that evening, they hosted a small reception at the house for me."

Birgithe's eyes widened. "A party! Was there dancing? And refreshments?"

Jessica laughed. "Yes. There was dancing and refreshments, both. I had a very nice time."

Birgithe carefully sat down on the edge of the bed. "Did you dance with a special beau?" she asked with a shy smile.

Jessica folded her hands in her lap and smiled back at her cousin. "Jeremy Hotchkins."

"Jeremy Hotchkins," Birgithe repeated breathlessly. "What does he look like?"

"I believe you'd think he's quite handsome. Dark, curling hair. Brown eyes. Tall and broad-shouldered." Jessica giggled and patted her cousin's hand.

"Ohh!" Birgithe squealed. "He does sound handsome. Are you smitten with him?"

"I thought so at the time," Jessica confided. "He was most charming at my birthday reception. But I haven't given him much thought since coming here to the valley."

"I'm sure he misses you very much."

Jessica cocked her head to one side. "Perhaps."

Birgithe stood and began gliding gracefully about the room as if dancing, while humming a tune. Jessica watched the younger girl, grateful to see her forget for the moment her sorrow over Billy's death.

Birgithe executed a curtsy to her imaginary partner. "Thank you for the waltz, Mr. Hotchkins," she said. "You dance divinely."

Joining in the charade, Jessica stepped to Birgithe's side. "Pardon me, but I believe you're dancing with my beau," she said, feigning a frown. She assumed a dancing pose with the invisible Mr. Hotchkins, and began to glide and turn in elaborate waltz steps. Then, suddenly, she grimaced and cried out, "Ouch! You just stepped on my toe, sir!"

Birgithe burst into laughter. Both girls settled onto the bed, giggling together. Sitting side by side, Birgithe asked, "Did both your sisters attend the birthday reception?"

Jessica nodded. "Yes. My younger sister, Clarissa, is quite spoiled and petulant."

"And Emmaline?"

Jessica smiled. "Emmaline is gracious, kind, and dutiful, except when she's in one of her moods; then she's stubborn and exasperating."

Birgithe sighed. "I wish I had a sister. Two brothers can be awfully tiresome at times."

Jessica chuckled. Although Birgithe voiced her occasional frustration with her two older brothers, her affection for them was obvious. Jessica liked that trait in her cousin. "I'd gladly trade one of my sisters for one of your brothers."

"Oh?" Birgithe said, grinning. "Which one?"

"Since I haven't met Samuel, I really can't say. Which one would you suggest?"

"Ethan can be sweet and thoughtful, and Samuel often says the most amusing things. I guess I couldn't part with either of them, after all." Birgithe stroked the skirt of the striped silk dress, a smile resting on her face.

"I'd like to meet Samuel," Jessica commented.

"Oh, you'd like him. Everyone likes Samuel." When Jessica didn't reply, she went on. "If you went with Ethan to the ranch, where he and Samuel are working, then you could meet Samuel. I heard Ethan say he wants you to visit there."

A frown darted across Jessica's brow. She picked up the maroon dress and began to fold it in preparation for putting it back into the trunk. "No, I can't, Birgithe. I'm going on to Sacramento, now that I have my trunk."

Birgithe watched her pack the stylish dress carefully inside the trunk. "You'll be leaving soon?" she asked.

Jessica glanced up into her cousin's face. Birgithe's expression was crestfallen. "Yes, I am."

Birgithe took Jessica's words as a cue to remove the silk dress she had on and replace it with her own plain gingham. After she'd changed, she laid Jessica's dress on the bed. "I'm glad your trunk and traveling bag got here safely, Jessie," she said.

"Yes, I'm glad, too. I thought I might have lost them both."

Birgithe straightened the bow fastened to the collar of the striped dress while Jessica continued packing. As she watched Jessica place a lace-trimmed petticoat inside the trunk, she remarked, "Although you didn't know where they were for awhile, Heavenly Father knew all along."

"What?"

"He knew where your belongings were and helped you get them back."

Jessica sat forward, feeling a wisp of annoyance. "Why do you believe that, Birgithe? Why wasn't it just plain luck, along with the sheriff doing his job?"

"Maybe it was, but faith and prayer always helps. I know that." Birgithe was nodding her head like a flower on a stalk in a stiff breeze.

"How do you know?" Jessica insisted.

"Through Enos' testimony of prayer, for one thing," Birgithe answered without hesitation. "Did you read the verses in 'The book of Enos?'"

"Yes, I did. But I don't see how Enos' prayer in the forest has anything to do with the return of my bags."

Birgithe scooted closer to her cousin. "After Enos had prayed to receive a blessing for himself, he prayed for the welfare of his brethren, the Nephites and the Lamanites. The Lord granted Enos' desires because of his faith and prayers."

Jessica stared at her younger cousin. She couldn't grasp the connection Birgithe was drawing between the two incidents.

"Enos remembered the Lord's promise," Birgithe said earnestly, trying to make Jessica understand. "'Whatsoever thing ye shall ask in faith, believing that ye shall receive in the name of Christ, ye shall receive it.' That's God's promise to each of us."

Jessica was silent as her mind wrestled with Birgithe's words. She wasn't sure if she believed Enos' story about prayer and faith, and the Lord granting Enos the desires of his heart. She doubted that God answered man's questions or clarified the personal conflicts and confusions of life. Yet her heart beat faster with the hope that such divine aid might be possible to ordinary mortals.

Jessica forced her thoughts into a more tangible channel. She took the plum and gray striped dress Birgithe had been wearing and held it out to her. "Here, Birgithe. I'd like you to have this."

"What do you mean?" Birgithe asked in confusion.

"It's a gift. From me to you. Here, take it. It's yours."

"But, Jessie . . . it's your birthday frock. You said your mother gave it to you specially for—"

Jessica interrupted by transferring the dress to her cousin's lap. "I want you to have it, Birgithe. As a token of my affection for you." She smiled, trying to set her cousin's mind at ease. "Besides, it looks better on you than it ever did on me."

Birgithe stared at the striped silk gown, then pressed it to her heart. "Thank you. Every single time I wear it, I'll think of you." She leaned over and kissed Jessica's cheek.

Jessica felt tears welling in her eyes. She blinked them back so Birgithe wouldn't see the emotion behind them. Boarding the train for Sacramento was surely going to be more difficult for Jessica than she had imagined.

That same afternoon, a messenger brought a telegram to the house. Jessica was the only one at home—the Kades had gone to visit Billy Fenton's family to offer their condolences.

When the knock sounded at the door, Jessica set down the book of Wordsworth's poetry she'd been reading. Ethan had given her the book he'd purchased several days before at the Quill and Ink, and she'd already read all of the poems through once and was in the midst of reading her favorite verses again. She hurried down the stairs and opened the front door. A messenger boy handed her the telegram. "Thank you," she said as she took the paper scrawled with black, printed letters.

Her eyes swept the page. The telegram was addressed to her, and the signature line read in bold letters— *"FATHER."* She gulped, and her brow broke out in a sweat. She sat down on the chair in the hallway and slowly read the few lines on the page.

RECEIVED YOUR LETTER. AM DISAPPOINTED AND ANGERED BY YOUR IRRESPONSIBILITY. RETURN HOME IMMEDIATELY. TRAIN TICKET IS WAITING FOR YOU AT STATION. FATHER.

Hot tears sprang to Jessica's eyes. Her father's harsh words cut her to the quick. He'd not offered a hint of sympathy or understanding, only cold condemnation. She dashed the tears from her cheeks with the back of her hand. Her father would not be sending her money. Without his backing, she could not go on to California.

She read the words lettered on the page a second time, then crumpled the paper into a tight wad. Bitter disappointment filled her heart. She'd been so close to her destination, to fulfilling her dreams; all her plans and goals were crumbling before her eyes. Tightening her fist around the wadded paper, she stiffly climbed the stairs to Birgithe's room and slumped down on the bed. Staring at the opposite wall, she could almost see her father's scowling face imprinted upon it. She heard his contentious tone in her ears; felt the sting of his accusations. The last thing she wanted to do was return home to that place of discord and turmoil.

She wondered what part her mother had played in this decision. If there was one thing Jessica had learned well from her mother, it was the notion that a woman had a right to enjoy the same opportunities as a man. Jessica didn't always embrace her mother's passion for women's causes, but her mother's views had fostered in Jessica an independent spirit. Jessica could be quick to throw convention aside, liberal in her thoughts and actions, and impulsive and impetuous.

She stood up from the bed and started pacing the room. She considered asking her Uncle James for a loan to cover the price of the ticket, then repaying him as soon as she received her first salary from teaching. He'd already offered to help her financially. But she couldn't bring herself to ask the Kades for money; her pride was too strong for that. Perhaps she should stay in Salt Lake City and work for a few months, just long enough to earn the money to take her to California.

She paused as a solution occurred to her. If there was a ticket to Illinois reserved for her at the train station, she'd simply exchange it for a ticket to Sacramento instead! Sweat collected along Jessica's brow at the thought of her father's reaction to such a deliberate act of defiance. She glared at the crumpled telegram in her hand. She wasn't going home, she promised herself. She would decide her own course.

At that moment she heard the front door open and then Ethan's step on the stairs. She listened as he walked up the hall and into his room, then shut his bedroom door. His presence triggered a sudden resolution to her dilemma.

She crossed the floor, leaving the telegram behind, and strode out of the room. Covering the distance from her room to Ethan's in a few steps, she knocked on the closed door.

"Come in," she heard her cousin say from inside.

She stepped through the doorway. Ethan was sitting on the bed, changing his shoes. The gash on his cheek stood out starkly, raw and red and swollen. A look of surprise flitted across his face when he saw Jessica standing inside the doorway.

Jessica's eye traveled briefly to the collection of wood carvings resting on the bedside table and the handsome watercolor hanging on the wall. "Ethan, did you mean what you said about taking me with you to the ranch?" she asked.

Ethan straightened, one foot partially inside a brown leather boot. "Of course," he replied. "Why?"

"Because if you're serious about the invitation, then I accept. I want to go with you to the cattle ranch in South Willow Creek."

Ethan stared dumbly at her; it took a moment before he recovered his voice. "All right," he said slowly. "We'll leave tomorrow at daybreak."

"That's perfect. I'll be ready." Jessica whirled and left his room as abruptly as she'd entered it.

# CHAPTER TEN

Ethan steered the buckboard into the yard, reined in the horses, and jumped down from the seat. Jessica was waiting for him on the porch. Beside her stood his mother and sister. "Is this everything?" he asked, grasping the handles of his cousin's bulging traveling bag.

"Yes," she answered as Ethan lifted the bag into the wagon bed.

"Okay." He pushed the heavy bag to one side of the wagon bed and tossed in his own saddlebag and bedroll beside it. "Ready to go?"

Jessica nodded.

"I think you'll enjoy staying at the ranch for a few days," Inger said to her niece. "And I'm sure Sister Bartlett will like having some female company." She smiled and gave Jessica a hug.

Ethan glanced up at the sky. The sun had peaked and was starting on its downward track. Ethan would have preferred getting an earlier start, but he'd wanted to attend Billy Fenton's funeral that morning with his family. Jessica had declined to go, and Ethan could hardly blame her. The services for Billy had been comforting, but the shock and sorrow he'd felt over the boy's death was still so raw that Ethan almost wished he'd stayed away, too. "If we start now, we should reach the ranch before nightfall," he said, clamping on his hat. "Let's get going. I'll be back when I can, Mother." He bent to kiss her cheek.

"Take care of yourself, Ethan," she said. "Give my love to Samuel and watch over your cousin."

"I will."

"Goodbye, Aunt Inger," Jessica said. "Birgithe, I wish you were going with us," she added, turning to her cousin.

"Me, too," Birgithe replied. "Have a good time, Jessie."

Jessica offered the girl a quick hug, then Ethan helped her up into the wagon seat. He climbed in beside her and shook the reins. "Gid up," he called to the pair of horses hitched to the buckboard. As the vehicle lurched forward, Jessica turned to wave at her aunt and cousin.

Ethan clucked his tongue, urging the animals to pick up their pace. His bay wasn't used to the harness, and the other—the family's plow horse—was plodding and slow. Bartlett's ranch was about 23 miles from town. A horse and rider could cover the distance in a few hours' time, but traveling by wagon would take much longer than that.

As the buckboard rattled along the rutted road, Ethan felt every bounce and jolt. He noticed his cousin studying the landscape as they drove south toward the point where the eastern foothills sloped down to meet level ground. The Running W Ranch occupied a tract on the slopes of the foothills, at the base of craggy, purple mountains.

"Why is the ranch called the Running W? Is 'W' significant for something?" Jessica asked.

Ethan squinted in the harsh afternoon light. "The 'Running W' is the brand name that Brother Bartlett's cattle wear. But it stands for the ranch's name, which is The Willows."

"The Willows," Jessica repeated. "That sounds nice. I picture a snug, little cottage tucked among the willows beside a shady stream, with cattle grazing nearby."

Ethan smiled. "It's not exactly like that. The ranch is located in an area referred to as South Willow Creek. When the Saints first arrived in the valley, they discovered the area to be good pasture land. They've been herding cattle and sheep on the foothills every since."

"Are there any towns nearby?"

Ethan considered the question. "There's a town called Draperville three or four miles north of the ranch. I wouldn't be surprised to see range lands eventually give way to more towns."

"You sound disappointed about that."

"I hope it doesn't happen. I like the wide open spaces with plenty of elbow room." Ethan turned to glance at his cousin. "I hope to have my own cattle ranch some day," he added.

"You would? I thought you liked living in town."

"I like being with my family in town, but I'm happiest on the ranch."

Jessica didn't offer a reply.

They rode in silence for a time, enjoying the scenery and the feel of the sun on their faces. Beneath a clear, cloudless sky, the cultivated fields were the color of amber. Traces of snow lingered on the high mountain peaks, but the valley was bursting with spring; emerald-leafed trees and patches of wildflowers, bright as jewels, dotted the wayside. The trill of birds and the smell of freshly-plowed earth drifted in the air. Ethan felt eager to return to his work on the broad, grassy range lands.

Jessica stirred in the wagon seat. "You'd rather become a rancher than a physician, like your father?" she inquired, apparently still reflecting on their earlier conversation.

"A physician? What gave you the idea I'd like to be a doctor?"

"I thought you might take up the profession because your father did."

Ethan slapped the reins across the horses' broad backs, and the animals quickened their step. "No, I haven't the inclination for that sort of work. Father had to apprentice with a physician and then attend medical college. I'd rather be in the outdoors."

Jessica listened without commenting on his response.

"After Father finished his term at the medical college in Chicago, he stopped in Nauvoo to see your parents before returning home to the valley. I think your older sister was a baby at the time," Ethan said.

"Yes, I knew your father came to Nauvoo once to visit Mother. That was the last time they saw one another."

"That's been a lot of years."

Jessica looked at him. "You're right. They've never seen one another since then. I wonder why not. What happened between them, do you know?"

Ethan lifted his shoulders in a shrug. "I don't think anything in particular happened between them. Just time and distance."

"No, something went wrong between them," Jessica replied, shaking her head. "Mother's never said anything specific about it, but I know from the tone of her voice when she speaks about your father that the two of them had some kind of falling out years ago. Mother has never forgiven your father for it."

"What?" Ethan exclaimed. "Forgiven my father? What did he do?"

"I don't know what he did. Offended my mother in some way, apparently."

Ethan straightened in his seat. "Now, wait a minute. My father would never deliberately offend anyone. You must be mistaken about that."

Jessica's gray eyes darkened, signaling an oncoming storm. "I'm not mistaken, Ethan. My mother and your father are estranged, and it must have stemmed from something that happened when your father visited Nauvoo."

Ethan felt a flash of anger. "If there was trouble between the two of them, it wouldn't have been my father's doing."

"You're suggesting that my mother was at fault?"

Ethan grimaced. He hadn't intended to start an argument. "I didn't mean for it to sound that way." He looked over at his cousin. Her mouth was pulled down at the corners. "Come on, Jessica. Let's not carry a misunderstanding our parents had into our own generation." Ethan paused, then added under his breath. "That would be similar to what fueled the war between the Nephites and the Lamanites."

"I don't know what you're talking about," she retorted.

Ethan's shoulders heaved with a sigh. "Let's forget about it, all right? I want you to have a good time at the ranch. Let's not spoil it with disagreements between us."

He sensed Jessica's unyielding displeasure. The cut on his cheek where he'd been slashed with the broken whiskey bottle suddenly started aching. He rubbed the injury with his thumb. He could feel Jessica sitting stiffly beside him, lips pressed together. Now he wasn't so sure it had been a good idea to invite his cousin to the ranch. Her visit might be more of a problem than he'd bargained for. What exactly was he going to do with her once he got her there? She couldn't stay in the bunkhouse with the hired hands. He'd have to depend on Sister Bartlett's hospitality to provide a bed for Jessica at the ranch house. And how would Jessica occupy herself while he was busy with chores on the ranch? Ethan frowned. He wished he'd thought through the situation a little better before extending the invitation to his cousin, he concluded glumly. The next few days would be complicated and confusing, of that he was certain.


Ethan dropped his saddlebag onto the bunk, stifling a yawn. Everyone else in the bunkhouse was asleep for the night; he could hear the cowhands snoring and snorting in their sleep. He yawned again, arched his back in a deep stretch, then plopped down onto the bed. He'd gotten Jessica squared away for the night; Sister Bartlett had been gracious about welcoming Jessica to the ranch house and offering her a bed. And, he had to admit, Jessica had been a good traveler throughout the entire trip to the ranch, never once complaining about the long ride or the bumpy road.

Ethan unfastened the strap on his saddlebag and lifted out the few items of clothing packed inside, then set the saddlebag on the floor beside his bed. He pulled off his boots, removed his shirt and trousers, and climbed under the blanket on his bunk. A pale ribbon of moonlight rippled through the window above his bed, illuminating the faded colors of the patchwork quilt. Clasping his hands together underneath his head, he lay staring up at the ceiling of the bunkhouse, thinking about the day's ride with his cousin. Jessica had continued to be ill-tempered for a time after the argument regarding their parents, but eventually she'd shed her bad humor and warmed up again to Ethan. The rest of the journey had passed pleasantly with the two of them conversing about ranching and school teaching and other topics.

Ethan turned onto his side and gazed at the figure in the bunk next to his. The sleeping lump that was his brother brought a smile to Ethan's lips. He wondered what Samuel's reaction would be when Ethan introduced him tomorrow to their cousin—his smile stretched wider as he pictured Samuel's surprise. The muted moonlight flowing in from the window was soothing. Ethan closed his eyes, basking in its soft glow. In another moment, sleep smoothed every line from his face.

The following morning Ethan awoke at sunrise. The other cowhands were already up, dressing or preparing their gear for the day. Ethan yawned noisily and stretched his arms.

"It's about time you got up."

Ethan felt a pillow slam into his head. "Hey, watch it, little brother." He grabbed the pillow and fired it back at Samuel.

Samuel caught the fluffy missile handily and tossed it onto his bunk. "Did you have a good trip? How's everyone at home?"

"Everyone is fine," he replied, rubbing the sleep from his eyes.

"Did you remember to bring me some of Mother's sourdough biscuits?" Samuel wanted to know. He grasped his spurs from off his bunk and slung them over his shoulder.

"I did. And I brought something else, as well." Ethan could barely suppress a grin.

"Yeah? What is it? More of Mother's home cooking, I hope."

Ethan got to his feet. "You'll have to wait and see, little brother."

"What do you mean by that?"

"You'll know soon enough. Where's my hat?" Ethan said, glancing at the clothing on the floor beside his bunk.

Samuel stooped at the foot of Ethan's bed and scooped up the rumpled, felt hat. He gave the hat a toss, sending it sailing toward his brother.

Ethan snatched it from the air. "Thanks." He slapped the hat on his head, then stood scratching his sides as he surveyed the clothing and other items on the floor. He heard Samuel start to chuckle. "What?" he asked his brother.

"I hope you're planning to wear something more than just your hat and your longjohns into the house for breakfast."

Ethan glanced down at his faded, red, cotton underwear and grinned at the picture of himself.

"See you inside," Samuel said, turning to leave.

"Wait a minute. Where's Rory? Is he out at the corral already this morning?"

"No. He spent the night tending cattle in the south pasture. He thought there might be trouble brewing."

Ethan felt a knot start in the pit of his stomach. "What kind of trouble?"

"Rory didn't say. He'll probably be back for breakfast; you can ask him then."

"Okay. I'll meet you in a few minutes," Ethan said as he reached for his shirt and trousers.

Samuel started toward the door of the bunkhouse.

"Hey," Ethan called after him. "Comb your hair. I want you to make a good impression."

"Huh?"

Ethan just laughed and began pulling on his trousers.

After Samuel left for the ranch house, Ethan hurried with his clothes. Then he headed toward the house with the other ranch hands for breakfast. When he entered the kitchen of the single-story, stone home, he spotted Jessica beside the iron stove, turning flapjacks in a shallow, flat-bottomed pan. He caught her eye and smiled.

Ethan took a seat at the large, oblong table. The kitchen was warm from the heat of the cooking stove, and the Bartletts' children darted to and fro in the morning's stir of excitement. Sister Bartlett greeted each ranch hand as she set the food on the table.

"What happened to your cheek?" Samuel asked, nudging Ethan in the shoulder.

"I had a squabble with a broken whiskey bottle."

Samuel squinted at the cut on his brother's face. "It improves your looks."

Ethan laughed.

"Now if you'll all quiet down, we'll have a blessing on the food," Brother Bartlett announced.

The room immediately fell silent. Each person bowed his head in preparation for the prayer Brother Bartlett pronounced. When he was through, everyone added their "Amen."

The men began to help themselves to the mountain of food Sister Bartlett had prepared. There was a heaping pile of fried potatoes, a stack of steaming flapjacks, and fat sausages. Ethan spooned a mound of potatoes onto his plate. He was just reaching for the flapjacks when Samuel nudged him in the shoulder. "Who's that, do you suppose? Has Sister Bartlett hired a girl to help her in the kitchen?"

Before Ethan could reply, Sister Bartlett took Jessica's arm to introduce her to the ranch hands. "This is Miss Jessica Scott," she said. "She's visiting the ranch for a few days."

Ethan's gaze slid to his cousin. He saw a spot of color redden her cheeks because of the attention drawn to her. She stood at the stove, ready to pour more batter onto the griddle.

"Miss Scott is Ethan's cousin. That makes her Samuel's cousin, too," Sister Bartlett added.

Ethan looked over at his brother just in time to see Samuel's jaw go slack. "Say hello to your cousin," Ethan said. "Jessica, this is my younger brother, Samuel. Samuel, meet Jessica Scott."

Samuel stripped away the napkin tucked in his shirt collar, stood up, and extended a hand across the table to Jessica. She placed her hand in his for an awkward handshake.

After the introductions were completed, Jessica went back to the stove and Samuel dropped onto his chair. He turned to his brother, his face a question.

"Jessica is Aunt Elizabeth's daughter," Ethan explained to him. On seeing his brother's confused expression, he added, "Father's older sister, Aunt Elizabeth."

"The one who lives in Illinois?" Samuel asked, stealing a furtive glance toward the stove.

"They're one and the same."

"But how did she get here?" Samuel rasped.

"It's a long story. I'll tell you about it after breakfast."

Sister Bartlett took over the task of cooking the flapjacks, and Jessica sat down at the far end of the table. Ethan saw her glance at Samuel as she dished herself a plate of food.

"Why didn't you tell me she was here?" Samuel hissed in his brother's ear.

"And ruin the surprise?"

"It's some surprise, all right." He turned to stare at Jessica. "What's she like?"

Ethan shoveled in a mouthful of potatoes before replying, then wiped his mouth with a corner of his napkin. "She's nice. At first I didn't think so, but she is." Ethan's attention returned to his plate of food. He was hungry after eating from a knapsack the day before. But the breakfast was disappointing; the flapjacks were soggy in the center, the sausage was fatty, and the potatoes greasy. Sister Bartlett's kitchen fare was a poor substitute for his own mother's tasty cooking. Ethan ate the lot without complaint, however.

Brother Bartlett and the ranch hands were discussing the day's work, while Sister Bartlett paced from the stove to the table with plates of food and kept an eye on her flock of children. Ethan was nearly finished with his meal before noticing Rory was absent from the table. That meant his friend was still riding herd on the southern boundary of Bartlett's property, where it bordered with Travers' ranch. He hoped Rory hadn't run into any trouble, for he didn't trust Travers' men one speck further than he could throw a stick at them.

He wolfed down the remainder of his breakfast, nudged his brother in the ribs to let him know he was leaving, then excused himself from the table. Before exiting the kitchen, however, he stepped over to speak with Jessica. "I'm going to put my gear away in the bunkhouse, then go on outside," he told her. "When you're finished here, why don't you join me? Samuel and I will be rounding up strays this morning. You can ride with us, if you like."

"All right. Where shall I meet you?"

"By the bunkhouse. It's the double cabin down by the stream. You can't miss seeing it."

Jessica nodded.

After thanking Sister Bartlett for the meal, Ethan returned to the bunkhouse. He tidied up the space around his bunk, tucking away his clothes and straightening the blanket on his bed. At the sound of the bunkhouse door opening, he lifted his head.

"Why didn't you tell me about her?" demanded Samuel as he strode inside.

Ethan sat down on his bunk. "Were you surprised?"

"Stunned. You should have given me some warning."

"Not a chance. It would have spoiled all the fun," Ethan said, grinning. "What did you think of her?"

"Well, I don't know. She's pretty."

"You think every girl is pretty."

"No, she's really pretty. Her hair's redder than a fiery sunset."

Ethan chuckled at his description.

"Why is she here? How did you meet her?" Samuel sat down on the edge of his bunk. "How long is she planning to stay?"

"Which one of those questions do you want me to answer first?" Ethan said with a grin.

"Stop fooling around. Tell me."

Ethan related the story, explaining how Jessica's baggage was stolen from the train as she was traveling to California, the telegram she'd sent to their father, and his trip to the train station to fetch her. He told Samuel, too, about the week's activities while Jessica had been staying at the Kade home.

After he finished rehearsing all the details, Samuel let out his breath in a low whistle. "Well, that's pretty amazing. I don't think I've ever given more than a fleeting thought to our relatives in Illinois."

"Me, either."

"You haven't told me yet why she's here at the ranch."

Ethan shrugged his shoulders. "It was my idea. I thought she'd enjoy seeing the ranch."

"How long is she planning to stay?"

"Until she gets tired of it, I guess." Ethan stood up and began gathering his gear for the day's ride. He pulled his hat over his forehead and tightened the knot in his neckerchief.

Samuel rose to his feet, too. "What are you going to do with her today?" he asked.

"Take her with us."

"Take her with us?" Samuel repeated incredulously. "Out on the range?"

"Yeah. She assures me that she knows how to straddle a horse."

"Ethan, we can't do that. What if she can't ride? And even if she can, she'll slow us down, and we have a lot of work to do."

"She won't be any trouble—at least not the kind you're thinking about. Come on, let's tack up. I told Jessica we'd meet her outside with the horses."

"But, Ethan . . ." Samuel protested as he followed behind his brother.

"You'll relish the experience, little brother. That red hair isn't the only fiery thing you'll notice about her."

# CHAPTER ELEVEN

Jessica slipped out the kitchen door leading to the yard behind the house. The stone ranch house was small, and this morning at breakfast it had been filled to its seams with children and hired men. Mrs. Bartlett had given her a room to share with her two oldest daughters; though the room was cramped, Jessica appreciated the bed, which she had to herself. She started across the yard, eager to join Ethan and Samuel. She smiled as she thought about her newly acquainted cousin. Samuel seemed pleasant; he was a few inches shorter than his older brother, she'd noticed, and stockier in build, with light brown hair and brown eyes that reflected an affable nature.

Behind the house, Jessica noticed a number of outbuildings and fenced pens dotting the open ground. Ethan wasn't in sight, but she easily spotted the double cabins that he had appointed as the meeting place. They were constructed of adobe and connected by a roofed porch between them. The sod roof was sprouting spring grass. Jessica headed toward it, intending to wait for her cousins under the shaded porch.

The morning was warm, and the scent of spring drifted on the breeze; but another odor permeated the air as well—the pungent, hardy smell of cattle. She spied the animals in their holding pens; there seemed to be hundreds of them milling around the big enclosures, bawling their discontent in being penned up. A sea of sharp-tipped horns made Jessica wonder how the cattle avoided poking their horns into the hides of their fellows.

In the shade of the porch the air was cool, and she reflected on the day before her. Ethan had said they would be rounding up stray cattle. She had no idea how far the ride would take her, or how lengthy it would be, but she looked forward to the experience and was determined to keep up with her cousins.

Just then she spotted them coming from the direction of the corral; Samuel was mounted and leading a saddled horse, a sleek-coated, speckled gray. Ethan was astride his bay gelding; he'd put on a pair of chaps over his trousers, and his hat was slung low over his brow.

Jessica was about to step from the porch to join them when the sound of galloping hooves coming from the south caught her attention. She spotted a rider on a brown and white pinto, and when he drew closer she saw that the young man on horseback was about Ethan's age. As he reined his paint toward Ethan and Samuel, Jessica noted the ease with which the rider sat in his saddle. His person seemed to be an extension of the horse; both moving in perfect symmetry.

"Ethan, good to see you back," the man on horseback said as he brought his mount to a stop.

"Howdy, Rory. Are you just getting in?"

Jessica hung back, not wanting to disturb the men while they talked.

"Yeah, I spent the night in the south pasture. Travers' men have been handy with the branding iron. I counted half a dozen calves nuzzling the wrong cows."

Ethan issued a low whistle.

"You sure they were Brother Bartlett's cattle?" asked Samuel.

"The brands were altered, and they did a sloppy job of it, too."

"Did you run into any of Travers' ranch hands?" Ethan asked, frowning.

"No, but I wouldn't go riding fences without a six-shooter strapped to my leg."

Jessica felt a shiver ripple down her spine. Cattle rustling? Here, at The Willows? Though she didn't know much about ranching, she was aware that stealing cattle was a serious offense—with dangerous consequences. She stepped out from the shadow of the porch and into the plain view of the men.

The cowhand who had just ridden in looked at her with a startled glance. Ethan and Samuel, too, turned toward her.

"Jessica, there you are," Ethan said, his mouth softening into a smile.

Samuel whisked off his hat. "Hello, again," he said.

Jessica's eyes moved from her cousins to the cowboy astride his paint. He had his hat off, wiping his forehead with the sleeve of his blue cotton shirt. A blue and red bandana was tied loosely around his throat. His look of surprise gave way to a curious smile.

Ethan dismounted from his horse. "Jessica, meet Rory McKellar, one of the cowhands here. Rory, this is Jessica Scott, our cousin. She's staying at the ranch for a few days."

"Pleased to make your acquaintance, Miss Scott," the cowhand said. He climbed off his horse and extended a hand to Jessica. She accepted the cowboy's firm handshake. "I hope you have a nice stay while at the ranch."

Jessica's attention centered on the young man's eyes, which were a dusky blue. His hair was nearly as blonde as Ethan's, though longer, coming to rest on the collar of his open-necked shirt. Her glance took in a rawhide vest, big silver belt buckle set with turquoise stones, and leather chaps with fringe running down the outside seam. A gunbelt and holster was around his lean waist, with the butt of a pistol glinting in the morning sunlight. "Thank you, Mr. McKellar." She turned to her cousin. "Ethan, I was waiting for you beside the cabins and couldn't help overhearing your conversation."

Ethan passed a hand over his chin. "There's been some trouble between Brother Bartlett and a neighboring rancher named Charles Travers, but it should blow over," he told her.

From the corner of her eye, Jessica caught the hasty look exchanged between Samuel and Rory—a look that did not confirm Ethan's optimism.

"Here," Ethan said, handing her the reins to the speckled gray horse. "I borrowed a mare for you. The wranglers tell me she's as gentle as a lamb. Sorry there's no side-saddle available. Can you ride astride in your dress?"

Jessica nodded, although she was reluctant to abandon the topic Ethan seemed so anxious to leave behind.

"Let me help you up into the stirrup," Ethan offered.

"No, thank you. I can manage." Jessica grasped the saddle horn with one hand, stepped into the stirrup, and swung gracefully into the saddle. She smoothed the skirt of her yellow print dress, settling the hem in place to cover her buttoned shoes. She felt Rory McKellar's eyes studying her and flushed with a sudden onrush of self-consciousness.

"Are you heading back onto the range?" Samuel asked the cowhand.

"After I get some breakfast inside me—if there's any left after you ate your share," Rory replied with a friendly grin. "Which direction are you boys riding?"

Jessica saw his eyes flitter to her face before resting his gaze on Ethan.

"I thought we'd show Jessica around the ranch a bit, then head for the foothills where she can get a good look at the valley," Ethan answered. "You want to join us?"

"Yeah, maybe I will." Rory climbed back into his saddle. The paint whinnied and pawed the ground. "I'll eat, have a word with Bartlett, then catch up with you. All right?"

"Sure," Ethan said. Samuel nodded in agreement.

"You don't mind my tagging along, do you, Miss Scott?" He replaced his hat as he spoke, tugging the brim over his forehead. In the shadow of his wide-brimmed hat, the color of his eyes changed from smoky blue to gray.

"Whatever suits you, Mr. McKellar."

"Good. Then I'll see you later." He gave her a nod, then touched his heels to the pinto's flanks. Jessica watched the horse and rider move away.

"Let's mount up," Ethan said to his brother. The two men swung into their saddles, the spurs on their boots jingling. "You set?" Ethan asked his cousin.

Jessica nodded, settling into the saddle.

Ethan led out, but Samuel hung back so he could ride beside Jessica. "Have you ever been to a cattle ranch before?" he asked her.

"No, I haven't."

"Well, you've come at a good time. There's plenty going on at the ranch right now because of the roundup."

Jessica nudged her horse forward. The gray had a smooth gait and a gentle disposition. "What happens during the roundup?" she asked.

"The roundup generally takes place twice a year, in the fall and the spring," Samuel explained. "The cowboys round up the cattle from the range, herd them to the ranch, then sort them."

"What kind of sorting?" she asked.

Samuel adjusted the rope coiled over his saddle horn. "We sort out the new calves for branding, corral the three- and four-year-olds for market, and separate any diseased or undersized animals from the herd."

"And then the cowhands count the herd," Ethan added, reining in his horse to match stride with the other two.

"It used to be that all the cattle from various ranches in an area grazed their herd together on the open range," Samuel went on. "Then the main purpose of the roundup was to sort out your own cattle according to the animals' markings stamped on their hides."

"The rancher's brand," Jessica said, nodding her head.

"That's right," Samuel replied. "Each rancher has his own brand to identify his cattle from his neighbor's herd."

"But just this spring Brother Bartlett put up fencing to keep his cows inside a designated grazing ground, and to keep other ranchers' cattle out," Ethan related.

"If you look over there, you can see where we've corralled Brother Bartlett's cattle while sorting them," Samuel told her, indicating the brood of lowing cattle Jessica had noticed earlier.

They rode past the cattle pens, Jessica eyeing the beasts and wrinkling her nose at the strong odor.

"Over that way is where we keep the horses," Samuel informed her, nodding toward another corral adjacent to a large, red barn. "The wrangler tends the horses, keeping fresh ones ready for the cowhands to use."

"Are you finished with the roundup?"

Ethan answered her question. "Just about. We're in the process of bringing in the last of the strays. That's what Samuel and I will be doing today, and Rory, when he joins up with us."

"How many cowhands work on the ranch?" Jessica asked, thinking about Rory McKellar and his striking, blue eyes.

"Six of us at the moment. The number fluctuates, depending on the season of the year and the work to be done on the ranch," answered Samuel.

"That reminds me of something I wanted to ask you," Ethan said, turning to his brother. "Did Hodkins and Anderson pick up those new Durham steers Brother Bartlett purchased?"

"Yeah. They're with the herd."

Jessica listened as her cousins discussed the new steers. She remembered Ethan telling her how Bartlett wanted to upgrade his herd by introducing purebred Durham cattle, and guessed this was the gist of the conversation at hand. The two cowhands they'd mentioned, Hodkins and Anderson, she'd met that morning at breakfast.

By this time, the three of them had left the corrals and cattle pens behind and were traveling a dusty trail toward the foothills. As they climbed the grassy hillside, Jessica saw spread below her a wide, green valley. The pungent smell of sagebrush, mixed with the tang of cattle and horseflesh, permeated the air. Jessica breathed in the sights and smells of the land, feeling a thrill of exhilaration. Her desire to see the West firsthand, witness its rugged landscape for herself, was being realized in a way she had never expected, and she found herself reveling in it.

"There're a couple of strays behind that ridge," Ethan said, pointing to the spot. He and Samuel spurred their horses into a gallop. "Wait here. We'll be right back," Ethan called to her as they dashed toward a grassy knoll several yards away.

At first, Jessica could see nothing but green grass and low-growing brush, but as her cousins neared the top of the knoll, three steers suddenly trotted from behind a clump of sagebrush. Jessica was surprised at how easily Ethan had spotted the animals, when she hadn't noticed them at all. Her cousins split up their approach, circling on either side of the cattle. With the trio of steers between them, they deftly herded the animals down the hilly ridge.

Jessica noticed her cousin's skill in managing the cattle. As he drove them to the spot where she waited, Ethan's actions were sure and confident. "I'm impressed," Jessica said to her cousins when they reached her side.

"With what?" Ethan asked, waving his coiled rope at one of the steers that was attempting to head off in a new direction.

"Your cowboying skills. You had those cows right where you wanted them in seconds flat."

"That was nothing. Wait until you see how fast we can rope these critters for branding."

"I'm sure it's amazing," Jessica agreed with a laugh.

"Of course, I'm much better than Ethan at roping cows," said Samuel, grinning.

"You want to make a wager on that, little brother?"

"Yeah. I'll bet you two bits that come branding I can rope the first calf faster than you can."

"You've got a bet," Ethan replied promptly. "Two bits plus your share of dessert at supper."

"Deal," Samuel pronounced.

Jessica laughed. "I hope your skills are equal to your boasting."

"You can ask Rory about that. Here he comes," Ethan said, gesturing down the hillside.

Jessica shaded her eyes against the sun, watching Rory's pinto loping through the tall grass toward them. The sunlight shimmering on the animal's coat turned the patches of brown to gleaming copper.

He tipped his hat at Jessica in greeting as his paint pranced to a stop, and Jessica nodded in acknowledgment. "I see you boys have been busy," Rory remarked, eyeing the three steers. "Seen any others?"

"These are all so far. Let's ride further south," Ethan suggested.

Driving the steers before them, the four trotted their horses in a southerly direction across the foothills. As they descended into a steep-sided gully, Jessica shifted her weight in the saddle, and in doing so discovered the hem of her skirt was tangled in one of the stirrups. She lifted her foot from the stirrup and tugged at the folds of her dress, but the fabric was stuck fast and she was unable to free it.

"Please allow me." She heard Rory's voice and looked up to find his eyes crinkling with a smile. "May I?" he asked, as he leaned down and extended a hand to untangle her skirt from the stirrup. In an instant he had the task accomplished.

"Thank you," Jessica replied.

"It's my pleasure."

Jessica felt awkward clothed in her long skirt of printed cotton. If she intended to fully appreciate her experience on the ranch, she decided, then she would dress consistent with the style of clothing worn here. Tomorrow she'd ask Samuel if she might borrow a pair of his trousers and a flannel shirt. Samuel was a few inches shorter than Ethan, and his clothing would fit her better than Ethan's. She'd borrow a hat, too. The bun she wore at the back of her head had loosened during her ride and tendrils of auburn hair trailed down her neck. She felt Rory's eyes appraising her and wished for a broad-brimmed hat like the kind the men wore, so she could pull the brim over her face and avoid the cowboy's open gaze.

"Are you from the Utah Territory, Miss Scott?" asked Rory.

Jessica glanced at him. He held the reins loosely in one hand, his body moving in harmony with the horse. "No, I'm not. I grew up in Illinois."

"Is that right? I was born in that part of the country. Indiana."

"Oh?"

"I lived in Indianapolis until I was sixteen. My father is a mint farmer there," Rory continued.

"A mint farmer?"

"Yes. He grows spearmint and peppermint."

Jessica pictured a field of glossy green and could almost smell its fragrance.

"What does your father do in Illinois?" He offered her a ready smile.

"He operates a lumber mill."

Rory raised his brows in interest. "Have you brothers and sisters back home?" he asked.

"Two sisters. No brothers," Jessica replied. "And you?"

"I'm the eldest of six children. Sometimes I really miss my family," he added.

She found herself responding to his friendly and easy manner. "Why did you leave Indiana?"

"That's a long story," he began, smiling at her. "My grandfather left Ireland during the potato famine in '46, and—"

"You're Irish?" Jessica interrupted.

He put a hand to his chest and said in a thick Irish accent, "Aye, lass. I'm wearin' a wee bit of a shamrock over my heart."

Jessica suppressed a giggle. "Go on," she said. "What about your grandfather?"

"For generations, my father's family were dock workers in Dublin. That was the only life my grandfather knew. But he couldn't provide for his family during the years of the Great Hunger, and so he booked passage on a ship sailing for the United States." Rory paused in his narration to push aside an overhanging branch. "My father and the rest of his brothers and sisters came over piecemeal, as Grandfather could pay for their passage. The family lived in New Jersey for a few years."

"There're not many shamrocks in New Jersey, I'd imagine," she said, smiling. He laughed, and Jessica liked the deep, rich sound of it. "Did your grandfather work on the docks there?"

"Yes, he did, and so did my father for awhile. But farming suited Father's temperament better than loading freight, and so he took his new bride and moved to Indiana."

Jessica glanced at her two cousins, who were still deep in conversation. She smiled to herself, amused by their friendly rivalry with one another when it came to their responsibilities on the ranch. She wondered what the brothers thought of Rory, and if they were friends as well as working partners. "So what brought you out west, away from Indiana?" she asked Rory as they rode together along the hillside.

"Grandfather's the one who told me about the West. He'd heard stories about it from travelers while working the docks in Dublin. Grandfather wanted to see the West for himself, but couldn't because he had a large family to provide for. He instilled in me that desire. He filled my head with tales about buffalo, and Indians, and high mountain streams so plentiful with fish that a fellow only had to dip his hand in the water in order to catch them." Rory smiled, and a tender look crept into his eyes.

"So you came west because of the stories your grandfather told you," Jessica summarized.

"I was sixteen and had the wanderlust. In my imagination, the West was a place of mystery and excitement, and I wanted to see it for myself, as well as for my grandfather. Grandfather had died by that time, but I'd inherited his dream, and I was set on realizing it. I left home with only my horse between my knees and a knapsack on my back, and started making my way westward. I'd been gone about two weeks when—"

"Rory, look over that way. There're half a dozen cows down by the stream near the willows," Ethan said, indicating the spot with a nod of his head.

"Let's go," Samuel whooped.

"Don't go away," Rory joked, turning to grin at Jessica. He spurred his horse and the animal galloped off. Jessica watched the handsome paint surge ahead of the other two horses, its coat of dazzling white and burnished red gleaming in the morning light.

The cowboys quickly had the cattle corralled and moving back up the hillside toward Jessica and the three steers they'd caught earlier. Now a small herd surrounded her, mooing and bawling their loss of independence. The points of their horns glimmered in the sun, and their stocky, roan bodies shone with sweat from the forced run.

The men circled the cattle, shouting and waving their arms to get the beasts all moving in the same direction. The smell of cattle was strong in the air; Jessica crinkled her nose, not yet accustomed to the tangy odor.

"Gid up, there," Ethan hallooed, reining his bay in a hard left to box off a straying cow. Soon the cowboys had the herd under control, and Rory trotted his horse again to Jessica's side.

"Do you think you have all of the cattle now?" she asked him.

"Probably not. We'll be rounding up steers for another few days. You'd be surprised how far these animals can roam," he answered.

The two of them rode side by side. "What happened after you'd been gone from home for only a couple of weeks?" Jessica asked impulsively.

Rory smiled. "That's right. I was in the middle of telling you my history."

Jessica stole a glance at him. His face was brown from the sun, and the deep blue shirt he wore matched the color of his eyes.

"So I hadn't been gone long when I happened to meet some Texas drovers who'd just completed a cattle drive to the railhead in Abilene. They had plenty of money in their pockets and plenty of stories to tell about their time on the trail. Both aspects appealed to me. So I rode with them all the way to Texas and joined up with the first cattle drive heading north I could find."

"How did you like the experience?"

"I enjoyed it, which was surprising to me. I'd been thinking more in terms of becoming an Indian scout, not a cowpuncher." He chuckled to himself.

"An Irish Kit Carson, is that it?" she said with a smile.

He laughed. "I guess so," he replied, pushing his hat back from his forehead.

"Over there," Samuel called out. "See those three or four steers in the thicket of brush near the stream?"

Jessica looked toward the creek, where she caught a glimpse of hooved feet and sturdy legs through a gap in the brush. Rory and her cousins started off on their horses. They were just about to the stream when two horsemen burst out of the thick brush, driving half a dozen head of cattle before them, shouting and whistling to keep the animals moving. Jessica watched the cattle gallop madly on their short, muscular legs. It took a moment for her to realize that the two men driving the cattle were herding them *away* from Rory and her cousins, not toward them. Her eyes darted to her companions; they were urging their horses forward, racing after the pair of strangers.

At first, Jessica was confused by the drama playing out in front of her. She heard Rory's angry shout and saw Ethan spurring his horse. Rory and her cousins sped after the two horsemen, steadily closing the distance between them.

Suddenly, a shot rang out. Jessica recoiled in horror as she watched one of the strangers on horseback turn in his saddle and fire his pistol a second time. The sound reverberated against the hillside, echoing in Jessica's ears.

At the sound of the second shot, Ethan and Samuel reined in their horses, but Rory continued to give chase. Ethan shouted for him to stop, but it wasn't until a third shot burst through the air that the cowhand slowed his mount.

As the pair of strangers galloped away, driving the cattle before them, Rory rejoined Ethan and Samuel.

Jessica let out her breath in a strident gasp of relief when the three turned their horses and started back toward her. "Those men shot at you!" she cried, when they reached her side. "Why?"

Ethan removed his hat and wiped his brow with the sleeve of his shirt. "They're Travers' men. First they were cutting fences, and now they're stealing cattle," he answered bitterly.

"I didn't think they'd carry it this far," Samuel muttered under his breath.

"They were firing at you!" exclaimed Jessica. "And could have killed you." She was trembling with shock and anger.

Rory reined his horse closer to hers. "Everything is all right," he said soothingly to her. "Those drovers were just trying to scare us off; they were after the cattle."

Jessica wanted to believe him, but the concern in her cousins' eyes persuaded her otherwise. "Tell me what's going on here, Ethan," she demanded.

Ethan wearily leaned on the saddle horn. "Travers arrived here about four months ago and started up a cattle ranch. At first he was friendly with Brother Bartlett, but then he began complaining about water rights for his stock. He accused Bartlett of diverting water from the creek to bypass his property."

"Which wasn't true, of course," Samuel put in.

"No, it wasn't true. And I don't think Travers himself believed it. It was just a ploy to access more water."

A scowl darkened Jessica's face. "So this Travers wants access to more water for his ranch, and your Brother Bartlett won't give it to him. Is that correct?"

"Not entirely," Rory answered, taking up the narrative. "There's more to it than that. What Travers really wants is to increase his herd, which means he needs more land to graze his cows with easy access to water."

"His ultimate goal is to drive Brother Bartlett right out of the cattle business and increase his own holdings at Bartlett's expense," Ethan summed up.

Jessica ran a nervous hand across her brow. Her cousins were getting caught in the middle of this feud going on between Travers and Bartlett, and that was a perilous position to be in."

"Let's go back to the ranch," Samuel suggested, "and tell Brother Bartlett what's happened. He has legal recourse if Travers and his men are rustling cattle."

Jessica's head was buzzing with all she'd seen and heard. Erased was her image of The Willows as a peaceful, tranquil spot beside a gentle stream. She was beginning to understand that the West was a restless place, capable of inspiring in men raw emotion and unbridled passion and greed. As she rode back to the ranch house in company with the men, her mind reeled from the harsh encounter she'd witnessed on the open grasslands.

# CHAPTER TWELVE

As Ethan and Samuel strode to the corral to saddle their horses, and the gray mare for Jessica, they paused to eye a trio of wild mustangs snorting and stamping inside a gated section of the enclosure. Bartlett had been wanting to acquire more horses to use on the ranch, and yesterday when one of the ranch hands spotted the wild herd five miles to the west, near the Jordan River, Bartlett sent Ethan and a couple of the other cowhands to capture some of the animals.

"That black sure is a beauty," Samuel commented.

"Yeah, isn't he?" Ethan replied, admiring the coal black coat and coarse dark mane of one of the mustangs pacing the corral. "He's the most spirited of the three. He hasn't stopped kicking up his heels since we brought him in."

Ethan rested his arms on the top rail of the gate, studying the untamed horses. With the two men in sight, the mustangs began galloping around the corral, looking for an escape. Ethan watched the black toss his head and rear up on his hind legs.

"Come on, let's go. Jessica's waiting for us," Samuel finally said, elbowing his brother in the shoulder.

Ethan kept his eyes on the black mustang as he followed Samuel into the main portion of the corral. His hands itched to rub the mustang's muscled neck, and feel the power of the horse beneath a saddle.

"I hope all goes well at the meeting with Travers this afternoon," Samuel commented as he saddled his sorrel.

Ethan glanced at his brother. "I hope so, too. I feel better about it knowing Rory will be there." His thoughts went back to three days earlier and the incident with Travers' men at the creek. Bartlett had been upset to hear about the stolen cattle. In their report to him, Ethan and Rory had left out the part about Travers' men shooting at them; they didn't see any point in fueling the feud. Bartlett decided to pay a call to Charles Travers to discuss the problem, and Ethan hoped the two men would be able to resolve their differences.

As Ethan saddled the gray mare, his thoughts turned to Jessica. He was sorry she'd witnessed the ugly scene at the creek. He'd wanted her to have a good experience at the ranch, and instead her first impression was one of violence. He frowned as he tightened the cinch around the gray's belly.

"I think you should have told Brother Bartlett about Travers' men firing on us, though," Samuel said, slipping the bridle over his horse's nose.

"We will, if it happens again. In the meanwhile, we'll keep a sharper eye out when we're on the range." Rory's earlier admonition about packing a gun was probably good advice, but Ethan hadn't strapped on his Colt this afternoon. And, he noticed, neither had Samuel. He shrugged, convinced they wouldn't run into any trouble from Travers' cowhands on the pleasure ride to the creek.

After saddling and bridling the gray, he turned to his own horse. He threw the saddle blanket across the gelding's back and patted the animal's rump. He'd purchased the handsome quarterhorse only six months earlier and hadn't once regretted his choice. The animal's coat was a glossy reddish-brown, with black mane, tail, and legs. Ethan had wanted the horse the moment he set eyes on him. He hefted the saddle onto the gelding's back and fastened the cinch.

"Do you think it's safe to take Jessica?" Samuel asked.

"I don't think anyone will bother us at the creek. She's set on having a picnic there, and maybe the herd of wild horses will still be in the vicinity. I'd like to show her the herd. They look pretty magnificent running free in the wild." Ethan bridled his bay and then climbed into the saddle, leading the gray by its reins. He waited for Samuel to mount up.

"You know, yesterday evening she asked me for the strangest thing," Samuel remarked as he swung into the saddle.

"Yeah? What was that?"

"She asked to borrow a pair of my old trousers, a shirt and hat. Now what do you suppose she wanted with those things?"

Ethan lifted his shoulders in a shrug. "Don't know."

They trotted their horses out of the corral and toward the ranch house where Jessica waited. "Are we going to do a little bronc busting when we get back?" Ethan asked his brother, glancing back at the wild mustangs penned in the corral.

"You bet."

"That black is a stick of dynamite."

"That should make it interesting."

"I'll bet that outlaw throws you inside of sixty seconds," Ethan said with a grin.

"Is that so? How much do you want to wager on that?"

"I'll bet you . . . hey, Samuel, who's that?" Ethan asked, interrupting his own sentence. He stared at the house, where a slight figure in brown trousers, flannel shirt, and wide-brimmed, floppy hat stood on the porch.

"I don't know," Samuel replied, squinting at the stranger.

"Must be a boy; he's too short and small to be a man."

"Why, that's my shirt and hat!" Samuel exclaimed. An instant later, his face broke into a smile, and a chuckle started in his throat.

"What are you grinning about?" Ethan asked, not grasping the reason for Samuel's amusement.

Samuel's brown eyes sparkled with laughter. "Take another look at that partner, Ethan, and I think you'll recognize who it is."

As Ethan stared at the young boy who was strutting toward them, he started in surprise. "It's Jessica!" he choked. "Why in tarnation is she dressed like that?"

"Afternoon," Jessica called. "You boys are a couple of slowpokes. I've been waiting for you."

"Jessica! What . . . Why . . ." Ethan couldn't get the words out of his throat.

"You look swell, Jessica," said Samuel brightly.

"Thanks, Samuel. I rolled the legs on the trousers a bit and cinched in the waist, but other than that, the clothes fit well enough. Thank you for lending them to me."

"Jessica, what are you doing? You're dressed like a man!" Ethan exploded.

"Do you like it?" She shot him a beguiling grin from beneath her low-fitting cowboy hat.

"Well, I'm surprised . . . that is, you look so different," Ethan answered, stumbling over his words.

"Stop gaping, Ethan, and hand me the reins to my horse."

Ethan passed the reins to her, conscious of the fact that his mouth was hanging open in astonishment.

Jessica gave him the picnic basket to carry, then took the reins and climbed into the saddle.

Ethan heard Samuel chortling at his side.

"This is much more practical attire for riding," Jessica said briskly, addressing both her cousins.

"Oh, I agree wholeheartedly," Samuel replied with a grin.

Ethan closed his mouth, at a loss for words. He followed behind Samuel and Jessica, nudging his horse onward with a flick of his heels. Ethan stared at his cousin's form-fitting trousers. He'd never seen a woman dressed in trousers and a flannel shirt before. His mother and sister always wore skirts, even when riding. The only women he'd ever heard about wearing men's clothing were the coarse, flinty girlfriends of outlaws who toted rifles instead of cooking pots. And Jessica definitely didn't fit that category. He gazed in amazement at the back of Jessica's small, slender figure as she rode beside Samuel.

The threesome left the yard and headed west toward the grassy flatlands near the creek. Samuel and Jessica carried on an easy chatter as they rode, but Ethan hung back, still startled by his cousin's change in appearance. As their horses moved through clumps of sagebrush, bunch grass, and desert weeds, Ethan kept an eye out for straying cattle wearing the 'running W' brand. He slowly relaxed as he sat in the saddle, the rhythm of the gelding's gait soothing his jangled nerves.

"Ethan told me the ranch runs about 1,500 head of cattle," Jessica said to her cousin.

"Yes, that's right. We'll get an accurate count this week after we have all the stock in," replied Samuel. "We always lose a few cows to injuries and accidents, and some to disease."

"Do you like ranching, Samuel," asked Jessica.

"It's all right, I suppose. Ethan's the one who urged me to come out here to the ranch to work with him for a season. I think he probably enjoys it more than I do, right Ethan?"

"I reckon," Ethan responded.

"If you don't particularly like ranching, Samuel, what kind of work do you want to pursue?" asked Jessica.

"I don't know for sure. Maybe apprentice as a carpenter or a blacksmith. Or perhaps farm." Samuel shrugged his shoulders.

"What would you think about becoming a schoolmaster?" Jessica asked, smiling.

"Oh, no. I couldn't wait to get out of school. I'm not about to enter the classroom again for any reason," Samuel replied emphatically.

"I'll bet you'd be good at it. You're congenial and have an easy way with people."

Ethan listened absently to the exchange going on at his side while he scoured the hills for stray cattle. It annoyed him just a bit that Samuel was paying more attention to his conversation with Jessica, than to keeping a lookout for strays.

"What made you choose teaching as a profession?" Samuel asked her.

"Well, as a teacher I can accomplish a lot of good and influence the lives of children."

Ethan glanced at his cousin, thinking about the textbook on arithmetic he'd purchased from the Quill and Ink and his intention to give the volume to Jessica as a parting gift when she boarded the train for California. She hadn't mentioned anything yet, however, about wanting to leave the ranch.

The three of them rode the grassy knolls and valleys for the next hour without spotting a single steer. Ethan was growing satisfied that all the cattle were accounted for and safely corralled back at the ranch. He had the stream in sight, where they planned to stop and picnic, when he noticed his horse was limping. He leaned over in the saddle and studied the gelding's right foreleg, but could detect nothing wrong. He let the bay continue its gait for a moment longer before pulling on the rein.

"Hold up," Ethan said. "My bay is favoring his right leg. He's probably picked up a rock." Ethan dismounted and ran his hand down the animal's foreleg, then lifted up the hoof to inspect the inside of it for any foreign material.

"I think I'll get down for a minute, too," Jessica said. "I'm getting saddlesore." She slipped from the saddle and raised her arms overhead, stretching her back.

Samuel, also, got off his horse and tossed the reins over a clump of brush. "Do you want to take a walk and stretch your legs?" he asked Jessica.

"Sure," she replied. "While Ethan's seeing to his horse, let's walk over to that patch of wildflowers. They're every color of the rainbow."

Samuel and Jessica drifted away, leaving Ethan with the gelding. He examined the horse's hoof and found a pebble embedded in the fleshy underside, lodged against the rim of the iron horseshoe. "Whoa, boy, take it easy," he murmured to the animal as he tried to pry out the stone with his fingers. But the stone was stuck fast.

He reached into his trouser pocket for his jackknife to dig out the pebble, and had just opened the blade when he heard an ominous rattling start near his feet. The horse heard it, too, and shied, lurching backward. Ethan grasped a tighter hold on the reins as the bay sidestepped and whinnied nervously. The rattle sounded again, louder and more insistent this time.

The gelding yanked its head, tearing the reins out of Ethan's hands. Already off balance from trying to hold in his horse, Ethan stumbled and fell backward onto the ground. The horse, freed from Ethan's restraint and spooked by the snake's rattle, galloped blindly off, dragging the reins in the dirt.

Ethan felt a sharp jab of pain in his hip where he'd struck against a rock embedded in a patch of brush. As he reached out to remove the rock, his hand froze in mid-air. Only inches away, partially obscured by the brush, the glistening, triangular head of a rattlesnake appeared, poised above its coiled body.

Ethan sucked in his breath. The snake's slitted, black eyes locked on Ethan, and its tongue darted in and out of its scaly mouth. The rattles on the reptile's tail made a whirring sound.

"Ethan?" he heard Samuel shout from a few yards' distance. "Where'd your horse take off to?"

"Ethan, are you all right?" echoed Jessica's startled voice.

Ethan carefully began to inch away from the snake. His forehead broke out in a sweat, and his heart was thrashing inside his chest. He saw the snake writhe into a tighter coil and hunker down, poised to strike.

Then he heard Samuel and Jessica running toward him, unaware of the snake. Any quick movement or sound from him would surely cause the viper to spring. Ethan felt panic rising inside him. He fought for control, forcing himself to think clearly. The snake's head remained motionless above its thick coils, but its tail rattled stridently. The cold, black eyes chilled Ethan to the bone. He sensed the snake was about to strike.

His brother and cousin came into sight, and in a voice barely above a whisper, he warned them, "Rattler. Next to my left hip."

Ethan saw his brother's eyes grow big with apprehension. Jessica, a few steps behind him, gasped when she spied the rattlesnake.

The snake slithered on its coils, its forked tongue licking the air. Ethan closed his eyes, certain the snake would hit.

At that instant, the sharp crack of gunfire filled the air. The loudness and nearness of the shot set his ears ringing. He winced, unsure of the bullet's target. Then he saw a spit of dust near his hip settle to the ground. His eyes fixed on the writhing body of the snake next to him. The rattlesnake wriggled and shuddered, then finally lay still, a gaping wound torn in its diamond-patterned body.

Ethan's breath rushed out in an audible gasp. His legs quivered as he scrambled to his feet. He bent over the dead rattler and shuddered when he saw the huge size of it. Driving his eyes away from the snake, he focused on his brother's ashen face. "Thanks, Samuel. I didn't think you'd brought your gun with you, but I'm mighty glad you did."

Samuel's voice was a squeak. "I didn't bring a gun. It was Jessica who shot the snake."

"What?" Ethan rasped. He stared at Jessica, who looked even more white-faced and shaken than Samuel. At her feet lay a bouquet of wildflowers, scattered by their abrupt fall to the ground, and in her hand she gripped a revolver. "*You* shot the snake?" Ethan gasped.

"I did it on impulse, Ethan, without thinking. Thank goodness you're all right." She came toward him with a stumbling step.

Ethan peered into her face. "Where did you learn to shoot like that?"

Jessica glanced at the Smith and Wesson in her hand. "From my father. He thought I should learn how to shoot a gun if I was coming out west by myself. He spent several hours with me in practice."

Ethan offered her a heart-felt grin. "You probably saved my life. Do you know that?"

She stared at him, blinking, then a slow smile smoothed the anxiety from her face.

Samuel stepped to his cousin's side. "May I see that pistol for a moment?" he asked Jessica.

She handed it to him hastily, almost with distaste for the weapon.

Samuel rolled it over in his hand. "A Smith and Wesson, and it's a beauty, too. Look at the markings on the grip, Ethan."

Ethan studied the gun resting in Samuel's hand. "Why did you bring it?" he asked Jessica.

"Like I told you, my father thought I shouldn't go out west unarmed and—"

"No," Ethan interrupted, shaking his head. "Why did you bring it today?"

"Because of the trouble with the rancher and because of Rory's warning."

"What warning?" Samuel asked.

"I overheard Rory telling you to wear a gun when working out on the range. So I took his advice."

"I'll be hog-tied," Ethan said with a laugh.

"That was a smart move," added Samuel. He returned the gun to her.

"Where were you keeping that thing all morning?" Ethan asked as he dusted off his trousers. His hip hurt where he'd fallen against the rock, and the rope burns from having the reins torn from his hand stung his palm and fingers.

"I carried the pistol in my handbag all the way from Illinois. Since I couldn't take the bag with me out riding, I put the gun under my shirt, tucked in the waistband of my trousers. Samuel's trousers, that is."

Ethan's brows rushed together in a scowl. "It's a wonder you didn't shoot yourself. What if your horse had shied or taken a fall? That gun could have easily gone off."

"I don't think she needs your criticism right now," Samuel advised his brother. "She just saved your life, remember?"

"You're right," he said to Samuel. He turned to Jessica with a smile. "Do you know what? I believe we've discovered your hidden talent, after all."

"What are you talking about?" she replied with a frown.

"Remember our conversation on my parents' porch when we were discussing talents? Well, I've uncovered yours. You're an extraordinary shot."

Samuel started to chuckle at that remark, and then so did Jessica. Ethan pushed the brim of his hat off his forehead and laughed heartily.


Ethan squinted in the fading sunlight as he sat outside the bunkhouse whittling a stump of wood. He shaved off a thin layer of wood with his pocketknife and smoothed the exposed surface with his thumb. He concentrated on his work, putting everything else out of mind as he carved the piece with short, smooth strokes of his jackknife. The sound of footsteps caused him to glance up from his work.

"Evening, Jessica," he said on seeing her approach from the house.

"Hello, Ethan." She came to his side and leaned against the adobe wall of the bunkhouse. "Nice night, isn't it?" she said to him.

"It is. Warm, for only the end of May."

"Yes."

Ethan watched her lift her chin to look up at the sky. The glow from a three-quarter moon shone on her upturned face.

"What are you whittling?" she asked after a moment of silence.

He held up the small stump of wood, turning it so the moonlight reflected off the smoothed surface. "I'm not sure yet," he hedged, smiling at her. "Let me get a chair from the bunkhouse for you." He thrust the piece of wood into his trouser pocket and went into the bunkhouse for the chair, then set it down next to his.

"Thank you."

From the direction of the horse corral came a fitful whinny and the sound of hooves pawing the dirt ground. "Sounds like those mustangs are resenting their confinement," Ethan remarked.

Jessica glanced toward the corral. Dark shadows moved restlessly in the enclosure.

"Brother Bartlett is anxious to get them saddlebroken."

"Are you going to do it?"

Ethan nodded. "Me, Samuel, and Rory, too. You can watch, if you want to."

"I'd like that. Is Rory a good friend of yours, besides being one of the cowhands, I mean?" Jessica asked after a pause.

"Yes, he and I are pretty good friends."

"I thought he seemed foolhardy the other morning, chasing after those men who were firing shots."

"Maybe. But Rory knows what he's doing. He's an experienced wrangler. He was a drover on a long cattle drive from Texas before coming here to work at the ranch."

"Yes, he mentioned that to me." Jessica threaded her fingers. "Have you known him long?"

"About a year. Since I've been working here at the ranch. Why?"

"No reason. I was just wondering, that's all."

Ethan leaned back in his chair and folded his arms against his chest. The moon was riding higher in the sky, spreading its glow in an ever-widening circle.

"Did you get to see Miss Hamilton again before leaving for the ranch?" asked Jessica.

Ethan shifted uncomfortably in his chair. "Yeah, I did. Just once."

"Are you going to see her again?"

"No. She dislikes me," he answered hastily.

"I don't believe that."

"It's true. When I went into the booksellers the next time, she didn't even remember my name."

"That doesn't mean she dislikes you."

Ethan shook his head. "No. I offended her, too."

"You offended her?" Jessica repeated, her eyes reflecting the moonlight.

"I didn't mean to; it just happened," Ethan explained miserably. He remembered the way Susannah had looked at him when he'd offered his glib compliment. It was a look laden with disdain.

"Ethan, why don't you simply talk to her, instead of hiding behind a book cover?"

"I tried to. It's no use." His hands stirred at his sides in a gesture of helplessness. "It doesn't matter anyway."

"Did she remember that you purchased a book of poetry the last time you were in the shop?" Jessica asked.

I think she mentioned that. She asked how I liked the Wordsworth."

"There, you see. She recalled your visit to the shop, and perhaps she doesn't dislike you as much as you think she does."

"Maybe." Ethan tried to sound indifferent, but he suspected he didn't fool Jessica for a moment. The memory of Susannah burned in his mind. He wanted to see her again desperately, but he was sure she didn't wish to see him. He slouched in his chair, feeling dejected.

"Susannah struck me as being a very cordial person. Perhaps next time you'll find her to be so," Jessica suggested.

Ethan didn't reply. Instead, he gazed up at the night sky, black now except for the countless pinpricks of starlight, and he envisioned Susannah's fair face in the twinkling configuration of light.

Jessica yawned and stretched her arms over her head. "I'm getting sleepy, so I guess I'll go inside. See you in the morning, Ethan."

"Goodnight. Right after morning chores we'll be saddling up those broncos."

"I'll meet you at the corral," Jessica replied. "Night."

After she left, Ethan slumped in his chair. He kept thinking about Susannah and couldn't get the image of her pretty face out of his head. He closed his eyes and let his mind wander. He imagined himself strolling under the stars with Susannah on his arm. She was gazing up at him in adoration, and her eyes were points of starlight, twinkling and shining. Her hair was black as the night sky and her face a luminous moon. The vision started Ethan's heart racing.

# CHAPTER THIRTEEN

Jessica tucked the shirttails of the blue-checkered flannel shirt into the waistband of the brown trousers Samuel had lent her to wear and studied her reflection in the mirror. The shirt, a checkerboard of navy and powder blue, hung baggy through the body and long in the sleeves on Jessica's small frame, but the blue colors complimented her complexion. She pushed behind her ear a wisp of copper hair and put on the wide-brimmed hat. Samuel's hat was too big for her head, but placing her knotted bun under the hat filled the gap nicely, so that it fit well enough. Given the makeshift style of the clothing, Jessica was fairly pleased with her appearance. She gave herself one last glance in the oval mirror, then left the bedroom Mrs. Bartlett had provided for her during her stay at the ranch.

As Jessica walked into the kitchen, she found Mrs. Bartlett there, preparing the noon meal. "It smells good," Jessica said.

Mrs. Bartlett turned from the stove, where she'd been stirring a pot of simmering soup, and gave Jessica a smile. "Do you like leek soup?" she asked.

"I don't think I've ever tasted it, but it smells wonderful."

"It's the onions and vegetables in it you smell," Sister Bartlett returned.

"You must grow nearly all the food you eat right here on the ranch, don't you?" Jessica asked, leaning over the pot of soup and letting its aroma tickle her nose.

"Yes, we do. We lay in a few store-bought supplies— flour, sugar, salt, and the like—but other than that, the ranch provides us with what we need."

Jessica nodded.

"Do you like cooking?" Mrs. Bartlett asked her.

"Uh huh. I used to do quite a bit of cooking back home for my mother."

"How would you like a job here at the ranch with us, Miss Scott? I need a girl to help me in the kitchen, what with all the hands to feed three times a day. I used to have a hired girl, but she got lonely being away from her family. You seem to have taken a liking to ranch life. I can pay you two dollars a week, in addition to your board and room."

Jessica was surprised by the woman's invitation. "That's very kind of you to offer me the position, Mrs. Bartlett, but

I'm afraid I can't accept. I'm planning to go to Sacramento, where I intend to teach school."

"A school marm, is it? Well, that's mighty nice, Miss Scott. I think you'll be real good at it."

"Thanks," Jessica replied.

"If it turns out that schoolkeeping doesn't suit you, remember you've got a place here at the ranch with us. You seem like a fine girl, and I can always use the help."

"Thanks, again." A smile surfaced on Jessica's lips as she pictured herself in a flour-sack apron, ladling out soup to the ranch hands. She could imagine her mother's reaction to that scene. Her mother was already firmly against her coming out west to what she considered a wild and barbaric place. If she believed Jessica was serving up vittles at an isolated ranch to a handful of rough cowboys, she would have been thoroughly appalled.

The smile faded from Jessica's face as an image of her father intruded into her thoughts. The telegram he'd sent her, demanding she return to Nauvoo, was in a crumbled ball in the bottom of her trunk back in Salt Lake City. The palms of her hands grew moist as she contemplated her father's state of mind when he discovered she had disobeyed his directive. She needed to write him a letter, telling him she'd decided not to return to Nauvoo. She'd been putting off the task because it was so distasteful to her. She had never blatantly defied her father before; pondering the action she'd taken sent a rush of stinging needles along her spine. She wiped the perspiration from her hands onto her trousers.

"I think I'll go outside and find my cousins. Ethan told me that he and Samuel are going to be breaking some horses this morning."

"Yes, the wild mustangs my husband acquired from the range. There's a whole herd of wild horses that run through here. They're as mean and ornery as a nest of rattlesnakes until they get saddle broken."

Jessica shuddered at the comparison Mrs. Bartlett had just used. The thought of the long, fat rattlesnake she'd shot yesterday afternoon gave her the shivers. When she saw the snake coiled and ready to strike, she'd nearly choked with fright. Her first instinct had been to reach under her shirt and draw the Smith and Wesson. She'd aimed, almost without thinking, and fired. It wasn't until afterward that she realized she could have easily missed the target and shot Ethan instead. That thought had left her shaking. She should have passed the gun to Samuel for him to use, but the whole thing had happened so quickly and unexpectedly that she'd had no time to think it through. She had only reacted. The sight of the dead snake, blown nearly apart by the bullet, had made her sick to her stomach.

"You might tell Ethan and the other hands that we'll be eating in an hour," Mrs. Bartlett said.

"All right, I will. And I'll be looking forward to tasting your leek soup."

Mrs. Bartlett patted her shoulder before turning back to the pot on the stove.

Jessica left the kitchen and stood outside on the back porch for a moment, shielding her eyes against the glare of the mid-morning sun. From the corral, she heard the sounds of men talking and of horses whinnying. She walked toward the horse pen, seeking her two cousins, and spied Samuel sitting on the top slat of the rail fence.

"Samuel," she called, as she hurried to him. He turned around and waved. When she reached the fence, he climbed down from his perch and stood beside her. All six of the ranch hands were gathered at the corral, some inside the fenced pen astride their horses and others sitting or leaning on the fence. Ethan was inside a gated area of the corral, struggling to fit a hackamore on a rearing, wild-eyed mustang stallion. Rory stood beside him, grappling with the horse's tossing head.

"Is Ethan really going to try to ride that thing?" Jessica asked her cousin, as she stared at the heaving animal.

"Yup," Samuel grinned. "Exciting, isn't it?"

"Crazy would be a more accurate word. That animal looks like it's going to chew up Ethan and spit him out."

Samuel chuckled. "He sure does. But Ethan will gentle him down some."

Jessica's gaze moved to Rory, who held the mustang in a headlock. She noticed how appealing Rory looked in the leather vest he wore over his red and white striped shirt, and his fringed chaps. A tingle started at the top of Jessica's spine as she stared at the young cowpoke.

"The boys have coined a name for that black," Samuel said, nodding toward the lurching horse in the pen. "Dynamite."

"Oh, that's encouraging. You boys are going to be killed if you try to ride that animal."

"Naw," Samuel responded. "We'll wear him down. Are you going to watch?"

"I wouldn't miss it."

"Hey, Ethan!" Samuel shouted to his brother. "You've got an audience. Try not to make a fool of yourself on that black." Samuel grinned at the cleverness of his remark.

Ethan glanced up at the sound of his brother's voice and so did Rory. Ethan lifted a hand in acknowledgement, but Rory stood stock-still, staring at Jessica. The mustang jerked loose from Rory's grip, and the hackamore that Ethan had nearly fitted in place slipped off.

"Hey," Jessica heard Ethan say. "I thought you were going to hold this cayuse."

Rory turned his attention back to the mustang. He grasped the horse's bobbing head and held it steady, while Ethan fastened the bitless bridle. Jessica smiled inwardly. Her appearance, dressed in men's clothing, had distracted Rory enough that he'd momentarily lost his concentration.

Samuel placed one foot on the bottom rail of the fence and stood grinning at the storming mustang in the stall. It took some moments before Ethan and Rory had the horse bridled and saddled. Jessica leaned against the fence, resting her arms on the rail. Her heart thudded with anticipation as she watched her cousin prepare to ride the snorting, black stallion. The horse's eyes were wide and wild, and his nostrils flared. His whole body quivered when Ethan eased into the saddle on his back.

"All right," Ethan said in a tight voice. "Let him out."

Rory swung open the gate to the stall, and for an instant the mustang stood motionless. Ethan gripped the rein, his body tense. Then, suddenly, the horse exploded into a ferocious kicking, bucking, frenzy. He rammed sideways into the pen, nearly turning an about face in the small, confined space in his fury at having a rider on his back. Jessica gripped the rail of the fence and held her breath. She was sure Ethan would be thrown and trampled in an instant. To her amazement, Ethan stayed atop the plunging, rearing horse as it rocketed out of the stall and into the open corral. Rory stood clear of the flying hooves and scaled the fence to watch the match between man and beast.

"Yeah!" Samuel shouted, his eyes fixed on the bucking bronco. He whipped off his hat and slapped it against his pant leg in excitement. "Stay with him, Ethan! That's it. Don't give him any head."

Jessica grinned in spite of the anxiety she felt for her cousin's welfare aboard the rearing horse. Samuel's shouts of giddy encouragement, joined by the whistles and calls of the other cowhands ringing the corral, created an almost carnival atmosphere that Jessica found herself swept up in. The black stallion bucked and jerked, nearly toppling over backward in its frantic attempts to dislodge Ethan from its back.

And then, abruptly, Ethan was on the ground. The horse continued to kick, flailing out with its hind legs. Jessica thought that her cousin would be stomped to death under the horse's rampaging hooves, but he rolled adroitly out of the way, then scrambled to his feet. The cowboys whistled and cheered, and Samuel hollered wildly. One of the mounted cowhands herded the bronc back into the narrow pen.

Ethan limped over to the split rail fence. Samuel hopped down from his perch and patted his brother eagerly on the back. "You got a little dirt there on your chin," he said, grinning at Ethan. "You did good work, though."

Ethan gave him a wan smile. "That hombre sure is a high roller."

"I'll say he is. He leaps like a salmon swimming upstream. We saw plenty of daylight between you and the saddle."

"Ethan, are you all right?" Jessica asked, leaning over the fence post.

"Yeah. Just a mite sore." He rubbed his thigh and winced.

"You want to try to ride that outlaw next, Samuel?"

Jessica's heart fluttered as she saw Rory approaching her cousin.

"Sure," Samuel answered him enthusiastically. "I'm ready."

Jessica put a hand on his arm. "Be careful, Samuel."

He grinned and patted her hand. "Now you're going to see some real riding."

"Watch out. He's a sunfisher," Ethan warned his brother.

As she watched her cousin stride to the pen, Jessica felt Rory's eyes on her. She glanced at him and briefly smiled.

"You look better in those clothes than Samuel ever did," he said in a husky voice.

Jessica felt her cheeks flood with color. "Is that meant as a compliment, Mr. McKellar?"

"You can definitely consider it a compliment."

His admiring glance left her short of breath. Instead of pursuing a conversation with him, she turned to Ethan. "What's a sunfisher?" she asked her cousin, carefully keeping her eyes from Rory's face.

"That's what we call a horse who twists his body in the air as he bucks." Ethan's attention centered on his brother, who was preparing to climb on the snorting mustang in the stall. "That horse didn't win its moniker without a reason, Samuel. Hang on," Ethan shouted.

Jessica chanced another swift glance at Rory. He, too, was intent on watching Samuel mount the stallion. Two other cowhands were assisting. One held the horse's head and the other stood ready to open the gate.

"Let's do it," Samuel said in a strained voice.

Jessica watched, wringing her hands nervously. The horse bolted out of the stall the moment the gate opened and immediately began leaping and lurching. A white froth collected along the animal's mouth, and his dark coat grew shiny with sweat. Ethan shouted and hooted at Jessica's side, while Rory stood silently studying the bucking horse and clinging rider. The horse gave a sudden, quick twist to one side, and Samuel flew from the saddle.

"Yowl!" Ethan exclaimed, waving a fist. "He's down. Get him away from those hooves, boys," Ethan shouted to the mounted cowhands inside the corral. One of the men leaned down from his saddle and helped Samuel to his feet, while the other chased the riderless bronc, trying to grab hold of its reins.

The mustang continued to elude the cowboy, kicking and bucking, the empty stirrups flapping at its sides.

"That's one explosive animal," Ethan remarked. "I think even you, Rory, will have trouble taming that stick of dynamite."

"I'm ready to give it a try. Get him in the shoot, Hodkins," he called to the cowhand still playing tag with the ebony stallion. "If you'll excuse me, Miss Scott," said Rory, tipping his hat to her.

"Certainly, Mr. McKellar."

Rory started toward the stall, and Jessica thought she detected a swagger in his walk. She smiled secretly. This cowboy from Indiana, whose roots sprang from Irish soil, was more fascinating than any young man she'd known back home in Nauvoo. She watched with pleasure as he mounted the caged stallion, gained a firm grip on the rein, and nodded for Hodkins to open the gate.

The mustang's ferocity was at fever pitch now. He hopped and twisted, kicked and reared, but Rory stayed seated in the saddle. The horse came slamming against the fence where Jessica stood, nearly scraping Rory off its back. As the horse flailed inside the corral, Jessica noticed that not only did Rory remain in the saddle, but there was purpose to his movements. He seemed one with the horse, and for brief intervals when the horse was not thrashing about,

Rory deliberately leaned with his body in one direction or another.

"Look at him ride," Ethan observed, marveling at the other man's skill.

"He's very good, isn't he," Jessica murmured.

"One of the best bronc riders I've ever seen."

Samuel was leaning against the fence of the corral alongside the other ranch hands; Jessica read the admiration in his eyes, too, as he watched Rory tame the kicking, snorting bronco.

The bucking, black stick of dynamite began to tire. Longer moments of nervous prancing stretched between each burst of wild bucking. Finally, the mustang snorted, pawed the ground, and submitted to Rory's weight on his back. Rory walked him around the corral, the horse making occasional crow hops and lunges, and then settling back down again under Rory's masterful handling.

"That's a beautiful animal," Samuel commented as he stood beside Jessica.

"Yes, he is. How long will it take to get him used to the saddle and rider?" Jessica asked him.

"A couple of weeks. Rory will continue to gentle him, and train him to the bit and saddle. He should make a fine range horse."

Samuel's comment prompted a question from Jessica. "What happened at Mr. Bartlett's meeting with Travers? Did Rory tell you much about it?"

Ethan leaned against the rough wood fence. "Yeah, he did. Brother Bartlett was met with half a dozen rifles and a message from Travers."

Jessica felt her stomach lurch. "Oh, no. What was the message?"

"Travers is through talking. Either Brother Bartlett produces a legal land certificate showing his share of water rights or Travers is going to force him off the land," Ethan related, bitterness lacing his voice. "And that's repeating the message in gentler terms than it was originally delivered."

Jessica pushed back the brim of her cowboy hat and wiped her brow. The late morning sun was hot on her face, despite the hat's protection. "What is he going to do, Ethan?" she asked.

"Talk to the sheriff in Salt Lake City, to begin with."

"Can he get a binding land certificate to show to Travers?" asked Samuel.

"I don't know. But it doesn't really matter if he has one or not. Travers is after his land and will resort to some other ruse if this one fails."

Jessica frowned as she pondered Ethan's response. More trouble was sure to erupt, and her cousins would be entangled in the thick of it. And so would Rory. "I hope the sheriff will be able to help," she remarked.

"So do I." Ethan turned back to the corral to watch Rory work the inky, black stallion. As he stepped up onto the bottom rail of the fence, he winced. "Ouch," he muttered, rubbing his thigh. "I loosened a few nuts and bolts from riding that fella."

Jessica set aside her concern as she glanced at her cousin. She was glad she'd come to the ranch with Ethan. In spite of the dangers lurking in this wild, passionate part of the country, she liked it here. Very much.

Jessica helped Sister Bartlett with chores for the remainder of the day, and then after supper wandered outdoors to enjoy the approach of evening. The Bartlett children were playing in the yard, and she paused to talk with them for a time. Then she took the well-worn, dirt path leading to the horse corral. She stood beside the fence and watched the black mustang trotting restlessly inside the pen. The animal held his head high, and his nostrils flared as he whinnied in protest at being restrained from running free across the broad, green hills. For an instant, Jessica felt sorry for the spirited animal. The other horses in the larger section of the corral stood quietly in the receding light, switching their long tails.

Jessica reached out to pat the nose of a tall chestnut standing near the fence. The nose was velvety smooth to her touch. Back in Nauvoo, her father owned a handsome thoroughbred, which he was fond of racing, and her mother employed a gentle mare to pull the buggy. Her mother seldom rode horseback; in fact, Jessica could remember only a time or two seeing her mother sit a horse. But Jessica, herself, enjoyed riding. She and her sisters often rode the mare through the orchard behind the house or over the abandoned dirt roads on the flats outside of town.

She smiled, recalling those memories, and scratched the chestnut's chin as he nudged his head against the fence.

The thoughts of home brought on a spell of melancholy. She left the corral and strolled around the grounds behind the stone ranch house, letting her thoughts wander. She caught sight of two of the ranch hands tending cattle in the pens. The evening was still and quiet except for the lowing of the cattle and an occasional whickering from the horses, and Jessica felt lonesome in being so far away from her family.

Often, when she felt lonely or unhappy, she turned to a book for solace. She had brought two books with her to the ranch, packed in her traveling bag—the book of poetry Ethan had given her and the curious volume with the title "Book of Mormon" stamped across the spine of it. She decided to read from one of the books while it was still light enough outside to see. She hurried back into the house, to the bedroom, and opened her satchel. Buried beneath a pile of clothing were the two books. Holding one in each hand, she studied their titles. She hadn't intended to bring the religious book, but Birgithe had pressed it into her hands the morning she and Ethan left for the ranch, urging her to find a few moments to read it. She would have refused the book except for Birgithe's earnest entreaty, and so she accepted the volume and packed it in the bottom of her bag, planning to leave it there untouched.

Not that the book didn't interest her, for it did. The unusual story of the man, Enos, praying in the forest for forgiveness of his sins had stirred her heart. She had thought about Enos' story several times since reading it, and although it was a remarkable tale of faith and answer to prayer, the account did not fit into any context of meaning in her own life.

The choice of which book to read this evening was simple and quick—Jessica replaced the Book of Mormon in the traveling bag. She took the volume of poetry and strode out of the house. The day before, she had noticed a small, secluded dell by the stream, which ran behind the house. With the book in hand, she hastened toward that spot. As she drew near, she heard the gurgling of the clear stream as it rippled over smooth-washed pebbles. She made her way through a tangle of willows growing beside the brook, and exited into a small clearing. The grass beneath her feet was a carpet of green, soft and downy. She smiled to herself and sat down, tucking her long skirt beneath her.

She had changed from trousers and shirt to a soft dress before supper. As she sat cross-legged upon the grass, with the book in her hands and her blue skirt billowing like a cloud around her, she felt a peace and contentment she had not experienced in a long while. She opened the slim volume and slowly turned the pages. She had read all of the poems through once already, and now was searching for her favorite verses to read again.

She read several of the lines penned by Coleridge and then turned to a lengthy poem written by Wordsworth. This particular poem was a familiar one, but it seemed to take on deeper significance as she read through it once more. Or perhaps it was that it raised more questions in her mind. The poem was entitled "Ode on Intimations of Immortality." Her eyes scanned the opening lines:

> There was a time when meadow, grove,
>     and stream,
> The earth, and every common sight,
> To me did seem
> Appareled in celestial light,
> The glory and the freshness of a dream.
> It is not now as it hath been of yore;
> Turn where so'er I may,
> By night or day,
> The things which I have seen I now can
>     see no more.

Jessica paused, thinking about the message cloaked in the words on the page. Was Wordsworth referring to a primordial time? Did he believe in a life before this earthly one? Or was it only his own childhood he was revisiting? The possibilities raised by the poet's words intrigued her. She read on silently:

> But there's a tree, of many, one,
> A single field which I have look'd upon,
> Both of them speak of something that is
>     gone;
> The pansy at my feet
> Doth the same tale repeat;
> Whither is fled the visionary gleam?

Where is it now, the glory and the
     dream?

Jessica looked up from the page and gazed, without seeing, across the sparkling stream and to the grassy foothills beyond. Where, indeed, is fled the visionary gleam, the glory and the dream? The questions penetrated Jessica's heart. She yearned to discover the answers, but where to look for them was a mystery. Perhaps the solutions lay hidden somewhere in Wordsworth's poem. She read on, this time speaking the words aloud, as if by vocalizing them, she might capture and unravel the puzzle behind the poet's soaring rhetoric.

She read the entire poem through and then read it again. The quiet, green glen where she sat, beside the brook, was like a shining jewel set in a crown. The water was a river of gold in the waning sunlight, the grass a sparkling emerald, and the sky as blue as amethyst.

After reading the poem a third time, Jessica closed the book and reclined on the velvet grass. She shut her eyes and let the images from the poem shimmer in her mind. It was only when she noticed that the little glen had grown awash in shadow that she stood, smoothed her skirt, and left the willow-cloaked spot behind.

Clutching the book of poetry in her hand, she followed the dusty path leading to the house, past the cattle pens and horse corral. As she neared the bunkhouse, she heard Ethan call her name.

"Jessica! Wait up, and I'll walk with you." She slowed, and he fell in step beside her.

"I didn't see you when I passed this way earlier, Ethan."

"I've been in the bunkhouse playing cards with some of the boys," he returned. He pulled from his pocket a small, brown paper sack and opened it. "Care for a lemon drop?"

Jessica wrinkled her nose. "No, thank you. I don't like the taste of them."

Ethan reached into the sack, then popped one of the yellow candies into his mouth. "Umm. You don't know what you're missing."

Jessica gave him a smile. The two of them walked along the dirt path leading to the house. Dusk was gathering, and the moon was rising in the sky.

"What do you have there?" Ethan asked, pointing to the book in her hand.

Jessica held it out for him to see. "The book of poetry you gave me. I've been reading from it."

Ethan sucked noisily on his candy.

Jessica opened the book as they sauntered toward the house together under the moonlight. "There's one poem I particularly like," she began.

"Oh, no. I hope you're not going to recite poetry to me," Ethan grinned, rolling the lemon drop to one side of his mouth.

"It would be good for you. Do you actually know any poetry?"

Ethan spun his candy out of the way with his tongue, and began to repeat from memory, "She was a phantom of delight, when first she gleamed upon my sight; a lovely apparition, sent to be a moment's ornament. Her eyes as stars of twilight fair; like twilight's, too, her dusky hair." He paused and grinned at Jessica.

"That was very good, Ethan."

"And you thought I didn't know any poetry," Ethan returned, chuckling.

"Your schoolmaster would be proud of you," Jessica teased. They laughed together, enjoying the camaraderie of the moment, and then Jessica grew more somber. "Ethan, I'd like you to listen to part of this poem and tell me what you think it means."

"All right," Ethan replied, still smiling from his enjoyment of the moment before. "I'll listen, but I doubt I'll be able to shed any insight on the poem's message."

"Just listen carefully while I read it and give me your thoughts on it," Jessica replied, thumbing through the pages of the book to locate the poem. "Here it is. It's called, 'Ode on Intimations of Immortality,' by William Wordsworth."

She tilted the book to catch the rays of moonlight and began reading the first stanza. When she finished with it, she paused and looked up at Ethan questioningly.

"It has a nice sound to it," Ethan offered.

"Yes, it does. The rhyme and meter are lyrical, but what is Wordsworth trying to say?"

Ethan shrugged his shoulders. "I don't know. Why don't you read some more." He cocked his head, listening intently, as she chose the fifth stanza to read next.

> "Our birth is but a sleep and a forgetting;
> The soul that rises with us our life's
> Star,
> Hath had elsewhere its setting
> And cometh from afar;
> Not in entire forgetfulness,
> And not in utter nakedness,
> But trailing clouds of glory do we come
> From God, who is our home."

Jessica paused, overcome by the emotion intrinsic in the words. She was conscious of Ethan chewing the residue of his lemon drop and then swallowing it.

Ethan cleared his throat, then said quietly, almost reverently, "That sounds to me like a reference to our heavenly home, from which we left at birth."

"Do you mean heaven? What is your definition of heaven, Ethan? And if such a place does exist, isn't it where we go after death? Heaven is not a sphere we inhabited before our birth. This is all so confusing to me."

Ethan paused in mid-stride and thrust his hands in his pockets. For a moment, Jessica thought he was reaching for another lemon drop, and she felt a rush of exasperation at his inattentiveness. But instead of taking another piece of candy, Ethan turned and looked her squarely in the eye.

"Jessica, our religion teaches us of a pre-mortal existence, a place where we lived with our Father in Heaven and His son, Jesus Christ; a heavenly home where we all existed in peace, love, and happiness, and where we grew and developed as spirits. And, if we are righteous and obedient, we will return to our Heavenly Father when we leave this earthly life."

As Jessica listened to him, an image of the Fenton boy, who was killed in the wagon accident near the Kades' home, slipped into her mind. And then, with even stronger feeling, she thought of Zachary Kade, buried on the lonesome prairie. Though she knew both boys were dead, yet she received the unmistakable impression that they lived— lived somewhere in the realms of spirits; happy, whole, and progressing. The flash of enlightenment stunned her, yet she stubbornly refused to believe Ethan's explanation.

"Do you understand what I'm saying?" Ethan asked, when she didn't reply.

"You're telling me that you believe we were alive before we came to earth?"

"Yes. Exactly."

"I've never heard that doctrine before. How can you know that?" she asked with feeling.

"I've been taught it all my life, Jessica. And I believe it. Here." Ethan tapped a finger to his chest.

Jessica looked at him, her mind filled with doubt.

"You can know the truth of it for yourself, Jessica, if you want to. The Spirit will testify to you that what I've said is true," Ethan told her in an earnest voice.

Jessica's expression hardened. "The *truth*, as you've stated it, is surely nothing more than the futile imaginings of men. The vain musing of poets. Like Wordsworth, here." She held up the poetry book with an edge of defiance.

Ethan placed a steady hand on the book. "Then don't read men's words to learn of God. Read God's word."

Jessica lowered her gaze. "I've read the Bible. It answers few questions for me."

"The Bible is only one set of God's revelations to men. There's a second witness; it's called the Book of Mormon, and it testifies of Christ and teaches the doctrines of his kingdom."

Jessica shook her head. "I don't believe in your religion, Ethan. My parents know it's a sham, and so do I."

"Are you certain of that?" asked Ethan quietly.

"You and your family have been taken in by silly superstitions and the lies of Joe Smith." Jessica was feeling the heat of anger now, and hot words tumbled from her lips. "Has it occurred to you that your religion might be wrong? A hoax? That you've been deceived?"

Jessica stalked off, not waiting or wanting to hear Ethan's reply. She didn't quite believe, herself, the words she'd just spoken in her flare of passion, and so she didn't expect Ethan to believe them. Suddenly, she felt foolish and miserable.

"Wait a minute, Jessica," her cousin insisted, reaching for her arm.

Jessica pulled away from him. "I don't want to talk about it anymore," she said as she swiftly strode away into the moonlit night.

# CHAPTER FOURTEEN

Ethan set the foot of the branding iron in the fire and looked out at the sea of cattle penned on the ranch property. He and the other hands had been branding calves most of the morning. As he stopped to move one of the irons closer to the coals, a sharp pain racked his thigh. He grimaced and straightened his leg. When the wild mustang threw him yesterday morning in the corral, he'd landed hard onto his hip and thigh; his leg was black and blue this morning. He shrugged off the pain, dismissing his injuries as part of the job.

"I'm ready for one of those irons," Rory said to him. Rory had one knee on the belly of a belligerent roan calf. Grasping one of the heated irons, Ethan walked over to the calf with it and pressed the end of the stamp iron, formed in the shape of a running W, firmly against the calf's shoulder.

The familiar smell of burning hair and hide filled Ethan's nostrils, and the calf protested with a loud bawl. With the brand in place, Rory released the calf. It scrambled to its feet and trotted off to join its fellows.

From inside the cattle pen, Samuel isolated another calf from the milling, bellowing herd and threw his lariat. The rope caught the calf around the hoof. Under Samuel's direction, his sorrel dragged the calf near the fire where Rory wrestled it to the ground, and then Ethan applied the red-hot iron. A couple of the other hands were lassoing the calves yet to be branded and leading them from the herd to the fire. With each application of the iron, another calf was marked with the "Running W" brand.

"You seen Jessica this morning?" Rory asked Ethan.

"No, I haven't. Why?"

"I thought she was going to be out here watching the branding. She's been interested in everything else going on at the ranch."

"Aw, I think she's angry with me," Ethan grunted as he wielded the iron on another struggling calf.

Rory grasped and then pinned the flailing legs of a roan and white calf, securing it for Ethan to apply the brand. "Why is she angry with you?" he asked, peering over the legs of the calf.

Ethan seared the calf's hide with the brand, then Rory let the calf go free. "We got into a discussion about religion last night. She didn't like what I had to say."

"Oh."

Samuel cut out another calf from the lot, looping the lariat above his head in an arcing circle. He tossed it, but the rope missed its mark. He gathered in the length of rope and again started it swirling over his head.

"Hey, Samuel," Ethan called. "You seen Jessica since breakfast?"

Samuel turned in his saddle. "She's over there," he said, pointing toward the pens where the cattle were corralled.

Ethan followed along the end of his brother's finger until he spotted Jessica talking with one of the hands on horseback. She was wearing Samuel's trousers and shirt, and her head was bare. The sun sparkled on her copper hair, laced into one long, thick braid hanging down her back.

Ethan turned back to the calf Rory was tussling to the ground. He saw that Rory's gaze was focused on Jessica, too. "She sure does look good in trousers," Rory grinned, when he caught Ethan watching him.

"Why don't you call her over here?" Ethan suggested.

"She's your cousin. *You* call her over here."

"I told you, she's mad at me. Go on over and talk to her. I know you've been hankering to socialize with her all morning."

"Maybe a little later I will," Rory hedged.

"We can take a break from branding for a few minutes. Go ahead." Ethan nodded in his cousin's direction. He stood up from the fire and arched his back. "Besides, my hip is paining me something fierce. I have a bruise as big as a bear paw on it from my tangle with that old mustang yesterday."

"Too bad. Guess you'll have to leave men's work to those who can handle it."

"Go on; get out of here," Ethan returned, smiling. He watched Rory dust off his hands and then saunter over to the cattle pens. He'd noticed his friend eyeing Jessica ever since meeting her on Jessica's first day at the ranch. Ethan moved the trio of branding irons from the flames to a cooler spot in the fire pit, then eased down onto the ground, cross-legged. He delved into his trouser pocket and withdrew the candy sack he kept handy there. Only a few lemon drops remained in the sack. He'd have to purchase some more when he got back to the city, he mused. He tossed one of the pieces of candy into his mouth and glanced over to where Rory stood in conversation with Jessica, beside a pen of lowing cattle.

A frown rumpled his brow as he recalled his conversation with Jessica from the evening before. He had botched his attempt at explaining the message of the gospel of Jesus Christ. The opportunity for such a discussion had been ripe, and he'd failed to make a spiritual impression on her. And that wasn't the first time he had missed an occasion to broach the subject of the gospel with Jessica. She had asked questions once before, following the Fenton boy's death, but he'd been too upset himself to realize the moment was right for explaining about the plan of salvation. He wanted Jessica to know about the gospel and become acquainted with its principles, but he was unsure of how to present it.

Ethan shifted position, taking some of the weight off his sore hip and leg. He watched the cowhands separating the calves for branding, and sorting the four- and five-year-old steers for market. The cattle selected for market would be herded to Ogden, where they'd be loaded onto cattle cars and taken by rail to cities in the East. Ethan and his brother would participate in the cattle drive and help get the cattle onto the train. Then he could spend a few days at home in Salt Lake before coming back to the ranch. He might even work up the nerve to visit the Quill and Ink. He rubbed his chin, thinking about that possibility.

"Ethan, can I speak with you for a minute?"

Ethan lurched to his feet. "Sure, Brother Bartlett. What is it?" Ethan hadn't noticed the lanky rancher approaching. Brother Bartlett had been working alongside the cowboys all morning, sorting out under-sized and diseased cattle. The man was lean and wiry, and his skin was weathered from working outdoors.

"It's difficult for me to leave the ranch just now, in the middle of all the chores connected with the spring roundup. I wondered if you might ride in to Salt Lake City and visit the land office there for me. As you're well aware, Mr. Travers is stirring up a peck of trouble concerning my title to the land. If you could find out exactly what my legal position is concerning title to The Willows, I'd be mighty appreciative."

"You bet, Brother Bartlett. I'd be happy to do that. When do you want me to go?"

"Not for a few days. I need your help here with chores for the present. You come up to the house in a day or two and we'll go over together what records I have. You can take any paperwork concerning my ownership of the land with you and show it to the necessary official at the land office."

Ethan nodded in understanding.

Bartlett put a hand on Ethan's shoulder. "You're a good boy, Ethan. Honest. Trustworthy. That's why I'm asking you to do the job. You and your brother have been conscientious about putting in a full day's labor. Rory, too. But I need his experience in directing the roundup."

"Thanks, Brother Bartlett. I appreciate the kind words."

"They're not empty words, son. I meant everything I said."

"Well, I appreciate the opportunity you've given me to work on the ranch. I'm enjoying it."

"That's good, Ethan." Bartlett patted him on the back, then started to walk away. But before he'd taken many steps, he turned back around. "After we get through here today, I'd like you to ride out to the southwest quadrant. Hodkins told me a section of the fence is down out there."

"Sure. I'll do it right away."

"And Ethan—carry your gun. For protection."

Ethan swallowed hard. "I will, sir."

Bartlett nodded and then returned to his work.

Ethan watched him go, pleased with the compliments and the responsibility his employer had entrusted him with. He was ready to get back to his job of branding. He glanced at Rory. The cowhand was still engaged in conversation with Jessica. Impatient to get started again, Ethan strode over to the cattle pen, where the two of them stood talking.

"How are things going, Jessica?" he asked his cousin in a cordial tone.

"Rory is teaching me the art of cattle branding," she replied, chuckling.

Rory tipped back his hat so that the sun shone full on his forehead. "She's learned how to read a brand stamped on cowhide—from left to right, and from top to bottom—and how some brands are standing, others lazy or running."

"I can decipher whether a letter or number brand is flying, boxed, tumbling, walking, crazy, or underscored with a bar," Jessica reported. "Although the 'Running W' brand looks like nothing more than a squiggly worm, I know it stands for The Willows Ranch."

"You're a quick learner," Ethan said.

"She also knows the difference between a gaucho iron, a stamp iron, and a plain old saddle-ring heated in a cowchip fire to burn a brand," Rory added.

"That's great," Ethan smiled. "Think we can get back to work, now?"

"Your cousin is a strict taskmaster," Rory said to Jessica.

"But a patient one," Jessica amended. "I'm sorry about how I behaved with you last night, Ethan. It was wrong of me to speak as I did. I apologize."

"You don't need to apologize; we were just airing our views. But I would like to take a closer look at that poem you were reading to me. Maybe talk about it some more," Ethan suggested. His heart beat a little faster as he recognized a chance to reopen the discussion about religion.

"What poem is that?" Rory asked.

"A verse written by William Wordsworth. I was asking Ethan last night what he thought about it," Jessica answered.

"Oh? What's the name of it?"

Jessica told him the title of the poem.

"I'm not familiar with it," Rory admitted.

"You should read it. It raises some interesting questions," Ethan said quickly.

"All right, I'd like to."

*Perfect*, Ethan thought. With Rory's assistance, the two of them might be able to teach Jessica the rudiments of the gospel. Rory was a faithful member of the Church; while working together at the ranch, he and Ethan had engaged in several conversations about the gospel.

"How about tonight, after evening chores?" Rory volunteered.

Jessica laughed. "Since when did you cowpokes develop such an interest in reading poetry?"

"You never know when it might come in handy," Ethan replied.

"Exactly," Rory agreed.

Ethan smiled. Both he and Rory were eager for the opportunity to spend more time with Jessica, but for entirely different reasons.

After the branding had been completed for the morning, and the cowboys had eaten their noon meal, Ethan, Samuel, and Rory saddled their horses and set off for the southwest quarter of the ranch to repair fencing, with Jessica riding along with them. Though the morning had been bright and warm, this afternoon the sky filled with dark clouds, and the smell of rain was in the air. Ethan pulled the brim of his hat low over his forehead as protection against the wind that was whining through the tall grass.

He was riding beside Samuel, while Rory and Jessica traveled a few horse-lengths behind, talking together. He could hear Rory relating some of his experiences from the Texas cattle drive he'd taken part in the summer before. Jessica seemed to be enjoying the story.

"A cowboy uses his legs, hands, weight, and voice in controlling his horse," Rory was telling her. "Both horse and rider need skill for the job of herding cattle. It's tough work—long days on the trail, sleepless nights tending cows, moving the cattle across rivers, heading off stampedes that can scatter your herd for miles, and guarding against Indian attacks."

Rory's descriptions held a fascination for Ethan, as well. He yearned for the opportunity to experience the long cattle drive for himself.

"Trailing the herds is a cheap way of transporting them, and the cattle fatten up along the trail," Rory continued. "A longhorn steer that might cost five dollars in Texas, will fetch about forty to fifty dollars in Chicago. Some cattlemen in Texas make a fortune off their herd."

Ethan quickly computed in his head the profits resulting from moving five hundred head of cattle across the range to market. The figures made his head swim. "Samuel," he said, turning eagerly to his brother. "What would you think about riding down to Texas next spring and hooking up with an outfit driving a herd east?"

Samuel shook his head. "That's not for me, Ethan. I don't enjoy sitting in the rain on horseback all day or having the hard ground for a pillow under my head at night. Naw, when we're through here at the ranch, I'm going back to Salt Lake City and stay put."

"Where's your sense of adventure?" Ethan asked him.

"It's not tied up with four hooves and a tail, that's for sure."

"I see. You're more interested in the two-footed kind. Do you have your eye on some girl, Samuel?" Ethan bantered.

"Not at the moment. But even if I did, I wouldn't tell you about it."

"Now, that hurts my feelings, little brother." Ethan reined in his horse in order to ride beside Rory and Jessica. He wanted to hear more of what Rory was saying.

". . . and we bunked in a Texas longhouse, much like the one here at Bartlett's ranch."

"Texas longhouse?" Jessica repeated.

"That's the term for it. Two log cabins joined by a roofed space. The Texas rancher uses one cabin for cooking and eating and the other for sleeping. Then as the ranch grows, the rancher might build a house for his family, a cookshack and a bunkhouse for the hands."

"Did the Bartletts, with their many children, live in the longhouse when they first came to The Willows?"

"I suppose so. The bunkhouse was probably the first building constructed on the place."

The wind was picking up force now. It rippled Ethan's shirt against his chest and tried to snatch his hat from his head. Ethan bent into the gale as he rode his bay over the grassy trail.

"Mrs. Bartlett offered me a position here at the ranch," Jessica said after a moment's pause.

"She did?" Rory replied.

"Uh huh. Helping her in the kitchen and with other chores around the house. She offered to pay me two dollars a week."

"What did you say?" Ethan asked, hoping his cousin had accepted the job.

"I turned it down. You know I can't stay, Ethan." Her words sounded almost apologetic.

"I'm disappointed. It would have been real nice to have you here," returned Ethan.

Rory didn't comment, but in glancing at him, Ethan easily read his look of regret.

The wind groaned in the trees, and black clouds scudded overhead. Ethan felt a chill in the air. He sensed the need to quicken their pace and attend to the chore of getting the fences mended. "I think we're just about to the place where

Hodkins said the fencing is down. The cattle have probably knocked over the posts and trampled the wire," he said.

The four of them continued to ride along the fence line, buffeted by the wind and a sprinkling of rain.

"Look up ahead," Samuel said abruptly. "The fence posts all along that section are down." He spurred his horse, and the sorrel galloped ahead to a spot where a wooden post sagged against the ground.

Samuel and Ethan got off their horses to inspect the downed post, while Rory rode ahead to see how far the damage extended. Jessica dismounted and waited in silence.

"This post is split nearly in two," Samuel observed. "I don't think a cow did that kind of damage."

"These next few are, too," Ethan replied, walking down the line of fence posts. He frowned, troubled by what he was seeing.

A few moments later Rory returned. "Bad news," he reported. "Not only are the posts down for a quarter mile or more, but the wire has been cut."

Samuel whistled under his breath, and Ethan's frown hardened. "All right. Let's get the posts standing again and repair what wire we can. Jessica, will you hand me the wire stretchers from my saddlebag?"

While Jessica went to get the tool for Ethan, Rory dismounted and untied a long, straight bar of iron from his saddle. One end of the bar was sharpened, and Rory began jabbing the sharpened end into the hard ground where the post had stood.

Ethan tugged on his leather gloves, then he and Samuel dragged the post over to the hole Rory was carving in the dirt. The wire was still attached to the pole, but it hung limp and loose. Once they had the pole back in position, Rory hammered the top of it with his iron bar, while Ethan held the post steady and Samuel began kicking dirt into the hole around it. Then Samuel tramped on the dirt with his boots, packing it down tight.

Ethan tightened the wire wrapped around the post, using his wire stretchers to grasp the wire and give it a firm twist. Three separate strings of wire wound around each post, spaced equal distance from the top of the post to the bottom of it, and Ethan tuned each strand. Jessica stood nearby, watching the process.

"This bar wire is called 'Merrill's four point,'" Rory said to her, as he watched Ethan tighten it around the post. "It's new, patented by the Merrill brothers about a year and a half ago."

Ethan paused to inspect the wire's tension. The thick wire was dressed with four short barbs of wire wound around it at spaced intervals, two barbs pointing upward and two downward. And the wire barbs were sharp, as Ethan had learned by painful experience.

"A wire fence takes less time to put up than wood fencing and is more effective. The cows learn real fast to stay away from the barbs," Rory explained.

Jessica listened attentively.

"I've heard that a man named Glidden is experimenting with two strands of bar wire twisted together for added strength, with barbs. I'd like to get a look at that when it becomes available," Rory said to Ethan.

"Yeah. It sounds like a smart idea." Ethan gave the top strand of wire looped around the post a final twist. "We'll need to drive a few nails through this post if we don't want it splitting in two."

Samuel dug into his trouser pocket. "I brought nails," he said, producing a handful. Ethan picked a couple of square-headed nails from his brother's hand and pounded them into the post.

"How long ago did Mr. Bartlett put up this bar wire fence?" asked Jessica.

"Just this spring we've been working on it," Samuel replied. "We're not through yet. There're still some sections that need to be fenced in."

"Bartlett is a modern, progressive rancher," Rory put in. "He's not afraid to try new ideas, like this barbed wire fence here, and is always striving to improve his stock. I admire his style."

"Let's move on. We're through with this post," Ethan directed.

The four of them walked down the row of fencing to the next post, leaving their horses behind to munch the tall grass. The same process was repeated on this post and wire, and then the foursome moved to the next. Further down the line, the wire strung between posts was cut in two, as Rory had reported.

The men worked on the posts and wire for the next hour. Jessica followed them from post to post, making herself useful in any way she could. The sky was crowded with moving black clouds, and the wind whipped through the grass. A spattering of rain started to fall.

"Let's bring the horses up," Rory suggested.

"I'll go back and get them," offered Jessica.

"All right, thanks," Ethan replied, giving her a quick smile as he tugged at a section of wire. He turned back to his work as she walked away.

In less than a minute she returned, panting and out of breath. "Riders are coming," she warned them in an urgent voice. "Three of them. I saw them cross the ridge as I was starting back for the horses."

Ethan straightened up from his task, his blood surging. "Which direction?"

"That way," she answered, pointing south.

"I hear 'em," Rory said.

Ethan listened and the next moment he, too, heard the galloping of hooves on the hard ground. His fingers brushed against the pistol holstered at his side.

"Stay behind us, Jessica," commanded Samuel. There was no place of cover where they stood, only patches of sagebrush and bunch grass. Few trees broke the hilly terrain.

"It might be cattlemen with friendly intentions, but you stay back, Jessica," Ethan said, repeating his brother's warning. He saw her hand flick toward the holster he'd provided for her Smith and Wesson. He turned to Rory, who was squinting into the distance. "What do you think?"

"Let's not take any chances," answered Rory. "Have your pistols ready."

Samuel stood with his legs firmly planted and Jessica positioned behind him. Ethan glanced at him and nodded; Samuel gave a slight nod in return.

"Here they come," Rory said, frowning.

Ethan saw three men on horseback break over the rise of a hill and come galloping toward them. He swallowed nervously, his hands flexing at his sides. As the riders neared, he flinched with sudden recognition; his throat went dry and his heart hammered. "Texas drovers," he rasped. "Of the worst sort."

"What?" Rory asked, startled. His eyes darted from the riders to Ethan's white-lipped face. "You know 'em?"

"I had a run-in with two of them at the train depot while I was in Salt Lake. They're a bad bunch, Rory."

"Samuel, get your pistol out," Rory directed. "And be ready to use it." Rory already had his gun in hand, and Ethan quickly unholstered his.

The three riders arrived with a jangling of spurs and a creaking of saddles and then reined in their horses. "Afternoon, y'all," one of the men said in a slurred voice.

Ethan remembered him as the man named Peyton. Unconsciously, Ethan rubbed the healed cut on his cheek.

"Can I help you men with something?" Rory said evenly. His gun was in plain view of the Texans. Ethan felt his own gun hand quivering.

"Why, you sure can. I'm afeared you're trespassin', boys." Peyton's slitted eyes swept the four of them.

"This is Bartlett ranch land," Rory returned without hesitation. "And I suggest you best be getting off it."

Ethan felt his stomach clench. His hands were sweating, and his grip on the gun felt slippery. "You heard him," Ethan said in a hard voice, when Peyton made no immediate reply.

Peyton's squinted gaze moved from Rory's face to Ethan's. Ethan thought he saw a glint of recognition light Peyton's eyes as the Texan looked at him.

"Now, we don't want no trouble," one of the other riders said with a deceptive grin. Ethan identified this man as the Texan who had arrived by train at the station. All three men wore Texas ten-gallon hats and fancy stitching on their leather vests. The guns holstered at their sides were in clear sight. Ethan saw the one named Quaid move his hand nearer his holster, his fingers twitching.

"Looks like you ain't got no fence to back up your claim," Peyton said with a sneer. "Does he?" he added, turning to his partners on horseback.

The other two men snickered.

"We got orders from the boss, hisself, to clear off any trespassers," Peyton began.

"That wouldn't be Travers, would it?" Rory interrupted in disdain.

"Yeah, that be who it is, all right. And Mr. Travers don't take kindly to trespassers nor cattle thieves," Peyton shot back.

"Do these boys look like rustlers to you?" Quaid asked, glancing at his associates.

"They sure do look suspicious, what with them wire stretchers and sech layin' about," the third man returned.

"You ought to know a thing or two about rustling," Rory snapped, his eyes narrowing in anger. "It's your handiwork here we're repairing, isn't it?"

Ethan held his breath. Rory seemed without fear, and his brazen confidence was riling the Texans. Ethan could see that plainly on their faces. He heard Samuel breathing heavily from a few paces behind him.

Peyton glared at Rory for an instant, and then he gave a short, ugly laugh. "You sure are cocky for a man lookin' down the barrel of a rifle." With those words, Peyton whipped up the rifle that had been lying across his saddle and pointed it at Rory. Quaid and the other Texan trained their guns on Rory and Ethan with lightening speed. "Now, boys. I'd advise you to drop your weapons, seein' as how you're covered," Peyton drawled.

Rory lifted his gun and aimed it at Peyton before the other man had the words out of his mouth. Ethan and Samuel quickly followed suit. Six guns glinted under the stormy sky, cocked, and ready to fire. Ethan gulped, sweat gathering along his brow.

Peyton climbed down from his horse, keeping his rifle pointed at Rory's chest. "Maybe you didn't hear me, boy. This land belongs to Mr. Travers now, and you best get off it if you want to stay in one piece. Or maybe you'd like to participate in a little necktie party," Peyton growled, taking a step toward Rory. "Mr. Travers has a penchant for hangin' rustlers."

Rory didn't falter or back down an inch. Instead, he raised his gun eye level to Peyton. "Get back on your horse," Rory growled. "Or I'll blow your head off."

Ethan swallowed, nearly choking on the lump that had arisen in his throat. He moved to Rory's side and steadied his pistol.

Peyton's eyes fell on him. "Ain't you and I had the pleasure of meetin' somewhere before?" he said to Ethan.

Ethan saw a glimmer of recollection in the other man's eyes, but he guessed that Peyton couldn't recall where they'd crossed paths. "I'd never deliberately cross trails with vermin like you," Ethan spat out.

The sudden anger and wild abandon he felt surprised him. The fact that he and his companions were being threatened by a band of lawless scoundrels filled him with fury. He gripped his gun and stood shoulder to shoulder with Rory.

He saw Peyton hesitate and the other two Texans glance uneasily at each other. Without saying a word, Samuel stepped to Ethan's side, his gun level with Peyton's head; and then Jessica, in her trousers and low-fitting cowboy hat, stepped forward, too, with her Smith and Wesson aimed squarely at the Texans. The four of them stood toe to toe against the intruders.

"What this?" Peyton sneered. "A show of strength by a bunch of swaggering upstarts. Who do you think you're dealing with here?"

"Vermin and scum," Samuel replied in an icy tone. Ethan glanced at his brother. Samuel's face was blanched, and his lips were a stark white, but his eyes burned.

Peyton's jeering stare rested on Samuel's face, then shifted to Jessica. "And who's that little bit of a feller?" he hissed, nodding toward her. "Your baby brother?"

The other two Texans on horseback chuckled nervously.

"Believe me," Ethan said with grit in his voice. "None of us are strangers to a six-shooter."

"Now clear out of here," Rory commanded. "And tell Travers to keep his hands off Bartlett land."

Ethan saw the rifle in Peyton's hand waver slightly. "Come on," the Texan named Quaid said from astride his horse. "Let these pups be for the present. We'll settle this score another time."

"Yeah, mount up, Peyton," the other Texan agreed.

Peyton glared at the four of them. "I won't forget your faces," he growled. "Not by a long shot." He lowered his rifle, and with a menacing stare, returned to his horse.

"You best watch your backside," Quaid threatened as he holstered his gun. "Next time we meet, we won't be feelin' so cordial."

"Clear out," Rory repeated.

Peyton swung into his saddle, and then the three of them galloped off in a flurry of dust.

Ethan returned his pistol to its holster. His hands were shaking, when only seconds earlier they had been as steady as granite. Samuel, too, holstered his Colt. Only

Rory remained with his gun in hand, staring grimly after the Texans.

"I'm afraid we've made some enemies," he said, turning to the others. "Those men won't likely forget us."

Ethan swallowed. His dry throat ached, and his head pounded. The rain that had started as a sprinkle began falling in a steady sheet, quickly soaking him to the bone. He looked from Rory to Samuel and Jessica. Both of them were grave-faced and ashen. He wasn't afraid for his own self, but he feared for his younger brother and cousin; the responsibility for their safety weighed on his shoulders. He swallowed and wiped the rain away from his face with a shaky hand.

# CHAPTER FIFTEEN

The next morning after breakfast, Jessica stood on the back porch watching Mr. Bartlett and all six of his ranch hands ride off for the southwest corner of the range to finish repairing the broken fence posts and restring the barbed wire. Each of the men was armed and prepared if trouble arose. Shading her eyes against the morning sun, Jessica watched until they crested a hill and disappeared from sight, leaving a trail of dust in their wake.

She turned and went back into the house, covering her mouth to stifle a yawn, for she'd hardly slept the night before. Every time she closed her eyes, an image of the three Texans with their guns drawn loomed before her. What little sleep she managed to get was accompanied by terrifying nightmares of gunshots and death. She'd jerked awake long before dawn and lay in bed waiting for the sun to rise and burn away the dark visions lingering in her mind.

The day seemed to stretch indefinitely before her. At her cousins' insistence, she'd promised to stay near the house. Although yesterday had been blustery and cool, with periods of heavy rain, today's weather was muggy. It was the first day of June and the heat of summer seemed to be already upon them. The house felt uncomfortably warm, even with the doors and windows open.

After helping Mrs. Bartlett with chores in the house, Jessica wandered outside to the yard, pausing to watch the three, wild mustangs snorting in the corral. She studied the black stallion, which the cowboys called Dynamite, admiring the proud lift of his head, his sinewy neck and powerful legs. She remembered the way Rory McKellar had sat the mustang, despite the horse's bucking and thrashing, until he was able to calm the muscle-bodied animal. It had been a compelling sight—the fierce mustang and fearless rider paired in a dazzling display of partnership.

Although she'd known Rory only since coming to the ranch, thoughts of the tall cowboy never strayed far from her mind. His easy smile and genial, blue eyes became fixed in her memory; his bow-legged walk, with the hint of a swagger to it, brought a secret smile to her lips. As she watched the ebony mustang moving restlessly in the corral, she found herself feeling equally restless awaiting Rory's return from the range.

The men arrived home at dusk, after spending the entire day mending fences and riding the southern boundary of the ranch lands. After learning that they hadn't encountered any trouble from Travers' hired hands, Jessica breathed easier. Mrs. Bartlett warmed supper for them, and by the time the cowhands finished eating, it was late into the evening. Jessica was able to talk only briefly with her cousins and Rory before they left the table.

Though she was sleepy, Jessica didn't feel like going to bed yet. The room she shared with the two eldest Bartlett girls was stuffy and cramped, and Jessica was sure the girls would want to talk before extinguishing the coal oil lamp. She wasn't interested in chatting with the younger girls; instead, she looked forward to a conversation with Rory. Perhaps he might still be outside checking the stock or bedding down the horses.

Slipping out the door, she found Ethan sitting on the porch step, whittling a square of wood under a lantern's light. The lantern hung from the roof, splashing a circle of golden light onto the porch.

"Hello, Ethan. I thought you'd be in bed by now, after the long day you had," she greeted him.

"Every bone in my body is sore, but I'm not tired," he responded, glancing up at her.

Jessica gathered her skirt underneath her and sat down on the porch step beside her cousin. Rory wasn't anywhere in sight, but visiting with Ethan for a few moments was a nice diversion. She studied the small piece of wood he was working. "Still whittling that block of wood, I see. Have you decided what shape to give it yet?" she asked.

"You'll have to wait and see."

Jessica hugged her knees and sighed. The moon was riding high in the sky, and a whisper of a night breeze ruffled the leaves on the maple trees in the yard behind the house. Jessica watched Ethan wield his pocketknife, cutting away tiny slivers of wood.

"You like to do whittling, don't you?" she remarked, feeling at ease in her cousin's company.

"It's relaxing for me," Ethan answered, keeping his eyes on his work.

"That's good. Good to have something to take your mind off your worries." Jessica frowned, thinking about the frightening experience of the day before with Travers' men. She had been awed by her cousin's courage in facing the Texans. Ethan had been unflinching, though Jessica feared he'd be shot at any moment.

"Ethan?"

"Yeah?"

"I was proud of the way you stood up to Travers' men yesterday," she said quietly.

"It was mostly bluster," he replied with a smile.

"Nevertheless, you showed great daring."

The two of them sat in comfortable silence for a time as Ethan chipped away at the piece of wood.

"Were you afraid?" Jessica asked, still thinking of the encounter with the cattlemen.

Ethan paused, his knife in hand. "Afraid? Yes, I suppose so. But the strangest thing happened—while staring down the barrels of those guns, I was filled with a surge of righteous indignation in response to the men who were threatening me and mine," Ethan revealed in a low tone of voice. "I felt a bit like Moroni must have felt, facing the army of the Lamanites."

"Who?"

"Captain Moroni. He's probably the Book of Mormon prophet I admire the most."

Jessica sat silently staring at her cousin. He resumed his whittling, his eyes on the wood. An image of the book stuffed in the bottom of her traveling bag sprang to Jessica's mind. She knew something about the Lamanites from her reading in Enos, but who was this Captain Moroni? And why was he leading an army against the Lamanites? The comparison Ethan had drawn between himself and the Book of Mormon figure intrigued her.

"Why did your Captain Moroni feel righteous indignation? Which, by the way, is a very unusual term," Jessica said with a smile.

Ethan folded the blade of his pocketknife and set it aside. When he turned toward her, Jessica saw his sober expression by the lantern's light. "Moroni was a young man of twenty-five when he was selected to be the chief captain over the Nephite army," Ethan began.

Jessica sat forward, listening intently. The words "Nephites" and "Lamanites" were somewhat familiar to her from reading in the Book of Mormon. She concentrated on what Ethan was saying, trying to follow his explanation with what limited knowledge she had about the book and its cast of characters with their peculiar names.

"Captain Moroni fitted his soldiers with breastplates, shields, and thick clothing when they went out to battle the Lamanites, which was a great advantage because the Lamanite army was not prepared with such things. They had only their weapons and wore nothing but a skin girded about their loins."

Jessica pictured the scene—the Nephite men protected in their armor, and the Lamanites trussed only in animal skins. Together with the descriptions she'd read in Enos about the appearance of the Lamanites, she guessed the battle between the two must have been fierce.

"Captain Moroni was a brilliant commander, but he was also a man of great faith and righteousness. He heeded the words of Alma, the prophet, and this helped him in his campaign against the Lamanites. He was devoted to defending the lands, rights, and liberties of his people, the Nephites, and their religion."

"Did Captain Moroni and his army of Nephites win the battle over the Lamanites?" Jessica asked. The odd names fell clumsily from her tongue.

"That's the remarkable thing about Captain Moroni, and the quality I admire most about him, for he repeatedly tried to sue for peace with the Lamanites rather than continue to slay them in battle. He told Zarahemnah, the Lamanite commander, that the Nephites did not desire war and the blood of their enemies, and that his Nephite army would not slay the Lamanites if they would only lay down their weapons and make a covenant of peace."

Jessica said nothing as she listened, spellbound, to Ethan's explanation. The lantern's light cast a glow on their shoulders as they sat together on the porch.

"Finally, after Zarahemnah had lost a large host of his men and the outcome of the battle was obvious, he surrendered his arms to Moroni and made the covenant of peace, and Moroni allowed him and his men to depart to their homes."

"And then was there peace between the Nephites and Lamanites?"

"For awhile, yes. But then other problems arose because of Amalickiah, a Nephite, who aspired to become king over the Nephites."

"So Moroni had to put down this rebellion among his own people," Jessica surmised.

"That's right, but it wasn't that simple. Amalickiah joined the Lamanites and stirred them up to battle against the Nephites, his own people. Not only that, but by treachery and murder, Amalickiah became king over all the Lamanites."

"And Moroni again led a battle against the Lamanites?"

"There wasn't just one battle," Ethan answered. "Several wars between the Nephites and the Lamanites took place. Many times the Nephites became fainthearted because of the ferocity of the Lamanites, but Moroni always encouraged and inspired them to fight on, for their cause was just in protecting their homelands and their freedoms."

Jessica nodded, beginning to understand the righteous strength of Moroni.

"Moroni never delighted in shedding blood; but he was determined to preserve his people's freedom and keep his brethren from bondage and slavery."

"Now I see what you meant by Moroni's righteous indignation," said Jessica. "But there's one thing I don't understand. Why were the Nephites and Lamanites such bitter enemies to begin with?"

Ethan changed position on the porch step so he could face Jessica directly. "For most of the Book of Mormon period, the Nephites were more righteous and obedient to God's commandments than the Lamanites. The Lamanites liked to place the blame for the two peoples' difficulties on what they traditionally felt was a wrong committed against their fathers by the ancestors of the Nephites. But that was only an excuse; the truth was that they were a wicked people who wanted power and dominion over their brethren."

Jessica fell silent, pondering the things Ethan had told her. As she sat on the step beside him, she felt a desire to read the account of Captain Moroni for herself. "I think I'll go inside now, Ethan. I'm tired," she said.

Ethan stared at her as if he wanted to say something more, then he lowered his eyes. "Me, too. I'm ready to turn in. See you tomorrow." With those words, he leaned over and gave her a quick hug.

Jessica was startled by the physical contact, for Ethan had never hugged her before, but it felt good.

"I'm glad you came to the ranch with me," Ethan said.

"Me, too."

He got up from the step and started toward the bunkhouse. Jessica could see his silhouette in the moonlight as he walked away. She smiled, feeling a deep tenderness for him.

She went back inside the house, to the bedroom she shared with the Bartlett sisters. Both girls were asleep. Jessica quietly opened her traveling bag resting at the foot of the bed and rummaged inside it until she located the brown, hard-bound book. She held it up to the light. The moonlight streaming in from the window illuminated the lettering; "The Book of Mormon," she read in a whisper.

She took the book and went to the window with it, and seated herself upon the wide sill, turning the book to catch the moonlight. The lantern hanging from the porch gave additional light, sufficient to read the words printed on the page.

Jessica had no idea where the story of Moroni and his brave Nephite soldiers was to be found in the book, and so she turned first to the table of contents page, thinking perhaps the story would be located under the heading of "Moroni." She discovered a chapter so titled, but in glancing over the few pages of the chapter, found no mention of the odd names Ethan had used in relating the story to her and concluded the episode must be situated elsewhere.

She frowned, but was undeterred by the delay and determined to find the account Ethan had narrated for her. She flipped through the pages slowly. When she was about two-thirds of the way through the volume, the word suddenly jumped out from the page. MORONI. She held the book closer and scanned the printing beginning at the top of the page. Finding it to be a continuation from the page before, she turned to the previous page and started reading. After a bit more searching, she came to what she thought was the beginning of the story of Captain Moroni, located in a chapter bearing the title, "Alma." Yes, Ethan had mentioned the name, Alma. She read with curiosity to begin with, and then more avidly as she became caught up in the story of Moroni and his struggles with the Lamanites. She continued to read as the moon rose higher in the sky, eagerly absorbing the account and the stalwart character of the man named Moroni.

The following morning Jessica arose with the sun. She had read late into the night by the lantern's light, and then her dreams had been filled with images from the book. As she finished dressing, she smelled breakfast cooking, and muffled sounds from the kitchen indicated the ranch hands were filing in for the morning meal. She fastened the buttons on her shoes, combed her hair, and went to the kitchen to help Mrs. Bartlett serve breakfast. The morning passed with little opportunity to share a private word with Ethan. She had dozens of questions to ask him from her reading in the "Book of Alma," but Ethan was occupied with his chores on the ranch.

The ranch hands spent the afternoon branding calves, and then later gathered at the corral to watch Rory break the second of the three mustangs they'd captured from off the range, a sturdy buckskin. Jessica joined the men clustered around the corral, delaying her questions concerning the book in her excitement over seeing Rory tame the wild buckskin. Both of her cousins sat on the top rail of the fenced corral, cheering on Rory as he rode the bronc. Samuel had his hat off, waving it exuberantly above his head.

The mustang reared, its front hooves clawing the air, but Rory stayed firmly in the saddle. Jessica watched breathlessly, every nerve atingle. Rory's body was controlled, and his face a mask of concentration as he worked with the horse. After another few moments, the mustang grew weary of fighting the saddle and rider and settled down to a nervous walk. Rory stayed on his back while the animal pranced and sidestepped inside the corral, and then when he was ready, handily slipped from the saddle and led the reluctant horse to the fence where Samuel and Ethan sat.

Samuel mounted the buckskin next, while Rory held the lead rope taut. Jessica watched her cousin astride the mustang; the horse was still jittery and making little crowhops. As Samuel trained the horse to the saddle, Ethan drifted away to talk with one of the other men, and Rory turned his attention to the saddle rope he was coiling into a loop. Jessica saw him glance up, and as their eyes connected, Rory's face broke into a smile. He strode toward her carrying the rope in his hand.

"Afternoon, Mr. McKellar," she said as he approached. She took in at a glance the red striped shirt he wore, open at the neck, and his fringed chaps. The jinglebobs on his spurs rang jauntily as he walked up to her.

"Hello. I figured you'd be nearby watching the bronc riding."

"I wouldn't miss it."

"We've gotten that second bronco pretty well broken," he said, nodding toward the mustang Samuel was attempting to control.

"Yes, I saw you do it. You're quite a cowboy." Embarrassed by her candid remark, Jessica felt the color rush to her cheeks.

But Rory seemed pleased with her comment. He grinned and replied, "Well, I've had my share of eating dirt without stooping."

Jessica smiled at his cowboy jargon. She watched him fidget with his saddle rope, coiling it up into a loose circle, then letting it out again, and realized he was just as nervous around her as she was with him. That simple fact helped to set her at ease.

"A few hours more of work with that buckskin, and we'll have ourselves a good saddle horse," Rory said.

"And what about Dynamite? Will he make a good saddle horse eventually, too?" Jessica asked teasingly. She'd overheard Rory and the hands discussing the volatile, black mustang that morning at the breakfast table. The horse, apparently, was as wild as ever even after Rory's ride three days before.

Rory gave a short laugh. "That mustang is as feisty as a polecat. But I reckon we can talk some sense into him."

Jessica dug the toe of her shoe into the dirt, trying to think of something more to say. "I don't know how you manage to stick to the saddle on those untamed horses."

"I keep one leg on each side and my mind in the middle."

Jessica chuckled. "That's the secret?"

"Yup." Rory flicked his wrist and the rope dangling from his hand spun.

"Are you able to do rope tricks, too?" Jessica asked, still grinning. If only her heart would settle down and stop beating so furiously, she thought, she'd feel more relaxed around him.

Rory looked at her with laughter in his eyes. He made another quick turn of the wrist and his lariat surged into a twirling circle.

"Remarkable," Jessica said, smiling. She watched as he maneuvered the whirling rope first to one side of his body and then to the other.

"Watch this," Rory told her as he stepped with one foot into the moving circle of rope. He looked at her and grinned like a school boy.

"That's truly amazing."

Rory snapped his wrist again, and the rope went flying in a ring above his head. And then the circle of rope whirred from his head to his feet, and back to his head again. "Yippy-ki-o," he quipped.

Jessica's laughter was genuine. As he twirled the rope, he began singing a few bars of a cowboy song in a deep, resonant baritone. Even though he was joking with her, Jessica realized he possessed a fine singing voice.

After another moment, Rory reeled in his lariat, looping it in his hand. "Did you like that fancy roping?" he asked with a sparkle in his voice.

"Immensely."

"I can teach you how to do it, if you'd like."

"You're joking. I could never learn to do that."

"Sure you could," Rory returned, slapping the loop of rope against his thigh. "I'll teach you after supper. How would you like that?"

"Now, what possible use could I have for learning rope tricks?"

"You never know. You might have to hog-tie an unruly school pupil."

Jessica laughed. "I never thought of that."

"And who's to say? You might someday want to become a cowgirl."

"A cowgirl? I don't think so."

"Anything's possible, isn't it? Look at me. I wanted to become an Irish Kit Carson."

His reference to their earlier conversation brought a glow to Jessica's cheeks. "You never let anyone forget that you're of Irish descent, do you?" Jessica teased.

"Are you accusing me of kissing the blarney stone?"

"The Irish are famous for tall tales and a quick tongue, aren't they?" she returned, cocking her head coyly to one side.

"Aye, lassie," he responded, breaking into his imitation of an Irish brogue. "Shall I sing you an Irish tale?"

"You sing Irish songs as well as cowboy ones?"

Rory let out a length of rope and sent it spinning and dancing at his feet. "You'll find I'm a man of many talents."

Jessica felt a chuckle tickle her throat. "Then by all means, please do so."

Rory cast a glance toward the corral where most of the cowboys were still gathered. Then he reached for Jessica's hand and started walking with her toward the stream behind the house.

Jessica's hand tingled at his touch, and her heart cartwheeled in her chest. She let Rory lead her along the dirt path to the grove of willows growing beside the creek. As they walked hand in hand, he started singing a somber Irish melody.

> "O Paddy dear, did you hear the news
> that's going round,
> The shamrock is forbid by law to grow
> on Irish ground;
> And Saint Patrick's day no more we'll
> keep, his color can't be seen,
> For there's a bloody law against the
> wearin' of the green."

He sang the words mournfully, full of feeling, in a clear, quiet voice.

"Then since the color we must wear is
England's cruel red;
Sure Ireland's sons will ne'er forget the
blood that they have shed;
You may take the shamrock from your
hat and cast it on the sod,
But 'twill take root and flourish still, tho'
underfoot 'tis trod."

Jessica was moved by the sober lyrics, which reflected a people's proud love for their homeland and their lost freedoms. Rory's strong baritone was embellished by a hint of Irish brogue as he sang the haunting words.

"When the law can stop the blades of
grass from growing as they grow,
And when the leaves in summertime
their verdure dare not show,
Then I will change the color I wear in
my corbeen,
But till that day, please God, I'll stick to
wearin' of the green."

Rory finished the song as the two of them reached the grove of willows growing beside the creek.

"That was really beautiful. What do you call it?" asked Jessica softly.

"'The Wearin' of the Green.' It's an Irish street ballad I learned as a boy from my father. The song dates back to the seventeenth century. There are more verses, but I can't recall the words to them."

Rory paused near a stand of willows fringing the stream—the very spot, Jessica realized, concealing the quiet dell where she'd sought solitude a few days before to read from Birgithe's Book of Mormon. He let go of her hand and squatting down ranged through the wild grass with his fingertips. Then he stood, holding a single, long-stemmed clover in his hand.

Jessica smiled quizzically at him.

"For you, Jessie," he said, taking her hand and placing the three-leafed clover gently onto her palm. "This is as close to a shamrock as I'm able to find."

Jessica held her breath. The wispy feel of the clover in her hand, and the magical sound of her name falling from Rory's lips, left her trembling. She closed her fingers around the bit of clover and looked up into his face.

Color flooded Rory's cheeks until they were nearly the same shade as the red stripes on his flannel shirt, and when he spoke, his voice was hoarse. "I guess I'd better be getting back to my chores."

"Yes," Jessica squeaked. "I need to get back, too."

Rory tipped his cowboy hat and then strode away, swinging the rope in his hand. Jessica thought she heard him whistling.

After supper that evening, Mr. Bartlett asked Ethan to stay a moment to talk with him. Jessica kept one ear tuned to the conversation taking place at the table as she dried the supper dishes, and by the time the two men had finished speaking, Jessica was wiping the last dish.

She followed Ethan out of the house. "Ethan, wait a minute," she called to him.

He stopped and turned toward her. "What is it?" he asked when she reached him.

"I heard your conversation with Mr. Bartlett. Are you going back to Salt Lake City soon?"

Ethan nodded. "The day after tomorrow. I was going to talk to you about it in the morning. Brother Bartlett needs me to obtain a document from the land office in Salt Lake to verify his ownership of the ranch lands. That way, he hopes to satisfy Travers and avoid any more trouble."

Jessica bit her lip. Just thinking about Travers and his Texas cowhands made her shiver.

"Are you ready to go back? Do you want to go with me to Salt Lake?" Ethan asked her.

Jessica wrestled with the question. She'd been at the ranch for a little over a week and hadn't considered leaving. She was enjoying her stay—especially since meeting Rory. "I don't know, Ethan," she said after a pause. "I haven't thought about it. Can I tell you in the morning?"

"Sure. You don't have to leave the ranch just because I'm going. I'll only be gone a couple of days, and then I'll be back. Samuel will be here, and so you won't feel alone while I'm gone."

"All right."

Ethan bent to look her in the eye. "If you do stay, I want you to stick close to the ranch house. You never know what Travers' men might take into their heads to do."

Jessica nodded.

"Promise me you'll stay put and let Samuel watch out for you," Ethan said sternly. "And this time, listen to what I'm telling you. You should have stayed behind us for protection during that quarrel the other day with the Texans. You could have gotten shot."

Jessica felt a swell of indignation. "Why, Ethan Kade, if you think I'm going to stand by and do nothing when I have a pistol at my waist, and my cousins are being threatened by thieving outlaws, you've got another—"

"Okay. Okay," Ethan surrendered. "I get the message." He turned and started toward the bunkhouse. "You probably could have plugged all three of them by yourself, without any help from us," he muttered as he strode off into the darkening night.

Jessica's anger left as abruptly as it had come. She stared after her cousin's retreating figure, shaking her head and smiling.

# CHAPTER SIXTEEN

Ethan affixed the three-cent stamp onto the letter Jessica had given him to mail for her and handed it to the mail clerk at the post office. The clerk added the letter to a stack of others to be delivered. Ethan knew the letter would take seven or eight days by train to get to the destination neatly printed on the envelope—Nauvoo, Illinois. He had noticed to whom the letter was addressed: "Mr. and Mrs. Alexander Scott," Jessica's parents. He wondered what Jessica had said to them in the letter concerning her stay with the Kades; he hoped it was positive.

He left the post office, located on Main Street, and walked down the plank sidewalk with his hands in his pockets. He was only a block from the Quill and Ink, but he had no intention of stopping there, although he ached to see Susannah. She disliked him—he was sure of that—and so he wouldn't press his company on her again, he'd decided in resignation. He withdrew a small, brown paper sack from his pocket, opened it, and dropped a lemon candy in his mouth. The tart taste pleased him, offering a bit of solace in his disappointment over Susannah.

His thoughts turned to the errand at hand—locating the land office and accomplishing the task Brother Bartlett had given him. He found the office without difficulty, a tiny place tucked between a tailoring shop and an undertaker's parlor. He glanced at the door of the undertaker's establishment. "That's appropriate," he mumbled to himself, thinking grimly about his encounter with the three Texans employed by Travers, and the rancher's efforts to usurp Bartlett's ranch land.

Pushing open the door to the land office, he went inside. The small room was cluttered with papers—a large map of the Utah Territory lying on a table, newspapers left forgotten on the seat of a chair, books and papers cluttering a writing desk. On one wall was a billboard, where a cluster of notices were tacked. Ethan glanced at the conglomeration of papers on the board as he walked to the desk, where a portly, balding man sat, rummaging through a sheaf of documents. Ethan stood quietly in front of the desk, waiting for the land official to notice him. When the man continued to thumb through his papers with a frown of concentration, Ethan stepped a pace closer and deliberately cleared his throat.

The man glanced up. "Can I help you with something?"

"Yes, thank you. I've come to inquire about the legal title to some ranch land owned by Mr. John Bartlett. Here is the document Mr. Bartlett asked me to show you."

Ethan took the copy of the homestead claim Bartlett had given him from his pocket and laid it on the desk. The land officer bent over the paper to read through it. He and Ethan discussed the document belonging to Bartlett, then Ethan told him about the difficulties Bartlett was having with the neighboring rancher.

The official listened to Ethan's tale and then said, "If you'll wait for a moment, I'll check to see what written verification we have on file here." The stout officer stood up from the desk and lumbered into a cramped back room.

Ethan remain seated until the official returned. The man explained to Ethan about the nature of the claim Bartlett had filed in the land office, which, indeed, showed Bartlett's legal title to the ranch lands, and then offered to draw up a copy of it for Ethan to take back to his employer.

"It will take me about twenty minutes to copy the documentation, Mr. Kade. If you wish to wait here, you're welcome to do so," the official said.

"All right. I will," Ethan replied. He leaned back in his chair and folded his arms against his chest, watching the land officer withdraw from his desk a clean sheet of paper and begin copying the information from the original onto it with a quill ink pen.

After a few minutes, Ethan grew tired of watching the official scribbling onto the paper. He stood up and went to the table where the territorial map was spread and bent over it, studying the map with interest. After a time, he wandered away from the table and picked up the newspaper lying across the seat of a chair. It was a section of the *Deseret News*, dated June 1872. Ethan glanced over a piece devoted to the upcoming presidential election in November. Running against President Grant on the Democratic ticket was the popular editor of the *New York Tribune,* Horace Greeley. The Greeley supporters had nicknamed Ulysses S. Grant "Useless Grant," and their rallying cry was "Turn the rascals out!" Grant's presidency had been marred by graft and political corruption perpetrated by some of his appointees, and by a disappointing performance of duties by the president himself. Ethan wondered if the former Civil War hero would win a second term in office.

After putting aside the paper, he stepped over to the billboard on the wall, where a variety of advertisements were posted. He glanced over them as a means of passing the time while he waited for the official to finish copying the document. A notice printed in big, black letters, telling of a silver strike in the Oquirrh Mountains, captured his attention. "RICH SILVER VEIN UNCOVERED IN WEST MOUNTAINS!" The advertisement described the discovery of silver in glowing terms, and promised miners wealth and fortune. Another notice announced "LAND FOR SALE! A PARADISE OF GREEN GRASS AND SPARKLING STREAMS!!" Ethan read over the advertisement detailing the land for sale in the northern part of the territory.

After perusing the two advertisements, his eyes moved on to a third one. "LYCEUM. TONIGHT ONLY. WORLD

TRAVELER BERNARD HINES WILL SPEAK ABOUT HIS EXPERIENCES IN EGYPT. 8:00 P.M. SOCIAL HALL." Ethan read the brief words a second time, his interest piqued.

"Here you are, Mr. Kade. This should be sufficient for your purposes." The land officer laid down his quill pen and blew on the paper to dry the ink, then handed the document to Ethan.

"Thank you. Mr. Bartlett would want me to extend his appreciation for your help."

The official nodded.

Ethan left the office and paused on the porch to glance over the document the official had copied for him. It carried the official's seal, testifying to its authenticity. Carefully folding the document, Ethan tucked it into his pocket. He was about to start down the porch step when he spotted Susannah Hamilton standing across the street with a male companion beside her. Ethan's breath wheezed in his throat as he stared at the couple. Susannah's dark hair glistened in the morning sun, and the blue dress she wore hugged her slender waist.

Ethan shrunk against the building, trying to make himself invisible. From his vantage point on the porch, however, he could plainly see Susannah's agitated expression and her companion's surly frown. The man was tall and slender, and stylished dressed; he sported side whiskers and a mustache. Ethan dropped his gaze, ashamed of himself for spying on the couple; but he couldn't stop his ears from hearing their raised voices. Although he couldn't make out the gist of the exchange, Ethan felt certain it was a lover's quarrel he was overhearing. *Edward Grayson,* he thought, feeling a stab of jealousy. This was probably the man Susannah's mother had warned her to avoid.

A moving flash of color caused him to lift his eyes just in time to see Susannah stalk off, her head bent and a handkerchief pressed to her eyes. Ethan watched the young man reach for her, but Susannah shook off his hand and continued down the plank sidewalk. The man let out an exasperated groan, then turned and strode away.

Ethan stepped down from the porch and gazed after Susannah as she retreated into the distance. It took all of his willpower to refrain from dashing after her and offering comfort. When she was out of sight, Ethan sighed and started in the opposite direction toward his horse tied at the hitching post up the street. He kept thinking about Susannah and the fellow who had been with her. If the man was Edward Grayson, why was Susannah still seeing him, knowing full well her parents' feelings on the matter? And what were they quarreling about? Ethan knew the affair was none of his business, but he couldn't get the sight of Susannah, crying and upset, out of his mind.

He was nearly to his horse when he stopped abruptly in mid-stride. He longed to see Susannah again, talk with her, try to befriend her. Perhaps his cousin had been right when she suggested that Ethan simply *talk* to Susannah, rather than hide from her between the covers of a book. He stood biting his lip, deciding on a course of action. Then he turned and strode back the way he'd come, past the land office and toward the building housing the Quill and Ink. His breath was coming in short, fast bursts, and his heart was hammering in his chest, but he continued on until he was standing outside the bookseller's shop.

He drew a deep breath to steady himself and pushed open the door. The little bell overhead tinkled, signaling his entrance. He found Susannah sitting on a stool behind the counter, dabbing her eyes with the handkerchief. Ethan swallowed and walked over to her.

When she caught sight of him, Susannah quickly composed herself and got to her feet. "May I help you?" She self-consciously tucked her wet handkerchief into the folds of her skirt.

As Ethan stood looking at her, he realized she was even more beautiful than the countless number of times he had imagined her in his thoughts and dreamed about her in his sleep. He took note of her red-rimmed eyes, and her pain and hurt went straight to his heart. "Hello, Miss Hamilton. It's nice to see you again. I'm Ethan Kade?" He ended his sentence with a question, in case she didn't remember him.

"I know who you are, Mr. Kade."

In spite of Susannah's curt reply, Ethan felt giddy over the fact that she recognized him this time. No one else was in the book shop, which pleased Ethan. He shoved his hands in his pockets and rocked back on his heels, nervous, but excited to be alone with her. "I'm in town just for today and wanted to stop by and say hello to you," he said sincerely.

Susannah wiped her cheek with the back of her hand, perhaps to make sure there were no stains from her recent tears. "I thought you lived here in town," she replied. Ethan could see her struggling to hide her recently ruffled emotions.

"I do. I mean, this is my home when I'm not working at the ranch," he explained.

"You work for a cattle rancher. I recall you telling me that."

Ethan's heart missed a beat. She remembered that about him, too. The revelation thrilled him, as insignificant as it might seem. "Yes, in South Willow Creek. In fact, that's the reason why I'm in town today. I'm taking care of some business for my employer."

"I see."

Ethan's fingers nudged the sack of lemon drops, stashed in one pocket, that he'd just purchased at the mercantile. He pulled out the sack, opened it, and held it out to Susannah. "Would you care for a lemon drop?" he asked with a smile.

She looked at him hesitantly, then reached into the sack and withdrew a candy. "Thank you," she returned, placing the lemon drop in her mouth.

He took a candy from the sack, too, and popped it into his mouth. "My cousin, Jessica, is staying at the ranch for a few days," Ethan remarked in an effort to make conversation.

"How is she liking it?

Ethan grinned. "I'm not sure."

"She seems very nice."

"She is. I'll be sorry to see her leave for Sacramento."

Susannah nodded as she sucked on her lemon drop.

"Have you ever visited California?" Ethan asked.

"No, but I've read about it. I like learning about people and places."

An idea leaped into Ethan's head. "In that case, perhaps you might enjoy attending the lyceum being held tonight. A fellow who's been to Egypt is speaking about his experiences there."

"Indeed?" Susannah's dark brows lifted in interest.

"Yes. This evening at eight. Would you do me the pleasure of accompanying me to the lyceum?" Ethan was amazed at his own boldness. He could hardly believe that he'd just extended an invitation for an evening out with Susannah Hamilton, the most enchanting girl he'd ever met.

Susannah looked startled, and Ethan felt sure she would decline his invitation. He'd offered it on the spur of the moment, without thinking, because he knew he'd be in town only for the remainder of the day. Early tomorrow morning he'd have to start back to the ranch. She said nothing for a moment, and then in an even voice she replied, "Yes, I would. Thank you, Mr. Kade."

"You would?" Ethan blurted. "You want to go with me?"

"Of course. I'd enjoy going to the lyceum very much."

She neglected to add "with you," but Ethan didn't care. His heart was soaring. "May I come for you about twenty minutes before eight?"

"That would be fine."

Ethan couldn't believe his good fortune. The grin on his face stretched from ear to ear.

"When you arrive this evening, come around to the side door of the building. That's the entrance to our house."

"All right, I will." Ethan stared at her with a widespread grin. "Here," he said eagerly, holding the small paper sack out to her. "Will you have another lemon drop?"

"Thank you. Actually, lemon drops are my favorite."


As Mr. Bernard Hines took a final bow behind the podium where he'd spoken that evening in the Social Hall, Ethan applauded enthusiastically. He glanced at Susannah, seated at his side, and saw that she, too, was smiling with approval. He sighed in relief—Susannah had apparently enjoyed the lecture on ancient Egypt. He, also, had liked the presentation, which surprised him. History was not his favorite topic, but Mr. Hines' animated style of delivery and the fascinating artifacts he'd exhibited to the audience, intrigued Ethan.

When the applause concluded, and Mr. Hines took his leave from the stage, the audience began to dissemble. Ethan stood up from his chair and offered his hand to Susannah in a polite gesture to help her to her feet. Susannah placed her hand in his, and a tingle rippled along his spine. Just sitting beside Susannah throughout the lyceum discussion had thrilled him. She smiled at him as she briefly took his hand.

"Did you like the lecture?" he asked her as they filed out of the room with the rest of the crowd.

"Oh, yes. Very much so," she answered eagerly.

He held open the door for her to exit the building. As he stepped outside, a slight evening breeze fanned his face, and the night sky sparkled with stars. "Are you warm enough?" he asked Susannah, helping her pull her fringed shawl around her shoulders.

She nodded.

In the starlight her eyes changed from emerald green to silver, and the striped brown and beige dress she wore shimmered in the moon's glow. Ethan felt his breath coming in short, little gasps just looking at her.

"What a remarkable presentation. The description of the pyramids was fascinating, wasn't it?" she said to Ethan.

"Absolutely. And what a feat of engineering to build one of those structures," he added, giving a low whistle.

"Yes, with all of its chambers and tunnels. And I liked seeing the artifacts Mr. Hines brought from an Egyptian tomb."

"Me, too," he agreed. Ethan smiled in contentment as he walked with Susannah along Main Street toward her home. The hours before his appointment with her had seemed endless. He had spent the time at home with his parents and sister, which was an agreeable diversion, but he hadn't been able to keep his mind off Susannah and their impending evening together. When at last he'd knocked at her door, his hand was shaking as if he'd been struck with an attack of palsy.

But Susannah's friendly manner had soon set him at ease. To his surprise, he found her to be more talkative than he had expected or had experienced from his brief encounters with her in the book shop. She seemed genuine and unpretentious, and she possessed a clever sense of humor. By the time they had reached the Social Hall where the lyceum was to be held, he was more smitten with her than ever.

"And the inscriptions carved on stone—I don't know how they ever decipher that stuff," Ethan remarked.

"It sounded almost like poetry, didn't it?"

"Poetry? I wouldn't know," Ethan answered with a sheepish grin.

"Aren't you the fellow who came into the shop looking for a book of Wordsworth?" Susannah's mouth curved into a rosy little bow.

"I have to confess that, generally speaking, I don't like poetry, much less understand it."

Susannah's smile widened. "I thought so, Mr. Kade."

"Are you disappointed in me?"

Susannah glanced up at him with a sweep of her dusky lashes. "Only slightly."

"Good. I'm glad. I hoped I wouldn't be a disappointment to you." Ethan meant to deliver the comment in a light-hearted tone, but the words came out sounding more earnest than he'd intended. He blushed and turned away.

Susannah made no reply, but a moment later Ethan felt her hand sneak softly into the crook of his arm. He glanced quickly at her face, but she had looked away. The feel of her hand on his arm sent a warmth rushing through him.

"When you go back to the ranch tomorrow, please give my regards to your cousin."

"I will," Ethan replied in a husky voice.

They strolled along Main Street, toward Susannah's home, under a canopy of starlight. Susannah chatted easily, while it was all Ethan could do to continue breathing in a normal fashion. The feel of her beside him stole his breath away. She inquired further about Jessica, and Ethan explained why his cousin had come to Salt Lake City and a little history of their two families, although it was accomplished in breathless spurts.

All too soon they drew up to Susannah's door. Ethan glanced at the hanging sign, featuring the depiction of a quill pen and an ink bottle, swinging lazily in the night breeze. They paused outside the door to the house. Susannah withdrew her hand from Ethan's arm and stepped a pace away from him. "Thank you for escorting me to the lyceum, Mr. Kade. I enjoyed it."

Ethan didn't know if she was referring to the presentation or to being with him. His heart was beating so hard that he felt its throbbing rhythm in his temples. He knew he had to start back to the ranch at first light because Brother Bartlett was expecting him with the land document, but he was desperate to see Susannah again.

Perhaps he could manage to steal away from the ranch the following weekend.

"Miss Hamilton," he began in a quavering voice. "I'd very much like to see you again. Perhaps I could call on you next Saturday evening, if you are agreeable to that." He paused, feeling suddenly vulnerable.

Susannah lowered her eyes, and Ethan thought she would surely decline his clumsy invitation. His shoulders drooped with disappointment.

"I have a confession to make to you, too, Ethan," she began softly.

Hearing her speak his given name sent a swell of feeling through him. "What is it?" he asked breathlessly.

"I haven't been entirely honest with you. I accepted your invitation for this evening for the wrong reason. I . . ." Susannah's glance wavered. "I had a disagreement with a gentleman friend of mine earlier today, and I wanted to strike back at him by making him feel jealous."

Ethan froze. The image of Susannah arguing with the man in the stylish clothing sprang into his mind.

"I'm so sorry, Ethan. Please accept my apology," she said sincerely.

It took a moment for Ethan to gather his senses again. He managed a smile and asked, "Are you sorry you went with me?"

Susannah stared at him for an in stant. "No. No, I'm not."

Ethan felt a renewal of hope. His smile broadened. "Does that mean you'll see me again next Saturday night?"

A smile started across her face. "Perhaps," she answered.

"Perhaps," Ethan repeated, nodding his head. "That's good enough for now. I'll leave the ranch after chores on Friday and come to the book shop to see you on Saturday afternoon. You can give me your answer then. All right?"

"All right," Susannah returned. "But I'd feel badly if your trip turned out to be a waste of time because of me."

Ethan gently took her hand, and the warmth of it started a fire in his soul. "Nothing I could do for you would ever be a waste of time, Susannah."

Ethan saw her face pale, or perhaps it was only the moonlight that made her complexion look translucent. At that moment, Ethan would have given nearly anything to kiss her ruby lips.

# CHAPTER SEVENTEEN

"That's it. Just turn your wrist a little more."

Jessica concentrated on the wrist motion, and the saddle rope whirled into a perfect circle at her feet. "I did it!" she exclaimed to Rory, who stood beside her.

"You sure did. I knew you could. All it takes is practice," he replied with a grin.

Jessica twirled the rope and the circle went round and round. "I've been practicing this for two days, and now I've finally gotten the hang of it. I can't wait to show Ethan when he gets back tonight."

"I doubt he'll be too surprised. You're a natural when it comes to cowboying skills." Rory cocked his head to one side. "I hear you're quite a shot with the pistol, too."

Jessica tried moving the circling rope to one side, but the rope tangled on itself and fell limp. She shook it out, preparing to try again. "Ethan was perturbed with me for drawing my pistol when we were up against those Texans," she said, glancing at the tall cowhand.

"He was?"

"He was being protective, I guess." She began flicking her wrist and hand, and the rope swung into a whirling circle.

"Even so, I was proud to have you standing shoulder to shoulder with me."

Rory's words started her heart beating double time. She tried to stop her hands from shaking, but the dancing rope wavered, wobbled, and then fell into a heap on the ground. As she coiled the rope, she looked up at him. His eyes were crystal blue under the morning sky; so bright and clear she felt she could see eternity in their depths.

She harbored a new concept of eternity, in part due to Rory. The evening before Ethan left for Salt Lake City, Rory had sought her out to teach her a simple rope trick, as he'd promised. When he'd handed her the rope, she was hesitant and nervous, but he guided her hand until she got the knack of spinning it. While she was practicing with the rope, he reminded her about the poem she'd promised to show him. At his urging, she brought out the book of verse and they sat outside on the porch step, under the lantern's light, to read Wordsworth's "Ode on Intimations of Immortality" together.

Rory had shown an intuitive insight into the poem's meaning, unveiling a level of interpretation she'd never considered. He used some of the same terms as Ethan had in talking with her about the poem; such words as "pre-mortal existence," "celestial glory," and "the witness of the Holy Ghost." Discussion of the poem had evolved into a conversation about Rory's religion, and Jessica learned he was a recently converted member of The Church of Jesus Christ of Latter-day Saints.

The following day, she'd asked Rory to tell her more about his beliefs. They took a long horseback ride together into the foothills east of the ranch, and Rory explained to her the basic tenets of the gospel. She told him that she'd read the story of Enos and the chapters about Captain Moroni in the Book of Mormon, and been stirred by the account. "The Book of Enos" and "The Book of Alma" were not merely chapters, he'd taught her in response, but actual books or histories written by individual authors and then abridged by a man named Mormon. Rory suggested that she read the entire Book of Mormon from beginning to end in order to gain an understanding of it, and then they could discuss further any questions she might have.

And so she had started that process. She'd taken the Book of Mormon from her traveling bag and gone alone to the secluded dell beside the creek, and begun to read the text starting with "The First Book of Nephi."

"Try it again," Rory said, nodding toward the rope.

As she let out the slack, she spotted Samuel coming toward them.

"Are you planning to help us rope cows for branding?" he asked, pointing to the saddle rope in her hand.

"She could easily do that," Rory responded before Jessica had a chance to reply. "Show him how you can make the rope dance, Jessie."

Jessica readied the rope.

"You've taught her how to throw a rope?" Samuel grinned. "Next she'll be wanting to cut cattle with us."

Jessica smiled at her cousin as she coaxed the rope into a whirl. In an instant, it was twirling at her feet like a pirouetting ballerina.

"Now move the rope from side to side," Rory directed.

"I can't. I'll lose it," giggled Jessica.

"Go on and try," Rory urged.

She did. Without interrupting the motion of her wrist, she moved the circling rope from one side of her body to the other.

"Good job!" Samuel cheered.

"That's perfect, Jessie," Rory congratulated her. "You've got it down pat now."

Jessica's smile grew as she moved the twirling rope from side to side without a hitch. After a moment, she let the circle collapse and reeled in the rope. "What did you think of that?" she asked Samuel.

"You're without compare, cousin." He leaned over and pecked her cheek.

"You cowpunchers better get back to work before Mr. Bartlett finds you standing around," chided Jessica with a grin. She handed the coiled rope back to Rory.

"Oh, all right," Rory replied, slapping the rope against his thigh. "Sounds like she's tired of our company, Samuel."

Jessica watched them walk away, smiling at the picturesque figure Rory presented dressed in his fringed chaps, collarless plaid shirt, vest, and bandana. His big, silver belt buckle set with turquoise stones glittered in the sun. Jessica liked the way he looked, the way he walked, and the way he made her feel when she was with him.

Later in the day, Jessica removed the Book of Mormon from her satchel and walked to her special spot beside the stream. She sat down on the soft grass and opened the book to "Third Nephi," where she'd been reading the night before. She grew unaware of the passing hours as she read of the signs given on the night of Christ's birth, the miracle of Nephi raising his brother from the dead, and the devastation across the land accompanying the crucifixion of the Savior. In reading the account of the resurrected Christ appearing to the people, she felt a profound sense of humility. Christ's words to the Nephites took root in her soul and caused her heart to swell within her. She didn't understand everything she read concerning the Savior's message and ministry to the people, but she sensed that the words on the page were true. She sat in the small clearing, reading thoughtfully, until supper time.

Ethan wasn't back yet from his trip to the land office in Salt Lake City. Jessica sat at the table between Samuel and Rory to eat her meal, then afterward helped Mrs. Bartlett with the dishes. Ethan still hadn't returned by that time, and so she took the opportunity to retire to her private niche beside the stream and read until dusk. She finished "Fourth Nephi," and the following "Book of Mormon," and got part way into "The Book of Ether" before it became too dark to see. Then she closed the book, her head and heart brimming with its remarkable teachings.

When she was nearly to the house, she heard a familiar voice call out, "There you are. I've been looking for you."

She turned, a smile springing to her face. "Ethan! When did you get back?"

"About an hour ago. How have you been?"

"Fine. I've kept busy."

Ethan smothered a yawn with his hand. "Glad to hear that. I have good news to tell you, but I'm so worn out tonight that it's going to have to wait until tomorrow."

"Oh, that's not fair. You have to tell me now, since you brought it up," Jessica pouted.

"I'll tell you one thing to whet your interest." The tired lines on Ethan's face transformed into a smile. "It concerns Susannah Hamilton and the evening we spent together."

"What?" Jessica squealed. "You called on Susannah? Tell me all the glorious details."

"Tomorrow."

"I can't wait until then."

"You'll have to."

"First thing in the morning, directly after breakfast," Jessica demanded.

"Not until after morning chores. Then we'll talk."

"All right. And I have something wonderful to tell you, too." Jessica gripped the book in her hand more tightly.

"Okay. We'll exchange stories tomorrow. Night." He turned toward the bunkhouse and strode away into the gathering darkness.

The next morning Jessica dressed in trousers and cotton shirt and joined the Bartletts and ranch hands at the breakfast table. Afterward, when the dishes were washed and put away, she went outside to find Ethan. He wasn't in sight, but she spied Rory at the horse corral, where he had the black mustang tied by a halter to the fence post.

"Morning, Rory. Dynamite looks as docile as a lamb," she said to him.

"Don't let appearances fool you," he returned, smiling. "He's still head shy and hasn't yet grown a mellow hide."

Jessica watched the soot-colored stallion paw the ground. He shied as Rory waved a horse blanket near his head. "You're spooking him," Jessica grinned.

"This is called 'sacking.' As part of gentling and training him, we slap him on the body with a sack or saddle blanket, or wave it at his head, to get him used to sudden movements. Helps make him easier to handle in the saddle."

Jessica nodded.

"He's learned to neck-rein, but he's still fighting the bit most of the time." The horse whinnied and side-stepped as Rory slapped his haunches with the blanket.

Jessica studied the animal's lean, sinewy body and shiny coat.

"What are you up to this morning?" Rory asked her, tossing the blanket over the split-rail fence. He moved closer to her, until only the fence separated them.

"I'm looking for Ethan. Have you seen him since breakfast?" Her heart quickened with him standing so near.

"He rode out a little while ago to check on the stream flowing through the north pasture. It's been running low. He should be back soon. Can I help you with anything while he's gone?"

"I just wanted to talk with him about a matter." Jessica felt herself blush under Rory's steady gaze.

"When I see him, I'll tell him that," offered Rory.

"Thanks. I appreciate it." She reached out to stroke the mustang's ebony mane, her cheeks hot and prickly with the rush of blood.

Rory patted the horse's rump. "Have you had a chance to read any more in your Book of Mormon?" he asked.

"Yes, I have. In fact, I've read all the way to 'The Book of Ether.' But there's a lot I don't understand."

"'The Book of Ether' is kind of sandwiched into the record of the Nephites and Lamanites. Chronologically, it takes place much earlier than the rest of the records Mormon is abridging. That's sometimes confusing."

Jessica threaded her fingers through the mustang's coarse, black mane. "That part is not what confuses me," she replied slowly. "I want to know what happened to the church Christ organized among the Nephites?"

"That's where the Prophet Joseph Smith comes in." Rory leaned his arms on the top rail of the fence, looking her in the eye.

"Joseph Smith? He started his own church, not Christ's church," she replied, perplexed by Rory's answer.

"No," Rory responded, shaking his head. "Joseph Smith didn't start his own religion. He restored the Church of Jesus Christ."

"What do you mean? I've lived in Nauvoo my whole life. I heard the stories about Joseph Smith."

"Then you know that Heavenly Father and Jesus Christ appeared to him in answer to his prayer concerning which church he should join."

"I know he claimed to have seen God and angels, too." Jessica's heart was racing, but this time it wasn't because of Rory's appeal. Her heart beat faster with the desire to learn the truth.

Rory bent nearer. "His claim was based on fact, Jessie. He did see God and angels. Angels ministered to him and instructed him concerning the gospel of Jesus Christ; and it was the angel, Moroni, who directed him to the Hill Cumorah in New York State to the spot where ancient plates lay buried. These plates were inscribed upon by prophets of old and described a people who lived on the American continent—a people who called themselves Nephites and Lamanites."

Jessica held her breath as she listened to Rory's account.

Rory took her hand. "Joseph Smith obtained the plates at Moroni's direction, translated them by the gift and power of God, and published the ancient record as the Book of Mormon."

"I want to believe that, Rory, but how can I know for certain? How can you convince me?" she asked, yearning to know the truth.

Rory paused before answering. "I can't convince you; I can only teach you about the Prophet Joseph and The Church of Jesus Christ of Latter-day Saints, which he restored under the Savior's direction through revelation."

Jessica felt bewildered and troubled. If Rory couldn't help her believe and show her the way to Christ, then who could? She felt his fingers curling around hers.

"It takes faith on your part, Jessie, to believe what you have been taught and to believe what you have read for yourself in the Book of Mormon. And if you have faith and ask Heavenly Father in humble prayer if those things are true, he will send the Holy Ghost to testify to you of the truthfulness of the gospel. You have Moroni's word on it."

Jessica stared into Rory's eyes, searching for the assurance that it was possible to gain a knowledge of those things for herself. His eyes shone with a light that came from within, as if a fire burned in his soul.

Faith. Prayer. A desire to believe. Were these the keys to finding Christ's church as established anciently among the people of Nephi? Her cousin, Birgithe, had talked with her about these same things and had urged her to read the Mormon book of scripture. If Joseph Smith truly did restore the gospel, then had she been misled all her life concerning this fact? Was the true gospel of Jesus Christ embodied in the religion practiced by Rory and her Kade relatives? The questions made her head dizzy with possibilities.

Suddenly, she realized Rory was still holding her hand. She lowered her gaze and awkwardly removed her hand from his, feeling self-conscious about her display of emotion.

Rory dropped his hand to his side. "If you feel like talking more about this, I'm always available to listen," he said quietly.

Jessica glanced away, her thoughts jumbled. "I've kept you from your work much too long. Look at Dynamite. He's practically asleep."

Rory chuckled softly. "I'm sure I can light a spark under him."

Jessica watched him untie the mustang's halter from the fence and step into the stirrup. He smiled at her and tipped his hat, then reined the black horse into the center of the corral to continue the animal's training.

While she waited for Ethan to get back from the north pasture, Jessica decided to take her Book of Mormon to the glen beside the creek and finish reading it. Then she planned to do as Rory suggested and ask God in prayer if the book was true. She removed the volume from her traveling bag and headed for the stream.

When she parted the willows growing thick along the embankment, she noticed something odd. No quiet gurgling of the stream greeted her ear. Pushing past the willows screening the creek, she saw to her surprise that the streambed was nearly dry. Only a trickle of water flowed through the bottom of it. Shading her eyes with her hand, she stared upstream, then downstream in the opposite direction. As far as she could see, the channel contained a thimbleful of water.

"What's happened here?" she muttered aloud. She stepped to the edge of the dry streambed, her hands on her hips and a frown on her brow, trying to determine why the water was not flowing. She walked upstream several paces looking for the source of the problem. Seeing nothing amiss, she retraced her steps and walked the other way.

Perplexed, Jessica returned to the grassy glen and sat down with her book. She opened it to the place where she'd been reading in "The Book of Ether" and bent over the page. But she couldn't concentrate on the words. Her mind kept wandering back to the puzzle of the dry creekbed. She tried again to fix her attention on the page. A moment later she heaved a sigh of frustration, set the book down on the grass, and got to her feet. She began pacing the secluded dale, feeling uneasy about the situation at the creek. She knew the Bartletts depended on the water running in that stream for use in the household, as well as on the ranchlands. It wouldn't just suddenly dry up by itself. That meant something was blocking the water's flow.

She decided to investigate the cause. Shouldering through the willows, she set off toward the stable to saddle the gray mare; she thought about asking one of the hands to go instead, but abandoned the idea. Rory was busy with the mustang, Samuel and the others were knee deep in chores, and Ethan was away working on the range. As she fit the saddle and bridle onto the mare, she wondered if Ethan had already noticed the dry streambed and that was why he'd gone to check the water level in the north pasture.

She determined to follow the stream north, hoping to run into Ethan. She mounted her horse and urged the mare into a trot, riding the line of willows growing beside the creek. A dozen yards away from the house, she noticed a pile of debris spilling over into the streambed. A broken branch, leaves, and small rocks partially clogged the channel. She got off her horse to inspect the rubble, but quickly concluded this was not the reason for the stream running dry. She cleared away the branch and kicked aside the stones, then climbed back on her horse and continued northward.

By now the sun was riding high in the sky, beating down on her head and shoulders. She pulled the hat Samuel had lent her snugly over her forehead and fastened a button that had come undone on her coarse flannel shirt. The baggy shirt, floppy hat, and brown cotton trousers shielded her from the sun's wrath. She nudged the mare into a canter, keeping her eyes on the creek.

She'd been riding close to an hour when she finally spotted the problem. Up ahead a few yards, a thick tree branch straddled the stream, buttressed by a pile of rocks. As she slowed her mount, she felt the hairs on the back of her neck prickle. This was no natural pile of debris like she'd spied earlier. Someone had deliberately dammed up the creek and gone to some effort to do so.

She reined her horse to a halt and warily looked around. Ahead was nothing but wide open ground broken only by an occasional rise or low hill, and to her rear the land was empty and silent. A chill crawled down Jessica's spine, and she sensed danger lurking.

A flash of movement caught her eye. As she turned to look toward the creek, a figure came barreling out of the brush. Before she had a chance to react, the attacker yanked her from her horse, and she hit the ground with a force that knocked the wind out of her. Landing on her side and gasping to catch her breath, she felt a heavy foot clamp down on her shoulder, pinning her fast to the ground.

"Well, well, well. What do we have here?" a man's guttural voice growled. "If it ain't one of our friendly neighbors." The man gave a snort and pressed his foot harder into Jessica's shoulder. She winced with pain and wanted to cry out, but she didn't have the breath to do so.

"Nice of you to come visitin', baby brother. We got a little reception all planned out for you and your friends."

Jessica recognized the man's voice, and her heart nearly stopped. Though she couldn't see his face because he still held her trapped to the ground, she knew who he was from his Texas drawl.

She felt a gun thrust against her temple as the Texan lifted his foot, grabbed Jessica by the arm and jerked her to her feet. The rough yank knocked off her hat, and her hair streamed down her shoulders.

The Texan's eyes widened in surprise. "What this?" he stammered. "A girl?" The cowboy stared at her as if he couldn't make sense out of what he was seeing.

"Take your hands off me," Jessica sputtered.

"I wasn't expectin' no girl!" the Texan snapped. A coldness settled over his face. "I thought you was with Bartlett's boys. I seen you ridin' with them."

The recognition glinting in the man's eyes was reflected in her own stare—this was one of the cowhands who had confronted Rory and her cousins at the creek. She swallowed, fighting off a swell of panic.

"Since you're here, you might as well make yerself useful," the burly man in the Texas ten-gallon hat snarled. He gripped Jessica's arm so tightly that his fingers gouged into her flesh.

Jessica struggled to break free. "Let me go!"

The Texan reholstered his gun. "Not a chance. You'll make perfect bait." Keeping a tight hold on her arm, he turned and shouted, "Quaid! Get over here."

"Let go, you're hurting me," Jessica demanded, still fighting to escape him.

The Texan dragged her toward his horse, tethered in a stand of willows along the stream. He took a rope from the saddlehorn and tied her wrists together. "We're settlin' this score once and for all," he drawled. "With Mr. Travers' compliments, a' course." He forced Jessica to a spot beside the creek, concealed from sight by the willows, pushed her onto the ground and bound her ankles with rope.

"You can't keep me here!" Jessica cried. She kicked and squirmed, trying to wiggle out of the rope.

"What's goin' on here, Peyton?" A second man with a whiskered chin and squinty eyes stepped into sight. Jessica realized he, too, was with the party of Texans who had threatened them.

"A little mouse found its way into our trap," the other man replied, grinning. He kicked at the rope binding Jessica's ankles as if to emphasize his point.

The second man, Quaid, stood staring at Jessica. "What are you goin' to do with her?"

Jessica glared at the two cowboys. She was frightened, more frightened than she'd ever been in her life, but she was also angry. She fought the ropes until sweat beaded her brow.

Peyton laughed as he watched her struggle. "Might as well make yerself comfortable, missy. You ain't goin' nowhere." His eyes hardened into stone as he looked at her. Then he nodded to Quaid to follow him, and the two men strode away.

"Where are you going?" Jessica shouted after them. "Come back here and untie these ropes!"

Quaid turned for an instant to look back at her, his expression implacable.

The two men moved several yards downstream and stood talking. Jessica strained to hear their conversation, but they were just out of earshot. Alone and vulnerable, she became aware of the throbbing in her head. Her shoulder was sore where the Texan had pinned her to the ground. She tasted blood from a cut on her lip.

She squinted at the two men. They had moved deeper into the willows so that all she could see of them was a patch of Quaid's faded red shirt and Peyton's tall cowboy hat. Up ahead a few yards, she saw where the creek had been diverted into a narrow, man-made channel. The water gurgled and swirled as it flowed into a little eddy before emptying into the artificial ditch.

She flayed herself for having used such poor judgment in riding out here alone, knowing the volatile situation between the two ranchers. The memory of the grim encounter with Travers' cowhands in the south pasture and the Texans' threats of revenge returned with full force. Now she understood what Peyton meant about a reception being planned; he was laying a trap for Bartlett's men. An ambush.

Jessica moaned in despair. Her cousins would surely come searching for her and when they did, they'd walk right into Travers' snare. She knew now the creek had been deliberately plugged—a ruse to lure the men into the open where Travers' cowhands could attack them. She strove to think of some way to warn her cousins, but every idea that came to mind seemed unworkable.

Except for one. With a start, she realized that the only help available would have to come from her Father in Heaven. Jessica knew God *could* help her. *Would* help her if she had the faith. Hadn't He helped to fight the battles for the righteous Nephites? Hadn't He given strength and wisdom to young Captain Moroni? Answered Enos' mighty prayer? She believed He had done all these things. She also believed that He could protect Ethan and Samuel from harm at the hands of Travers' treacherous band.

Jessica twisted and wriggled until she was able to get onto her knees. She closed her eyes. "Dear Father in Heaven," she whispered. She paused, unsure of the words she should use to communicate with deity. But her heart was overflowing with emotion, and so she simply said what she felt. She pleaded with the Father to protect herself and the others, to grant her courage and wisdom, to strengthen her faith. She poured out her heart, believing that God was listening to her and would answer her earnest supplications.

She was praying for help to escape her captors when she heard the Texans approaching, talking in low tones between themselves. She uttered a final plea for protection, then quickly concluded her prayer. The men's voices were clearer now, and closer. She shuddered when she looked up and saw Peyton and Quaid heading straight toward her.

# CHAPTER EIGHTEEN

It was nearly noon by the time Ethan returned to the ranch from the north pasture. He'd started out after breakfast to ride upstream to check on the creek's flow because the water was low. But as he was following the stream along the fence line, he'd come upon one of Brother Bartlett's steers entangled in the barbed wire fencing. A section of fence was down, and the animal had gotten its hooves caught in the wire. The more the steer had struggled to free itself, the more enmeshed it had become. By the time Ethan came across it, the animal was snarled in the wire up to its belly, with the spiked barbs biting into its hide.

Jumping off his horse, Ethan had tried to tear away the wire with his hands. He'd left his wire cutters at the ranch, and the rawhide gloves he wore were little protection against the thorny barbs. Ethan ignored the painful stabs of the barbs as he worked to free the steer. As he grappled with the sharp barbed fencing, the frightened steer thrashed about in a panic. The barbs jabbed the animal's thick coat and raked its hooves and legs, leaving deep, bloody gashes.

Ethan could see that the animal was tiring from its battle to escape the wire. The steer snorted and bawled, and its eyes bulged wide. Ethan redoubled his efforts to free the animal, knowing he had to accomplish it quickly if the steer was going to survive.

But it was already too late. The steer became more firmly ensnared; the barbed wire corded its body and crept up around its neck. Exhausted and losing strength, the steer bawled pitifully. Finally, Ethan pulled out his pistol and ended the animal's suffering.

Now, as he trotted his bay toward the corral, he spotted Rory inside the pen working the black mustang. For the moment, he put aside his thoughts of the dead steer. "How's the training going?" he asked as he reined in his horse.

Rory tightened the slack on the rope fastened to the mustang's halter. "I think we're going to have ourselves a good ranch horse."

Ethan stared doubtfully at the stallion. Its hide, black as ashes, twitched, and its coarse tail switched in agitation.

Ethan's bay nosed the mustang and snorted. Immediately, the stallion reared up.

"Whoa, boy," Rory shouted, gripping the rope. "Settle down." The mustang whinnied shrilly and lunged backward. Planting his feet in the dirt, Rory clung to the rope.

Ethan shook his head at the sight of his friend trying to calm the wild stallion. Even after all of Rory's efforts to tame the animal, the mustang continued to be unpredictable and hot-tempered. "A good ranch horse, huh?" Ethan said to him, grinning.

Rory shot him a wry look. He loosened the tension on the rope, trying to pacify the horse. The stallion snorted, and its ears quivered. "Settle down, now," Rory repeated to the animal. When Rory approached, the mustang lashed out with its hind legs. Its head pitched and its body twisted before finally easing into a nervous prance. "That's it, boy. No one's going to hurt you." Rory continued to talk to the mustang and to rub its neck.

"That's some firecracker," Ethan commented, dismounting from his horse. "You never know when he's going to explode."

"He's high-spirited," Rory agreed, easing up on the rope. He finally succeeded in getting the stallion quieted. He patted the horse's rump. "Was everything all right in the north pasture?"

Ethan unbuckled the cinch on his horse's belly and pulled off the saddle. "I stumbled across one of the cows. It was tripped up in a strand of barbed wire."

Rory glanced at him. "Did you get it untangled?"

"No, I couldn't. I ended up putting the steer out of its misery," Ethan replied, feeling a stab of sorrow for the animal.

"That's too bad. Barbed wire makes good fencing, but I've seen more than one steer get hung up on it."

"Yeah. I'd better go inform Brother Bartlett." Ethan swung his saddle onto the top rail of the fence, then removed the bridle and turned his horse into the corral. The bay whickered and shook itself, then trotted off. Ethan saw the mustang tense and pace nervously in place. He turned away and started for the ranch house.

"Hey, have you talked to Jessica yet this morning?" Rory called to him.

"No. Why?"

"She was looking for you after breakfast. She said she wanted a word with you."

Ethan smiled as he remembered his promise to tell Jessica about his evening in town with Susannah Hamilton. "I'll find her after I talk to Bartlett."

Rory nodded and returned his attention to the mustang.

Ethan went first to the ranch house, but Bartlett wasn't inside. He checked the barn and some of the other outbuildings, and finally located the rancher at one of the cattle pens. After he'd spoken with Bartlett about the steer, he started back to the corral, thinking he'd find Jessica there. On the way, he ran into Samuel. "Hey, little brother, have you been keeping busy this morning?"

Samuel took off his hat and wiped his brow. The glaring, June sun beat down on their shoulders. "Yeah. I've been helping Hodkins shoe horses. You?"

"Just getting back from the range. Do you happen to know where Jessica is?"

"I haven't seen her all morning. I thought she was with you."

"No, she's not with me."

"Then she's probably in the barn grooming the gray."

"I just came from there. She's not in the barn. Or in the house." Ethan felt a chill shimmy up his spine, despite the summer's heat. It wasn't like Jessica to disappear—she'd been in the thick of every activity taking place on the ranch. "Come on, let's see if she's at the corral with Rory."

When the two of them reached the horse pen, Rory was still inside, brushing the mustang's black coat. But Jessica was nowhere in sight.

"Rory, when did you see Jessica last?" Ethan asked him.

Rory paused, his hand resting on the horse's haunches. "After breakfast, like I told you." Rory looked from Ethan to Samuel, then back again at Ethan. "Can't you find her?"

Ethan shook his head.

"I haven't seen her all morning, either," Samuel said in a tight voice.

Rory set down the horse brush. "Then we'd better start searching for her."

"I've already looked everywhere around here," Ethan told him. He tried not to sound worried, but his heart was hammering. "Maybe she took the mare for a ride."

Rory straightened his hat, his eyes shaded beneath its wide brim. "She wouldn't go off on her own without mentioning it to someone."

Ethan started for the stall. "I'll saddle the horses."

"Wait a minute," Rory said, putting a hand on his arm. "I have an idea where she might be. Samuel, get the horses ready, and Ethan, you come with me."

Neither of them spoke as Ethan followed Rory to a thicket of willows growing along the creek bank behind the house. They plunged through the willows into a shady spot beside the stream. Ethan glanced around the little glen. "Why did you think she'd be here?"

"It was just a hunch I had." When Ethan gave him a puzzled look, he cleared his throat and added, "She and I were here together picnicking a few days ago."

If Ethan hadn't been so worried about his cousin's whereabouts, he would have teased Rory over that comment; but right now the only thing on his mind was Jessica's safety. The feud with Travers had him on edge. He crossed the small dale, pausing to stare at the dry streambed. Normally, the water would have been flowing freely downstream, but now only a trickle filled the sandy bottom of the creek.

"Ethan, look at this."

Ethan turned around just as his friend picked up off the ground a brown, hardbound book. "What is it?"

Rory brushed away a fallen leaf from the cover. "Jessica's Book of Mormon."

"What?" Ethan exclaimed. "Let me see that." He strode to Rory's side, took the book, and opened it. On the title page he recognized his father's handwriting; printed in neat, black letters was the word, "KADE." He looked at Rory in astonishment. "This belongs to my family. What's it doing out here?"

"Jessica has been reading it. She told me that your sister sent it along with her to the ranch."

Ethan's eyes grew round. "She's been reading it?"

Rory nodded. "She's nearly finished."

Before Ethan could say another word, Rory was already striding out of the grassy glen. Ethan joined him, clutching the book of scripture.

"Jessica wouldn't just leave the book behind or forget to take it back into the house," Rory said as he forged past the willows. "Something's happened to her."

Ethan's heart skipped a beat, for his worst fears were confirmed with those words. When they reached the corral, Samuel had their horses saddled and waiting for them. Ethan tucked the book into his saddlebag, then mounted the bay, "Let's ride upstream along the creek bank. Jessica may have gone that direction," he said in a tense voice.

Spurring their horses into a gallop, the three men rode abreast, following the stream as it wound into the foothills above the ranch. With his mouth fixed in a grim line, Ethan scoured the trail, searching for any sign of his cousin.

# CHAPTER NINETEEN

Jessica scrambled up off her knees just as the two cowhands strode toward her. They paused at her feet. "She looks like a trussed up turkey all ready for roastin', don't she?" Peyton laughed at his own joke.

"Looks like ya got yerself in a real situation here, that's for sure," Quaid said to her, doffing his hat and running a palm across his sweaty brow.

She didn't know if the men expected her to reply, but she remained silent, eyeing the two of them warily.

Quaid stepped closer and gazed at her wrists where the ropes bit into her flesh. "Maybe we oughta loosen them ropes on her hands some. Her wrists are gettin' cut up and bleedin'," he said to Peyton.

Peyton gave her a cursory glance. "Leave 'em be, Quaid. She's all right."

Quaid shrugged his shoulders. "Sorry, missy," he mumbled to Jessica.

Jessica watched the two of them walk to their horses. They talked together for a few minutes longer, then Peyton climbed into the saddle. "Crowther is on the back trail watchin'," Jessica heard him tell his partner. "I'll head downstream. You stay here. When I see 'em comin', I'll come back and warn you."

Jessica bit her lip to keep it from trembling. She guessed that the outlaws were tightening their snare, and she prayed that her cousins wouldn't be caught in it.

The two men talked some more in voices low enough that Jessica couldn't make out what they were saying. She shifted uncomfortably on the ground. Her hands and feet were beginning to go numb from the tight bands. She shook her fingers and toes, trying to get circulation into them. She watched as Peyton spurred his horse and sped off without a backward glance. Quaid ambled back to the makeshift camp, pausing to stare at her, then hunkered down beside a tree to wait for further orders.

The time inched by. Jessica was hot, frightened, hungry, and sore. The rope chaffed her skin, making her wrists and ankles burn. She sat nervously watching Quaid. The Texan got up to pace beside the stream, waiting for the signal from his partners.

"Will you loosen the ropes a little?" Jessica ventured. "I can't feel my hands or feet."

Quaid paused, considering her request. He walked over to her and studied the ropes. She saw the empathy on his face. "I'm sorry, missy. I can't do that. Mr. Peyton's orders."

Jessica hoped she could appeal to the man's sensibilities. "If you'd loosen them just for a moment, it would help so much."

He shook his head. "You'll have to wait til Peyton gets back." Quaid went to his horse and took a rope from the saddlehorn. For an instant, Jessica feared he'd use it to bind her even more securely. But, instead, he squatted on the ground and began fussing with one end of the rope where it had become frayed. She watched him wrap the end with a piece of twine to keep the rope from unraveling further.

When he was through, he tied the ends of the rope into a slipknot, then yanked them loose. Jessica could see he was restless. He kept tying the rope into a knot and loosening it again. Then he made a lasso and threw it at an imaginary target. As she watched him continue to throw the lasso to lessen his boredom while waiting for Peyton's signal, an idea popped into her head. She sat up straighter, wondering if the scheme would work.

"You're pretty good with that rope," she said to Quaid, her mind racing with the possibility of putting her plan into action. "Can you throw a fancy rope?"

Quaid looked at her. "What do you mean?"

"You know. Circle the rope overhead. Twirl it from side to side." Jessica held her breath.

"You mean like this?" The Texan made a poor attempt at whirling the rope back and forth.

"Can you step in the circle of rope while it turns, without getting tangled in it?" she pursued.

He tried, but his boots got caught in the rope.

She smiled deceptively. "I can show you how to do that."

"You?" he asked with skepticism.

"Yes. I can make the rope dance. Do you want to see?" She desperately hoped his curiosity would outweigh his better judgment.

"I dunno. It depends."

"On what?" she asked, giving him another inviting smile.

"I'd have to untie you. And Peyton said not to."

She shrugged. "Well, it's up to you. I should think you can make your own decision about that. Do I look like I'm able to escape, even if my hands were untied? I have no horse."

"Aw, Peyton's got it tied up in the brush over there." The Texan pointed with his finger.

Jessica sucked in her breath, trying not to let her eagerness show.

"You sure you know how to do fancy ropin'?" he asked, rubbing a hand over his grizzled chin.

She nodded. She could see the cogs turning in his head; he wanted to see the tricks she could do with the rope, but he hesitated untying her.

"I'll show you how, but I won't show your partner. I don't like him," she urged the cowboy.

She caught the glint of indecision in the cowhand's eye. "All right. I'll untie your hands for a minute so you can show me. But if you're lyin' . . ." He left the sentence unfinished, giving her a threatening glare.

"I'm not lying. I'm very good with a rope, and I can teach you how to do tricks, too." Her words came out in a breathless rush as he shambled to her side and unknotted the rope binding her wrists. "I can't show you if my ankles are still tied together," she smiled.

Quaid untied the rope from her ankles. He guarded her with a close eye while she rubbed the circulation back into her feet and hands.

"Thanks," she said finally. She held out her hand for the rope. Her heart was heaving in her chest as she started twirling the rope in a circle.

The Texan squinted at her, making sure she didn't try to bolt.

"It's all in the wrist motion. See? You flick your wrist like this," she explained, sending the whirling rope off to one side and then crossing it in front of her body to the other.

"Well, what do ya know," Quaid commented under his breath.

"Want to see how I can move the rope from my head to my feet?" she asked.

"Sure. Go ahead."

While she was whirling the rope, readying it for the trick, she darted a glance to the spot where Quaid had indicated her horse was tied. She could see the mare's gray rump in the shadow of the leaves, not more than six or seven yards away. Quaid's own horse stood closer at hand. A plan for escape formed more clearly in her mind.

"I'm watchin'," the cowhand reminded her.

With a quick movement of the hand, she swung the circling rope above her head, then down to her feet, keeping it whirling without interruption.

Quaid looked impressed.

"Now, I'll show you how to dance inside the circle of rope." She let the rope fall and gathered up the length of it in her hands, preparing for the demonstration. "You have to move your feet fast and keep your wrist moving smoothly at the same time."

Quaid eyed her closely, still not trusting her.

She drew up the slack and started it whirling in a circle along the ground. She'd never tried this particular trick before, though she'd seen Rory do it. Holding her breath, she hopped inside the dancing circle of rope with both feet. "How about that?" she grinned, glancing up at the Texan.

He chuckled, and Jessica sensed his watchfulness over her easing. As she readied her escape, her heart was hammering so hard that she thought it would burst. She stepped out of the circling rope with one foot, then back into it with a quick two-step. Quaid's eyes were trained on her feet.

With a catch in her breath, Jessica abruptly drew the rope into a loop above her head and tossed the noose at her target. Before Quaid could react, the noose caught him squarely around the shoulders; Jessica tightened the loop in an instant, pinning Quaid's arms against his body. He cried out in alarm. With her heart thrashing, Jessica raced to Quaid's horse and looped the lasso around the saddlehorn, then she smacked the horse's rump hard and let go of the rope. "Ya! Get up, there!" she cried. The animal sped off like a shot, jerking Quaid to the ground and dragging him behind its galloping hooves. He shouted and cursed, but Jessica didn't pause to listen. Running to her horse, she untied the reins from the willow branch and swung into the saddle. She lashed at the gray with her heels, sending the horse into headlong flight.

The escape happened so quickly that Jessica's head was reeling. She hunkered down against the horse's flying mane, forcing him on faster. Reining the horse due south, she kept to the high ground. Riding in the open exposed her to danger, but it also provided a clear view for miles around. If her cousins were in the vicinity, she'd be able to spot them.

She knew Quaid's horse would slow before very long, and the Texan would free himself from the rope. He was probably already on her trail or on his way to inform Peyton of her escape. Any moment a bullet might come flying toward her. She pressed her body against the mare's and hammered her heels into the horse's flanks.

The minutes ticked by as she raced southward, fearing that she wouldn't reach her cousins in time to prevent them from riding into an ambush. Then suddenly, she sighted three riders coming from the south. The copper and white hide of Rory's pinto flashed in the sun, and riding alongside him was Ethan and Samuel.

Jessica cried out a warning, but the trio were too far away to hear her. Realizing that she had to intercept them before they reached the spot where Travers' men waited in hiding, she lashed her horse and reined it toward a deep gully that cut across the hillside. Plunging into the hollow and up the other side would shorten the distance between her and her cousins. Her horse didn't miss a stride as it nosed into the steep-sided gully. Jessica nearly lost her balance in the saddle as the horse negotiated the rugged descent, the mare's hooves slipping and sliding down the loose dirt wall of the ravine. Jessica clung to the horse with her legs, relying on the animal to keep its footing. With a lunge, the gray leaped the last few feet to the bottom and started up the other side.

Just as the mare cleared the top of the ravine, Jessica saw her cousins heading for a stand of aspens near the creek. Catching them before they reached the grove would require a beeline across open ground, and she knew Travers' men were close enough to spot her. Holding her breath, Jessica urged the horse forward.

The gray sprinted over the ground, closing the distance between Jessica and her cousins. "Ethan!" she shouted. "Stop! Wait for me." The men didn't hear her warning; they kept riding toward the trees. "Ethan!" she screamed. "Samuel! Wait!"

Then a shot rang out like a clap of thunder. Jessica crouched against the mare's neck. Another crack of rifle fire followed, and the bullet passed so close she could hear it whizzing overhead. Her heart constricted with fear. The shots brought her cousins and Rory wheeling to a halt. They twisted in their saddles and spied her dashing toward them.

Another shot sounded from near the creek, and Jessica felt a sudden, sharp sting in her thigh. At the same instant, the gray whinnied frantically and reared up. Jessica slid sideways off the mare as it stumbled and fell, landing hard on her back. For an instant stars flashed in her eyes, and her head throbbed. She sat up groggily. Next to her lay the mare, blood streaming from a bullet hole in its neck.

Jessica's stomach heaved. She started to reach for the horse when a barrage of gunshots sent her sprawling to the ground. Gulping for breath, she inched up to the dead horse and used its body as a shield against the firing. It was then she saw Rory galloping on horseback toward her while Ethan and Samuel emptied their weapons at Travers' men, who were concealed in the willows.

Leaping from his horse, Rory sprang to her side, leaving his pinto to gallop away with the reins flapping in the dirt. "Are you hurt?" he rasped, his eyes wild with concern. He flung a protective arm around her as the crackling of gunfire echoed across the hills.

Jessica buried her head in Rory's shoulder, fear and shock nearly overwhelming her. "I'm all right," she stammered.

With guns roaring, Ethan abandoned his horse and scrambled for cover behind a large rock midway between the creek and where Jessica and Rory crouched. Samuel, too, jumped off his mount and headed for the willows beside the stream. With bullets flying at his heels, he made it to the safety of the low-lying trees.

Rory scrutinized her from head to toe. "You've been hit," he said anxiously, focusing on a ragged, blood-smeared tear in her trousers. Jessica stared at the wound in astonishment. Blood trickled from her thigh, and it was only then that she noticed the searing pain in her leg.

The firing ceased and an eerie silence hung in the air. Jessica glanced at Ethan, who was only a few yards away, behind the rock. Her cousin's face was pale and pinched. Mouthing the words, he asked if she was safe. She nodded and saw his shoulders sag in relief.

"We need to tie something around that leg to stop the bleeding," said Rory. He tore off his neckerchief, rolled it lengthwise, and cinched it snugly around Jessica's thigh.

Jessica saw the strain in his eyes. "Thank you, Rory. I'll be fine now."

"I think the bullet only grazed your thigh. The mare took the brunt of it."

Jessica lifted her head to gaze at the dead horse.

"Stay down," Rory ordered.

Before Jessica could comply, a bullet whistled overhead. Rory hunkered close to shield her. From the corner of her eye, she watched Ethan raise up and return the fire, then duck back down behind the rock.

"Hey, boys, throw down your guns and we'll let you go peaceable-like."

Jessica recognized Peyton's voice, and she shivered.

"Come on, lads. You ain't bein' real neighborly," Peyton called out.

Ethan fired his pistol at the Texans, who were hidden a few yards up ahead near the creek. Jessica covered her ears as Peyton and his partners responded with a volley of shots. She saw Ethan flatten himself against the rock to avoid getting hit.

"We need to get out of here," Rory said, glancing over his shoulder. "Can you walk with that wounded leg?"

"I think so." Jessica flexed her leg. The movement brought a wave of pain, but she felt able to bear weight on it.

Rory crouched forward. "Ethan," he called in a low voice.

Ethan looked over at him.

"Where's Samuel?"

Ethan pointed toward the willows near the creek.

"Is he safe?" Rory asked.

"Yeah. I can see him from here," Ethan whispered loudly. "He's wondering what we're going to do to get out of this. So am I."

Rory glanced upstream where the Texans were positioned. "Jessie," he said, "do you know how many of Travers' men are hidden up ahead?"

"At least three. Two by the creek, and a third near the trail," she answered. Her mouth felt as dry as powder.

Rory motioned to Ethan. "I'm going to circle around behind them," he said, keeping his voice low. "Can you and Samuel cover me?"

Ethan nodded.

"I want to get Jessie into the safety of the trees over there," Rory added, pointing toward the stand of aspens.

Again Ethan gave a brief nod. Then he turned and gestured to Samuel who stood cloaked in the willows beside the creek.

"Jessie, when I give the word, you head for those trees as fast as you can. I'm going to slip upstream."

Jessica swallowed hard. She would be out in the open, an easy target for Travers' henchmen. She looked into Rory's eyes for courage and nodded.

"You ready?" Rory asked, gripping his pistol.

"Yes." She gathered her strength, ready to leap from the tenuous safety of the mare's body.

Rory turned to Ethan and nodded. Ethan passed the message to Samuel, and an instant later all three of them began firing upstream toward the creek.

"Go!" Rory hissed. Jessica darted away, hugging the ground. The pounding of her heart seemed even louder than the roar of the guns. She raced on foot toward the trees, hearing the ping of bullets striking around her.

She sprang into the stand of aspens and leaned against a tall tree, gasping to catch her breath. Her thigh pulsated with pain, and her whole leg threatened to collapse beneath her.

Rory waited until he saw that she was safe, then he began a wide circle to get behind the Texans. As Rory skittered from cover to cover, Samuel and Ethan kept a barrage of bullets flying.

Jessica drew a deep, ragged breath, trying to still her hammering heart. She squinted through the trees to the rock where Ethan was protected from the Texans' view and watched him load bullets from his gunbelt into the chambers of his pistol. She couldn't see Samuel, hidden in the willows beside the creek several yards away, but she knew he was behaving as courageously as his brother.

When she turned her gaze back to Ethan, he glanced over at her and sent her a reassuring smile. A tide of affection for him swept through her. She watched him squat on the heels of his boots, his gun poised and ready.

She began worrying about Rory, wondering how far upstream he was and what his strategy would be once he succeeded in getting on the backside of the Texans. She shuddered as she anticipated the shootout that was sure to occur as Rory and her cousins tightened their circle around the outlaws.

Jessica didn't see the signal to close in. Samuel abruptly sprang into sight racing along the bank of the stream, heading directly for the Texans' position. Simultaneously, Ethan leaped from behind the rock and barreled toward the creek. Just as Ethan reached the fringe of willows growing along the bank, a shot sliced through the air. Jessica heard Ethan cry out, then saw him arch backward and slump to the ground.

"No!" Jessica shrieked.

From upstream came an explosion of gunfire, but the sound blurred in Jessica's ears as she bolted out of the grove of trees and darted across the open ground to where Ethan lay. Samuel reached him at the same moment. Up ahead, the roar of gunshots was concentrated near the spot where Peyton and Quaid had made their camp. Jessica ignored the bursts of gunfire, concentrating on Ethan. She lifted his head into her lap, her tears spilling onto his cheeks. "Ethan!" she cried. "Ethan!" In horror, her eyes fixed on the scarlet stain spreading across the front of his shirt.

"Let me take him, Jessie," Samuel rasped, kneeling beside her. "I'll get him to cover."

He lifted his brother in his arms and sprinted for the trees. Jessica followed behind him, her eyes swollen with tears and her gaze riveted on Ethan's limp body.

# CHAPTER TWENTY

Ethan managed to open his eyes a slit and found himself lying on his back in a darkened room. He turned his head toward the cracks of light coming in through the shuttered window, and a pain so sudden and severe that he gasped in surprise, ripped along his shoulder.

"Lie still, son. Everything is all right."

Ethan moved his head very slowly to avoid another piercing shaft of pain and stared at the speaker. "Pa? What are you doing here?" The words came out slurred, and it was an immense effort to speak them, though he didn't understand why.

Ethan felt his father's hand on his. "You're going to be fine."

"What do you mean, Pa?" His words sounded weak and rasping in his ears.

He felt his father's reassuring touch.

"What's wrong with my shoulder? It hurts." He wasn't sure if he spoke the words or merely thought them, but his father stood up from the chair at his bedside and bent over him. Ethan wanted to ask again about his shoulder, but he was suddenly overcome with weariness. He closed his eyes, feeling himself drifting back into sleep.

"Stay awake until I can get some medicine down you."

Ethan forced his eyes open, making them as round and big as he could. He swallowed noisily, and his throat felt dry and prickly.

His father gently eased Ethan's head from the pillow and put a cup to his lips. Ethan sipped the liquid, choked. "Just take it slow, son."

Ethan again sipped from the cup and this time was able to swallow a bit of the cool, medicinal-laced water without choking on it. He lay back, exhausted with the effort of swallowing.

His father pulled the quilt up under his chin. "Feeling a little better?" he asked.

Ethan nodded slightly. He realized now that the pain in his shoulder was a constant companion. It seemed to throb in rising crescendo and then recede to a level he could bear. He tried to fix his gaze on his father's face. "What happened to me, Pa?" he asked in a croaking voice.

"Can you remember anything about the shooting?"

"The shooting?" Ethan repeated, puzzled. He struggled to focus on a floating, ghostly image in his memory. It was like trying to snatch at air. He remembered something—something frightening—but he couldn't grasp it.

"We'll talk about it later, after you've slept."

Ethan closed his eyes and let his mind unwind. A shooting. A shooting. A shooting. The words played leapfrog in his head. Then suddenly he heard the sharp, loud bang in his mind and felt the sting in his shoulder. Shot! He'd been shot! His eyes flew open.

"You're safe now," his father said soothingly. "You took a bullet in the shoulder, but I've removed it, and you should heal just fine."

Ethan blinked, trying to assimilate all his father was telling him. "How long have you been here, Pa?"

"Two days. You've been unconscious most of the time."

"Two days?" Ethan repeated incredulously. He stared at his father, trying to make sense out of what he was hearing.

"Just rest now."

Ethan closed his eyes again, exhausted by the effort of the conversation. He felt his father's hand stroking his brow.

"Go ahead and sleep, Ethan. I believe we're out of the woods."

Ethan tried to nod in acknowledgment, but he was already dreaming.

The next day Ethan felt better. The pain in his shoulder was still rampant, but his head was clearer and his father's dose of medicine had taken the razor-sharp edge off his suffering. He began to remember more details about the shooting, even recalling his last thought before blacking out. That thought was of Susannah. And how, because he was shot and probably dying, he wouldn't be able to call on her the following weekend as he'd promised. He remembered how bitterly disappointed he felt over that fact. And then all he recalled after that was darkness, until waking up in the Bartletts' bedroom with his father at his side.

"Tell me again what happened after the ambush," he questioned Samuel, who had come to his bedside after breakfast. "Did you and Rory manage to overtake Travers' men?"

"Rory began circling behind the Texans—"

"Yes. I remember that much," Ethan said, nodding.

"He surprised two of them and held them at gunpoint. But a third one was hiding in the brush. He's the one who fired the shot at you."

Ethan shivered, hearing again the twang of the gunshot and feeling the slug rip into his shoulder. He closed his eyes, wanting to block out the memory of the gun fight.

"Jessica was grazed by a bullet, too, but she's all right. Jessica was trying to warn us about the ambush."

"And probably saved our lives—at the risk of losing her own," added Ethan in a quiet voice. "What happened to the Texans?"

Samuel swallowed and ran a hand across his brow. "Rory wounded one of them. Another got away."

Ethan stared at his brother. "And the third?"

"Dead."

Ethan lowered his head. The whole episode seemed surreal, as if he were only hearing about the incident and hadn't been a participant in it.

"They were laying a trap for us," Samuel muttered. "Cowards. Cowards and murderous thieves," he said angrily.

Ethan sighed and leaned back into the pillow. His shoulder ached, despite his father's concoction of powders and pills. "I understand you rode all night to get Pa, then turned around and came back to the ranch with him without a lick of sleep. Thanks, Samuel." Ethan's voice grew husky with emotion.

Samuel squeezed his brother's arm. "You'd have done the same for me."

Ethan turned at the sound of his father entering the room. "Morning, Pa."

James came to his bedside. "How are you feeling?"

"Better. The pain seems to have eased."

"His color looks better, don't you think, Pa?" asked Samuel.

"Yes, it does. Let's change those bandages for you, Ethan."

"I'll step outside," Samuel said hastily, glancing at Ethan's bloodied bandage. His face blanched when he saw his father begin to remove the cloth strips.

"See you later, little brother."

Ethan grimaced as his father peeled away the soiled cloth bandage from his shoulder.

"I was thinking, Ethan," his father began as he carefully lifted off the last of the cloth strips, "as soon as you're able to travel, I'll take you home to complete your recuperation. That way I can keep a close eye on the wound."

"All right," Ethan said through clenched teeth. Now that the bandages were off and the wound exposed to the air, the injury pulsed with pain.

His father was silent for a moment as he studied the bullet wound, then he rummaged in his black physician's bag and withdrew a small, round tin. When he removed the lid, the pungent odor of the salve filled the room with a noxious smell.

"Phew," Ethan said, wrinkling his nose. "The smell alone is strong enough to cure me."

His father chuckled. "That's the oil of camphor in it you smell, and other good medicinal properties."

His father applied the salve. In spite of his gentle touch, the open wound stung with a vengeance under the slight pressure of James' fingers.

"There. That should do it. I'll rebandage it for you." His father tied fresh cotton strips across Ethan's upper chest and shoulder.

"Thanks, Pa," Ethan breathed when James had finished his handiwork.

"I'll dispatch a message to your mother letting her know you're doing well, and that we'll be home perhaps as early as next week."

"How long do you think it will take before I'm completely healed?"

James scratched his chin. "Three or four weeks. Possibly sooner."

Ethan frowned. "This is the worst possible time to be laid up. Brother Bartlett needs my help to get the steers to market. And we're not finished yet with the sorting and branding."

"Don't worry about that, Ethan. It can't be helped. Brother Bartlett can hire another man if he needs to."

"It's not that easy to find someone who knows cattle." Ethan chewed on his lip. "Pa, will you ask Rory to come in here for a minute so I can talk with him?"

His father stood up from his chair. "I'll fetch Rory, but I don't want you getting all worked up over this, son. Other arrangements can be made. You concentrate on getting well."

Ethan nodded, but his mind was distracted, racing in several directions at once.

"Are you hearing me, Ethan?"

Ethan gathered his attention and centered it on what his father was saying. "All right, Pa. But it's awfully disappointing to have to miss the whole rest of the roundup."

"I know how much you were enjoying your work at the ranch, but it will still be here waiting for you. Cattle ranching isn't likely to go out of business anytime soon."

Ethan returned his father's smile. "Thanks, Pa. And thanks for taking care of me."

"I'll find your friend and ask him to come in." James patted his son's arm, then left the room.

Ethan sighed and settled deeper into the pillow. Although his father's words were reassuring, Ethan was frustrated over not being able to participate in herding the cattle to market. He gingerly rubbed the bandages covering his wound. The slight pressure made the pain in his shoulder increase dramatically. Three or four weeks. He looked up at the ceiling in discouragement and heaved another frustrated sigh.

"How you doing, cowpoke?"

Ethan propped himself up against the pillow. "Come on in, Rory."

"You look like you're going to live," Rory said with a grin.

"Yeah, I guess so. But ranching is out for the time being."

"You'd do anything to get out of a little work," Rory joked, taking a seat next to the bed.

"My pa wants to take me home to recuperate," Ethan said glumly.

Rory nodded without commenting.

"I'll have to miss the cattle drive."

"There's always next year. Maybe we can get our own cattle outfit going by then. We've talked about it—perhaps now's a good time to take action."

Ethan brightened, buoyed by Rory's suggestion. "You're right. I could do a little checking around on cattle prices while I'm in the city."

"Yeah. It'd be a perfect opportunity for that," Rory returned.

"I've been saving my pay, and perhaps my pa could help us get a loan from the bank to buy stock," Ethan offered eagerly.

"I can scout out the price of land for a spread."

"With the two of us working both ends, we might be able to come up with something."

"It's a sure thing," Rory replied. "Green grass flows through my veins instead of blood."

"Mine, too. You know what? Maybe I won't go home with Pa just yet. Maybe I'll stay here to recuperate, and in another week or two I should be able to get around just fine."

Rory shook his head. "You need to rest and regain your strength. Right now you couldn't ride a rail fence in a stiff breeze."

Ethan's gloomy mood returned.

"Don't look so down in the mouth, partner. Breaking into the cattle business takes time and a lot of preparation. You'll be able to do some of that while you're getting back on your feet."

"I guess so."

A silence stretched between them. Then Rory asked, "When do you think you'll be leaving the ranch?"

"In a few days. As soon as Pa thinks I'm well enough to travel."

Rory tented his fingers. "Do you think your cousin will go with you?"

"Jessica?"

"Yes, Jessica."

"I don't know. I haven't talked to her about it." He looked more closely at Rory. "Why?"

"Well, uh . . ." Rory changed position in his chair. "It's just that over the last little while, Jessie and I have sort of struck up a rapport."

Ethan stared at him. "A rapport?"

"Kind of a friendship, you might say." Rory squirmed in his seat. "Aw, heck, Ethan—I'm smitten with her."

Ethan gaped at his friend.

"Don't look so surprised," Rory said irritably. "Your cousin is a fascinating girl. And exceptionally pretty."

"Yeah, and also headstrong and tempestuous."

Rory grinned. "True, she's opinionated. And impulsive. You're never sure what she might do or say next. But those are the qualities that make her so intriguing."

Ethan rolled his eyes. "You sound like a love-sick calf."

"I guess so."

"I don't know what to say," Ethan began. "You and Jessica? It never occurred to me that you might be serious about her."

"Then you've been blind as well as rifle shot."

"How long have you felt this way?"

"As near as I can figure, from the first second I laid eyes on her." A lopsided grin rolled across his face.

"Why didn't you say something about it to me before now? Have you told Samuel?"

Rory shook his head. "I haven't mentioned it to anyone. Least of all, Jessie, herself."

"You haven't said anything to Jessica about your feelings?" Ethan asked incredulously.

"No. Are you kidding? I'm scared to death to broach the subject with her. She can be a wildcat."

Ethan burst out laughing, even though it made the wound in his shoulder throb.

"What's so funny?" Rory growled.

"You. You have fearless courage when it comes to a face-off with murderous cattle thieves, but you quake at the thought of telling one skinny-waisted girl that you care for her."

Rory looked at him with a hurt expression. "I'd like to see how you react around the woman you love."

Rory's words produced a sobering effect as an image of Susannah Hamilton darted into his mind. Ethan remembered shaking from head to toe in her presence and striving to form an articulate sentence. "You're right. I'm sorry for laughing. You took me by surprise, that's all."

Rory scowled at him.

"You have to tell her how you feel before she leaves the ranch, whether it's with me in a few days or not for several more weeks."

"I'm planning to tell her," Rory countered. "I'm just working up the nerve to do it."

Ethan gave him an empathetic smile. "Maybe she's in love with you, too."

"Do you think she might be?"

"I wouldn't know," Ethan replied. "Most of the time she keeps me in the dark when it comes to her personal feelings."

Rory nodded, saying nothing for a moment. "Were you aware that she's been thinking seriously about the gospel?" he asked in a subdued voice.

Ethan's brows rose sharply in surprise. "No, I wasn't. We've had a conversation or two about the Church, but I didn't think she had any real interest in it."

"It seems she does."

"She told you that?"

"Not in so many words, but I can feel the difference when I'm around her. She's calmer. More at peace."

Ethan issued a long, low whistle.

"She's been reading the Book of Mormon," Rory said.

"That's right, you told me that the other day at the creek." Ethan recalled putting the book in his saddlebag for safekeeping.

"I think she's gained a testimony of its truthfulness."

Ethan leaned back against his pillow, remembering his conversations with Jessica about the Church and the gospel of Jesus Christ. He'd felt backward about knowing how to present the gospel plan to her. He recalled thinking at the time that if she'd only listen with faith, she'd be able to hear the whispering of the Spirit, in spite of his ineptness. "Wouldn't that be something if she accepted the gospel and joined the Church," Ethan said quietly.

"It would, indeed."

# CHAPTER TWENTY-ONE

Jessica carefully folded Samuel's cotton trousers and flannel shirt into a tidy square and laid them on the bed. She avoided looking at them, afraid tears would start in her eyes if she did. She finished packing her remaining articles of clothing into her traveling bag, then placed her book of poetry and the Kades' Book of Mormon on top of the pile. Closing the bag, she glanced around the room she had shared with the Bartlett girls over the past few weeks.

The morning sun streamed in through the single window of the room. Jessica turned her face to the filmy beam of light, letting the warmth soak into her skin. She closed her eyes, basking in the sun's rays and thinking how remarkable these last weeks had been, how much they had changed the direction of her life. This morning she would be traveling back to Salt Lake City with Ethan and her Uncle

James. What she would do after that was an open question. She was content to wait and see how she felt.

She needed to say goodbye to Samuel. He was remaining at the ranch to help Rory and the other cowhands drive the cattle to the railhead in Ogden to be transported by train to eastern markets. Rory had said he'd come to the house to see her afterward—if she was still there and not gone on to California.

Rory's image filled her mind: his crisp blue eyes, his ready smile, his sun-gilded hair. She thought about how he looked dressed in his chaps and boots, vest and wide-brimmed hat, with the turquoise-studded silver belt buckle at his waist, and the picture brought a smile to her lips. She could have gone on thinking about him, but she needed to get her things loaded into the wagon for the trip back to Salt Lake.

From off the bed she gathered the trousers—laundered and mended where the bullet had left a tear—shirt and hat Samuel had lent her to wear while staying at the ranch, then grasped her traveling bag and carried both armloads out to the buckboard standing in the yard. Samuel was waiting there beside the rig, along with Rory. She cast a furtive glance at Rory.

"Here's the clothing you loaned me, Samuel," she said, holding out the little pile of garments to him. "Thank you for letting me borrow them."

Samuel took the bundle from her. "You're welcome. I'm going to miss you around here," he replied with a warm smile.

"I'll miss you, too."

"We'll be all through here in a few weeks and ready to drive the cattle into the city. After we get them to the railhead, I'll be home. I sure hope to see you there."

Jessica averted her gaze. "I don't know, Samuel. I can't say what my plans will be."

"I'm going to assume you'll be there. So I'll give you a hug now and another when I see you at home." Samuel encircled her in his arms.

She felt tears start in her eyes. This might be the last time she'd ever see her cousin. She hugged him tightly and kissed his cheek.

When Samuel released her, he smiled into her face. "I hope you had a good experience at the ranch, in spite of the troubles we ran up against."

Jessica didn't allow herself to dwell on the harrowing ordeal with Travers' ranch hands. "I did. I'll miss the Running W." She darted another glance at Rory. He stood with his head bowed, his face hidden under the brim of his hat. Jessica wanted to say something to him, too, but she didn't trust her voice. It was already cracking with emotion.

"Our work here was made brighter by your visit," said Samuel.

"Thanks, Samuel. I'd better get back to the house. Ethan may need my help with last minute preparations." Her eyes moved past Samuel's face to Rory's. She flushed just looking at him. "Goodbye, Rory."

Rory's head jerked up. He thrust his thumbs into his pockets and watched Samuel walk to the corral to get Ethan's horse for the trip. Then he turned to Jessica. "Maybe I'll saddle up Dynamite for the drive into the city. See how he behaves on a long ride," Rory remarked. "What do you think?"

"Sounds like a good idea." She smiled, thinking about the temperamental stallion. "I should apologize for being a little headstrong myself while I've been here. It's one of my worst faults. Like Dynamite, I'm fighting the bit most of the time."

Rory chuckled. "That's part of your charm."

"Oh, no, I'm much too impulsive and obstinate. My parents are always telling me so." She remembered the telegram her father had sent to the Kades' home, demanding that she return to Nauvoo, and her stubborn unwillingness to obey him. She still had that predicament to unsort.

"You and Dynamite. A pair of renegades," Rory grinned. He stepped closer to her.

Jessica's heart quickened. She offered her hand, concentrating on keeping it from trembling. "It's been nice to make your acquaintance, Rory."

He took her hand and held it fast. "When my pa left home as a young man, Grandfather recited an old Irish blessing as a parting gift for him. My pa passed it on to me when I left to seek my fortune in the West." He held tightly to her hand. "I'd like to leave that same Irish blessing with you. It's sort of a good luck saying, to wish you well on your journey."

He looked into Jessica's eyes, and she felt her knees buckling. "All right," she stuttered. "I'd be honored."

He moved closer, until his face was only inches from hers. His voice took on a wisp of an Irish brogue. "May the road rise to meet you. May the wind be always at your back. May the sun shine warm upon your face, the rains fall soft upon your fields, and, until we meet again, may God hold you in the palm of his hand."

Rory's words set her heart spinning. She returned his gaze, conscious of little else but him.

"I'll be seeing you again," he said, "if I have to go all the way to Sacramento to do it." With those words, Rory leaned forward and kissed her.

Jessica's uncle handled the reins, while Jessica sat beside Ethan on the bed of straw Mrs. Bartlett had arranged in the wagon. "Are you comfortable enough?" she asked her cousin.

He nodded. "This straw is as soft as a feather bed."

Jessica knew he wasn't telling the truth, because she could see the grimace on his face with every bounce and jostle of the buckboard.

Riding along under a cloudless sky, with the mountains to the east golden in the morning light, Jessica's thoughts turned to Rory McKellar and the kiss he'd given her that morning. She smiled to herself as she recalled the feel of his lips on hers. Already she missed him more than she had expected. She let out a soft sigh.

"Are you cold?" Ethan asked, mistaking her sigh for a shiver.

"No, I'm fine." She blushed with the memory of Rory's kiss.

"You can take one of these quilts to wrap around yourself if you're chilly."

Jessica patted his arm. "I'm plenty warm. The morning air feels good."

She settled back to enjoy the scenery passing within her view as the two horses pulling the wagon traveled the bumpy road. As the sun rose higher in the sky, Ethan dozed. Jessica bunched the straw to pad his shoulder, then climbed into the wagon seat beside her uncle. They conversed about Jessica's family in Nauvoo, and her uncle told her tales of his boyhood years there, living beside the wide Mississippi with his parents, sisters, and younger brother.

"Uncle James, may I ask you about something that's been on my mind?" she inquired, hesitantly.

Her uncle turned to glance at her. "Of course."

"Ethan and I were talking about the time you went back to Nauvoo to visit my mother, after your term of medical school." She paused, unsure of how to phrase the question she wanted answered.

"That's right. I saw your parents before coming home from Illinois."

"Well, we figured something happened between you and Mother at that time. Perhaps an argument?" She darted a look at her uncle's face. "Because to the best of our knowledge, the two of you have never been in contact since."

Jessica held her breath as her uncle sat in silence for a moment, apparently gathering his thoughts. "Your mother and I are different in temperament. We were not especially close while growing up, although I loved Elizabeth very much."

Jessica saw a brief frown cross his brow.

"When Elizabeth refused to come west with the rest of the family, it caused further friction. My parents delayed their departure until after your mother's marriage to your father so we could be in attendance."

She nodded.

"After we arrived in the valley, my father—your Grandfather Kade—wrote often to Elizabeth, urging her to come out for a visit and expressing his love for her. But she and Father had never gotten along well. Perhaps Elizabeth blamed him in some way for marrying our mother after our natural father died. In any case, the two of them did not see eye to eye on several key issues, including religion. That was part of the reason why Elizabeth refused to move west."

He paused, and Jessica watched the muscles in his jaw tense.

"On that occasion, when I'd completed my schooling in Chicago, I went to visit your parents. Your mother and I were glad to see one another, and I met your older sister, Emmaline, who was just a baby at the time. But an incident occurred while I was there that persuaded me to cut my visit short. Elizabeth was unhappy with me for leaving, and also for defending our father's character which ran counter to her perceptions of him, and for upholding my faith and my religion when she argued against it."

Jessica looked closely at her uncle. There was something he was leaving out—something about the incident that prompted his departure.

"I think your mother became increasingly bitter toward me over the years. I wrote her, and in the beginning she wrote back. But as time went on, she stopped writing any of us." His voice was tinged with sadness.

"Mother can be stubborn and quarrelsome, but I don't believe that was always her nature. She and Father have an unhappy marriage, which has caused contention at home for my two sisters and me. We've not had the harmonious home life you've cultivated, Uncle James."

"Whatever difficulties your parents have faced, Jessica, they remain your parents and deserve your devotion and gratitude," her uncle replied. "Resolve never to speak unkindly about them. You don't want to pass down to your own children a legacy of family hatred and bitterness."

Jessica felt a chill along her spine. "Like what happened between the Nephites and Lamanites."

Her uncle looked startled by what she'd said. "You know the story of the Nephites and Lamanites?"

"I've read the entire Book of Mormon, Uncle James. Birgithe lent me the copy on your mantle when I left with Ethan for the ranch."

Her uncle's eyes widened, and he seemed pleased with her response.

"Ethan was the one who pointed out to me the reasons for the Nephites' and the Lamanites' estrangement. It had to do with family, and bitterness and pride. Ethan told me that we shouldn't carry a misunderstanding our parents had into our own generation."

James nodded his head. "That's good counsel to follow."

"I want to know all about your religion, Uncle James. About the work of Joseph Smith, and the mission of the Holy Ghost, and repentance, and where our spirits go after leaving this life. And if I feel the same way about all of that as I do about the truth contained in the Book of Mormon, then I'd like to be baptized."

James gave her a hug. "Now seems as good a time as any to start teaching you the gospel of Jesus Christ."


"Birgithe said you received a letter from home while we were away at the ranch. Is everything well?" Ethan asked as Jessica plumped the pillow behind his shoulders as he rested on the parlor couch.

"Father is angry with me for not returning home to Nauvoo. After I lost my luggage on the train, he arranged for a return ticket. The ticket is still sitting at the depot."

"You never claimed it?" Ethan asked in surprise.

"No. I don't want to go back to Illinois."

Her father's letter, waiting for her when she arrived in Salt Lake, was filled with harsh words. He called her irresponsible and instructed her to leave immediately for Nauvoo. The tone of his letter was demanding and insensitive, exactly like the man himself.

"If you're not going home, what do you plan to do?" asked Ethan.

Jessica eyed his pillow to make sure Ethan was situated comfortably. "I don't know yet. But I wrote my father again this morning, telling him I'm staying in Salt Lake for the present and explaining my decision to join the Mormon Church."

Ethan issued a low whistle. "What will your parents say to that?"

"They'll be angry with me. And upset." Jessica shivered, fearing her parents' reaction to the news; but whatever their objections, she would not be dissuaded from her resolve to be baptized into The Church of Jesus Christ of Latter-day Saints.

Jessica's uncle had taught her the principles of the gospel as they'd traveled from the ranch to Salt Lake City and instructed her further since arriving at the Kades' home. She had spent much time on her knees, petitioning the Lord for an answer regarding the truthfulness of the gospel. And she'd received an undeniable witness—a burning in her heart and a peace in her soul—that this was Christ's true Church, organized as in times past with prophets, revelation, and saving ordinances.

Since Jessica had no intention of returning home, she needed to decide what course to take. Should she go on to California and teach school as she'd originally planned? That dream no longer seemed attractive. Did she want to stay in Salt Lake City and take up a teaching position? She wasn't sure. Thoughts of The Willows Ranch, nestled at the foot of vaulting mountain peaks, filled her head. She'd enjoyed her stay there, despite the traumatic episode with Travers' men, and the whole idea of ranching appealed to her. Would she be happy with that kind of life for herself?

Of only one thing she was certain, and that was her desire to become a member of Christ's church and let the gospel serve as the pattern for her life. If she did that, then she would be content no matter what course she chose to take afterward. After penning the letter to her parents, she had written Emmaline, explaining her feelings. Gentle, caring Emmy would surely understand her motives and support her decision to join the Church. And, in addition to that, she wanted to acquaint Emmaline with the gospel of Jesus Christ. She wanted to share the gospel plan and her personal testimony with her guileless, older sister. Her younger sister, Clarissa, would be less open-minded and inclined to pride, but Emmaline was humble and honest, and Jessica wanted with all her heart for Emmy to embrace the message of the gospel.

She felt Ethan take her hand. "I'm proud of you, Jessica. You're not afraid to do what you know is right. I don't think that I'd be as courageous."

Jessica appreciated his words. "Now there's something I want to ask you," she said, leaning forward in her chair.

"What is that?"

"After you'd completed the errand for Brother Bartlett in Salt Lake, you said you'd spent the evening with Susannah and that you would tell me about it. You haven't yet."

A smile settled on Ethan's face. "Well, I decided to take your advice."

"My advice?" Jessica replied, puzzled.

"Yes, about talking to Susannah, instead of hiding behind a book. And so I did. I visited the Quill and Ink and had a conversation with her. I invited her to a lyceum being held that evening and she accepted, much to my surprise."

"You see!" Jessica exclaimed. "She liked you after all, when you were sure that she didn't."

Ethan grinned. "Maybe. But she mostly accepted my invitation because she was angry with her beau."

"Her beau? I don't understand."

"Some fellow has been courting her. She got into a disagreement with him and went out with me to spite him."

"Oh, dear."

"The bright side is that we had a nice time together. I asked if I might call on her again, and she said perhaps so. I told her I'd see her the next weekend, but then this happened." Ethan gestured to his wounded shoulder.

Jessica frowned in empathy.

"She expected me to call on her two Saturdays ago." Ethan shrugged. "But it's just as well. She undoubtedly has patched up the quarrel with her beau by this time."

Jessica didn't reply. She sat on the chair next to Ethan, chewing her lip in thought.

"So let's get back to you. When do you plan to be baptized into the Church?"

She looked up at him and smiled. "When Samuel gets home. I'd like your father to baptize me and all of you to be in attendance. So hurry and get well."

"I'd be honored to witness your baptism."

Jessica smiled at him, but at the moment her thoughts were not centered on that important first step she would take in order to become a member of the Church. She was thinking about Ethan and what she could do to help him see Susannah again.

"Is Rory invited to the baptism, too?" Ethan asked her.

"Rory? Of course. If he wants to be there." She felt her heart pick up an extra beat.

"I'm sure he will."

An idea had begun formulating in her mind, and even the pleasant reminder of Rory McKellar was not enough to turn her thoughts aside. "Ethan, I told you that I'd written my parents a letter. I'd like to mail it today. Do you think I might borrow a horse to ride into town to post it?"

"Sure. You can take my gelding. Hitch him to the buggy if you prefer taking the buggy rather than riding."

"All right, I will, if you're sure you don't mind," she said.

"He needs the exercise," Ethan returned.

Jessica stood up from her chair. "I want to help your mother and Birgithe with chores, and then I'll be leaving."

"Will you bring back a few lemon drops for me from the mercantile? It's located two doors down from the post office."

"I'll be happy to do that."

"There's money on the bedside table in my room. Take what you need to purchase the candy and to buy a sweet for yourself and Birgithe, too."

"Okay. Thanks, Ethan."

"Have a good afternoon."

"I will. And you get some rest. Your father said that rest is the best medicine for your injury."

"I'll sleep for a couple of hours this afternoon."

Jessica wiggled her fingers in farewell and left the parlor. The plan taking shape in her head filled her with anticipation. She walked with a light heart up the stairs to help her aunt air the beds and sweep the bedroom carpets. Her Aunt Inger had braided the rag rugs herself, and Jessica wanted to learn the skill. She admired the dainty, lace doilies her aunt crocheted to cover the armrests of the chairs in the parlor, and the lovely, hand-woven picture hanging in Birgithe's bedroom, with its flowery patterns crafted from strands of human hair.

Jessica appreciated her aunt's creative handiwork and desired to learn the artistry for herself, but more importantly she wished to emulate Inger's other virtues—her kindness, gentleness, warmth, and compassion. Jessica wanted her own future home, in which she would preside as wife and mother, to be modeled after the Kade household. And she knew the outward beauty, as well as the peace and harmony that permeated the home, was achieved in large measure through the efforts of her Aunt Inger.

Two hours later Jessica was driving the buggy, pulled by Ethan's reddish-brown gelding, toward the center of town with the letters to her parents and Emmaline in her handbag, and with an idea regarding Ethan fermenting in her head. The June day was sunny and warm, and she was happy being outdoors to enjoy it. She mailed the letters, purchased the lemon drops, then headed for the Quill and Ink. Thirty minutes after that, she was on the road homeward, with a passenger seated beside her in the buggy.

When they arrived at the house, she found Ethan in the parlor carving the same piece of wood she'd seen him working before, only now the block of smooth wood was partially shaped into four legs and a tail. Ethan looked up when he heard her come in. "How was your trip into town?" he asked.

"Very nice. Your horse behaved himself beautifully."

Ethan smiled. "I'm glad he was a gentleman for you."

"Here are your lemon drops," Jessica said, reaching into her skirt pocket for the sack containing the candy.

"Thanks a lot. I've been hankering for these."

"I brought along something else for you, too," Jessica said, barely able to suppress a grin.

"You did? What is it? More sweets from the candy counter?"

"No. Something you like much better than sweets. Wait here, I'll go get her."

"*Her?*" she heard Ethan repeat as she hurried out of the sitting room.

She stopped in the hallway where Susannah Hamilton was waiting with Birgithe, after Jessica had introduced the two of them a few moments before. "Susannah, he's in the parlor," she whispered so that Ethan wouldn't hear them talking. "He doesn't know you're here. Do you want me to tell him before you go in?"

"I'll surprise him, if that's all right." The dimples in her cheeks winked as she smiled. She gave Jessica's hand a squeeze.

Jessica nodded toward the open door leading into the sitting room and grinned as Susannah stepped inside.

Birgithe covered her mouth to quash a giggle when they heard Ethan's astonished exclamation. "Susannah! How did you. . . . What are you doing here?"

After that, Jessica and Birgithe slipped down the hallway to the kitchen and took a seat at the table.

"She's so pretty," Birgithe squealed.

"Isn't she? Your brother thinks so, too."

"I've never heard him say a word about her. How do you know Ethan likes her?" Birgithe whispered in a conspiratorial tone.

"I was with him once when he visited the Quill and Ink. It was obvious from the way he behaved in her company that he had feelings for her. After that, we talkcd a few times about her. He took her out for an evening when he was here a couple of weeks ago," Jessica confided.

"He did? He didn't mention it to any of us."

Jessica rested her elbows on the table. "I'm not surprised. He thought she didn't care for him. But I believe she does."

"Really? How do you know?"

"When I went into the bookseller's this afternoon to tell her about Ethan's injury, she showed genuine concern. I suggested that she might visit him at the house, if she liked, and she decided to do so today. So she rode with me."

Birgithe's brown eyes grew big with the significance of being privy to such a revelation.

"We had a pleasant conversation on the ride here. She's very nice; intelligent and gracious, too. And a devoted member of the Mormon faith."

"She must have dozens of beaus besides Ethan," Birgithe remarked breathlessly.

"I imagine she does. But she seemed very anxious about Ethan." Jessica lowered her voice to a whisper. "I think she likes him as much as he likes her."

Birgithe clapped her hands together in delight.

"What are you girls giggling about?" Birgithe's mother asked with a smile as she bustled into the kitchen.

"There's a girl visiting with Ethan in the parlor," Birgithe announced with an air of importance.

"A girl? Who is she?"

"A friend of Ethan's, Aunt Inger. Her father owns a book shop in town, and she works there. That's where Ethan met her."

Inger joined the two girls at the table. "Really? Does Ethan think highly of her?"

"I'm quite sure he does," answered Birgithe solemnly.

"Well, my goodness," Inger replied. "I had no idea."

Birgithe and Jessica grinned at one another from across the table.

"Shall we invite her to stay for supper?" Inger asked.

"I think that would be a lovely idea, Aunt Inger."

# CHAPTER TWENTY-TWO

"How does your ice cream soda taste?" Ethan asked the young woman sitting beside him at the table for two.

"Umm, very good." She sipped a strawful of the frothy stuff, then wiped her mouth with a napkin. "Too good," she said, chuckling.

"You missed a little." Ethan reached over and wiped a dob of ice cream from off her chin. "There." Giving her a grin, Ethan turned to his own soda. The sweet combination of ice cream and soda water was a treat new to him. Wassom's Ice Cream Parlor had only recently opened for business. Located on Main Street, just a few doors down from the Quill and Ink, the parlor was a popular spot and an ideal place for Ethan to spend a few minutes with Susannah Hamilton away from the book shop. He didn't know which he was enjoying more, the smooth, cool taste of the confection on his tongue or sitting so close to Susannah.

"Oh, here," she mumbled, swallowing a mouthful of ice cream. "I brought a present for you."

"A present?" Ethan replied in surprise. "What is it?"

She took from her lap a parcel wrapped in brown paper and string and held it out to him. "Something to keep you occupied while you finish recuperating."

Ethan took the package. As he removed the string and paper, he smiled to think she cared enough about him to want to give him a gift.

"This book was only recently published, and we just got it into the shop," she explained as Ethan peeled away the last of the paper.

Ethan turned the volume around to see its title. *"Roughing It,"* he read.

"Yes. It's written by an author named Mark Twain who's becoming very popular." She borrowed the book and opened it to the first page. "It's a story about Twain's trip to the West and some of his experiences while traveling."

Ethan listened to her explain about the book. He liked the gift, but he was more interested in hearing her talk and watching the animated expressions on her face. "Thank you, Susannah. I appreciate the book, and I'll enjoy reading it."

"Perhaps it will keep your mind busy so you won't feel so anxious about returning to your work at the ranch."

"It was thoughtful of you to get this for me," he returned, taking the volume from her outstretched hand. "I'll read it all the way through before I leave for the Running W."

Susannah took a drink from her straw. "When do you think that will be?" she asked, her eyes on the soda glass.

"Soon, I hope. My shoulder is nearly healed. I'm just waiting for my father to agree so I can get back to work. Having a physician for a father isn't as convenient as it might seem."

She smiled at that remark.

Ethan's heart beat faster as he considered whether Susannah would miss him while he was gone. Ever since her surprise visit to the house with Jessica three weeks before, Ethan had worked up the nerve to call on her half a dozen times. Most of the visits had taken place at her parents' home, with her mother hovering close by. Today was the first time that he had an opportunity to spend an hour alone with her. He'd met her at the booksellers at noon and together they'd strolled down the street to the ice cream parlor to share a soda while her mother tended the store.

"When you get to the ranch, will it be time to drive the cattle to market?" Susannah asked, lifting her eyes from the glass to look at him.

"In a couple more weeks. That's why I'm in a hurry to go. There's a lot of work to do before herding the cattle up to the railhead in Ogden," he replied. He quickly reviewed in his mind the list of chores needed to get the cattle ready for market. It was already the second week in July and preparations at the ranch would be in full swing. "And I'm anxious to have a conversation with my friend, Rory, who's one of the cowhands at Bartlett's ranch."

"Oh?"

"Yeah. Rory and I are planning to start our own outfit. It will be a small ranch to begin with, of course. Just fifty head of cattle or so. I've been speaking with some cattlemen in town about buying a herd." Ethan glanced at her, wondering how she'd react to that information.

She arched one eyebrow and stirred her soda with the straw, but didn't comment.

"Once we get the ranch going, what would you think about coming out to see it?"

She finished her ice cream, then pushed the glass away. "I don't know about that," she replied, her green eyes teasing him.

"You might like it there," Ethan persisted.

"I doubt you could entice me away from the city," she said, laughing.

Ethan felt disappointed at her answer, though he didn't know what he had expected her to say. "The truth is, you couldn't bear to leave all those books behind, could you?" he asked in jest.

"It's not the book shop so much," she answered slowly, her voice taking on a serious note. "Living in town offers many advantages and opportunities."

Ethan nudged his empty glass aside. Her words resurrected the jarring memory of seeing Susannah in town with her beau. The man's smartly tailored clothes and stylishly combed hair brought a sudden stab of envy. Ethan felt like a rough peasant in comparison. "So you'll probably settle down with some wealthy gentleman and live a life of ease and grace in the city," he responded.

"Maybe."

When he looked up at her, he saw the dimples in her smile. "I don't suppose you'd like to tell me about that beau of yours? The one you wanted to make jealous?"

"Oh, Ethan, I thought you'd forgiven me for that," she said with a sudden look of chagrin.

"I will, on the condition that you tell me something about him," Ethan prodded.

"Why? You know that whole episode is over and done with."

Ethan leaned forward in his chair and grinned. "Do you want my forgiveness or not?"

"Oh, all right. His name is Edward Grayson, and he's from back East. I met him in the book shop."

"Go on," he encouraged.

"Edward and I had been seeing one another for awhile when I learned that he was courting another girl at the same time. When my parents found out about it, they forbid me to see him again."

Ethan sobered as he contemplated the embarrassment and hurt Susannah had undoubtedly felt.

"I was upset, as you can imagine, and wanted to hear an explanation from Edward. And I wanted to believe that what I'd been told about him was untrue." Susannah lowered her eyes. "I arranged, without my parents' knowledge, to meet

Edward, but somehow my father found out about it and was angry with me for disobeying him."

Ethan recalled the conversation he'd overheard at the book shop between Susannah and her mother. "So was that the end of it?"

Susannah shook her head. "No, I arranged to meet him one last time. He confessed to dealing cruelly with me, but promised that he would never see the other girl again if I would take him back."

"And what did you say?"

Susannah picked up her napkin and began twisting it in her hands. "I told him it was over and that I wished to never hear from him again."

Ethan nodded, feeling a sense of satisfaction.

"But then a week ago, he sought me out."

Ethan's heart missed a beat. "Oh?" he stuttered.

"He begged me to come back to him." Susannah glanced away. "Then he made a proposal of marriage."

Ethan was so stunned by this news that he couldn't utter a word.

"Aren't you going to ask what I said to him in reply?" She gripped the napkin in her lap.

"What did you say to him?" Ethan croaked.

"I told him that I'd met someone else. Someone who I cared for very much."

Ethan blinked, unsure if he'd heard her correctly. It was only when her hand tentatively sought his that he could form a response. He clasped her hand, his heart throbbing in his chest. "My feelings for you, Susannah, have ever been constant. You have always had my heart." He lifted her hand to his lips and softly kissed it.

"He's here," Samuel called from the front hallway. He walked to the staircase and hollered up the stairs, "Jessie, Rory's just ridden up to the house. Come on down and be sociable."

A moment later, a knock sounded at the door. Ethan hurried to join his brother in the front hall.

Samuel threw open the door. "Don't you look dapper?" he greeted Rory with a grin. "Come in, cowpoke."

Rory whisked off his hat and clutched it in his hand as he stepped into the hallway. "Good to see you, partner," he said to Samuel.

"I'm glad you're here," Ethan said, stepping forward to welcome Rory with a friendly clap on the back. "Wish I could have joined you on the trail ride."

"You didn't miss anything but eating a whole lot of dust," Rory replied.

Ethan had gone to Ogden ahead of the herd, at Brother Bartlett's request, to make preparations for the sale of the cattle. He hadn't seen Rory since leaving the ranch at that time. "Samuel told me that you've been scouting out some grazing land."

"Ethan's talked of nothing else," Samuel put in. "Did everything go smoothly in Ogden after I left?"

Rory nodded. "Before I saddled up, I talked to a couple of cattle ranchers, and they gave me some pointers on what to look for when we're ready to purchase land."

"Come in and sit down, Rory," said Ethan eagerly. "I want to hear all about it."

The three of them moved into the parlor. "Samuel brought you your pay from Brother Bartlett's sale of the cattle?" Rory asked.

"Pay? What pay? I haven't seen any money," Ethan said, lifting a brow in surprise.

Samuel jabbed his brother's arm. "He got his pay. He's pulling your leg."

Rory shook his head and smiled at the two of them.

"So tell me all about it. Samuel said the cattle drive to Ogden went well, and Brother Bartlett received a favorable price for the herd," Ethan said.

"That's right. We didn't have any problems on the trail, and Bartlett was pleased with the price he got per head." He turned to Samuel. "You've probably spent your wad already, haven't you Samuel, in just the three days since I saw you last."

Samuel put his hands in his trouser pockets and turned the linings inside out. "Not a penny left," he joked.

"You're sure you don't want to go into the cattle business with your brother and me?" Rory asked.

Samuel spread his hands. "Not a chance. I've bunked on the open ground singing lullabies to a bunch of bellowing cattle for long enough. Unlike you two, I'm a fellow who likes a soft bed."

"You could be a silent partner. Invest your money with us, then we'll pay you the dividends after market," Ethan suggested, leaning forward in his chair.

"No, thank you. I've other plans for my hard-earned cash. I'm thinking of enrolling at the university."

"Seriously? You haven't mentioned that before," replied Ethan.

"Jessie's been talking to me about it. I might give it a whirl."

"How is Jessie?" Rory asked eagerly. His inquiry brought a smile to the faces of both brothers. "What? Why are you two grinning?"

"We were wondering how long it would take you to ask," Ethan replied.

"And we noticed how handsomely you're dressed," Samuel teased him. He sniffed in Rory's direction. "Could it be you're even wearing sweet-smelling rose water?"

Ethan sniffed the air, too.

Rory's cheeks reddened. "It's just a little hair tonic."

"Spearmint, isn't it?" Samuel asked, lifting his nose. "Definitely spearmint."

"All right, you've made your point. Is Jessica here?"

"How about we discuss business first, and then you can try to impress my cousin?" Ethan replied with a grin.

Rory's glance lingered at the parlor door, as if he couldn't decide which course to pursue first. "Have you had any luck with finding a few head of cattle to buy?" he finally asked.

"As a matter of fact, I have. There's a fellow in Arizona who wants to sell his herd. I've written him about it, but haven't heard back yet. He raises Durhams and . . ."

"Hello, Rory."

All three men turned toward the parlor entrance, where Jessica stood in the doorway. Ethan's eyes widened as he stared at her. Her hair was swept away from her face and gathered into loose curls. The dress she wore was a deep maroon, with a bustled skirt and sleeves that fell past her wrists in wide, lacy cuffs.

Rory jumped to his feet. "Good afternoon, Jessie. It's nice to see you again."

Ethan saw his cousin blush under Rory's awestruck stare. She entered the room, her skirt rustling as she walked, and took a seat between her two cousins. She looked like a beautiful, red rose, plucked from the garden, Ethan thought.

"How have you been?" Rory asked.

"Very well. And you?"

Her coppery curls and wine-colored dress accented the pink bloom on her cheeks. Ethan smiled, thinking how Rory's poor heart must be racing.

"I was afraid you might have gone on to California by this time," Rory said to her.

"No, I've been trying to make myself useful here." She tilted her head to one side and laughed briefly, a little trill like a bird's song. "Ethan's been impatiently waiting for you to get here. I imagine he's told you already about the herd he wants to buy."

"He was just mentioning it," Rory replied.

"I was saying that the rancher raises Durham cows. He owns a small herd, about five hundred head. That would be a perfect base to build on." Ethan paused, realizing Rory wasn't paying any attention to his explanation; his friend's eyes hadn't left Jessica for an instant. He glanced at Samuel. His brother was leaning back in his chair with his arms folded across his chest and an amused look playing on his face as he, too, watched Rory and Jessica.

Ethan tried again. "If we buy the herd, we can ride out to Arizona and drive them back to the valley. Perhaps Brother Bartlett will let us graze them on his land until we're able to purchase a few acres of our own. We can ask him about that. By this time next year, we could increase our herd and—"

"He's not hearing a word you're saying," Samuel broke in with a grin. "Come on. Let's go get ourselves a snack in the kitchen." Samuel got to his feet.

"Just a minute. I've been waiting to tell Rory about this," Ethan said in frustration.

"Later," Samuel said, pulling his brother by the arm out of his chair. "Right now Rory's got his mind on more important matters."

"Please don't interrupt your conversation because of me," said Jessica, turning to her cousins.

"We'll be back later," Samuel replied. "We're hungry. Come on, Ethan."

Ethan grumbled as he followed his younger brother out of the room. Just before he turned into the hallway, he glanced back to the parlor. Rory had already left his chair and taken one closer to Jessica.

"I didn't even get a chance to talk to him about the Durhams," Ethan complained to his brother as he trailed Samuel into the kitchen.

"Are you blind, Ethan? All Rory and Jessica are interested in is each other. Give them a few minutes together. Want a sandwich?"

Ethan scratched his chin in annoyance. "What kind?"

Samuel went to the icebox in the pantry and opened it. "Chicken or . . . chicken. That's our only option."

"In that case, make it chicken."

Samuel came back from the pantry with a plate of cold chicken, left over from supper the night before. He put the dish onto the table, then reached for a slice of his mother's freshly baked bread. Ethan plopped down on a chair at the table.

"Do you suppose Rory is still interested in starting up a ranch of our own?" he asked Samuel.

"Sure he is. He talked about it the whole way to Ogden while we were trailing the herd. He even suggested a brand—'the double K'—for Kade and the K in McKellar."

Ethan envisioned the symbol in his head. "That's not bad."

Samuel spread a scoop of butter onto four slices of bread, and then layered pieces of chicken on top.

"The Double K Ranch," Ethan mused. "It has a nice ring to it."

Samuel passed a sandwich over to Ethan. "I suggested branding the cows with a shamrock. For luck," Samuel mumbled, after taking a bite out of his sandwich.

Ethan picked up the chicken sandwich Samuel had made for him. "A shamrock?"

"I was only kidding," Samuel returned, taking another big bite.

"No, wait a minute," Ethan replied. "A shamrock brand. That's a stroke of genius, Samuel."

"It is?"

"Of course." Ethan waved his sandwich in the air, excited with the idea. "We can call the outfit the Shamrock Ranch. It suggests good fortune and success. I like the name. And it reflects Rory's heritage."

"Which he's mighty proud of," Samuel grinned.

Ethan took a bite of his sandwich, the wheels churning in his head. "It's perfect," he said with his mouth full. "The Shamrock Ranch. I know Rory will go for the name."

"You might have to revise the brand a little, though. Maybe use a double shamrock."

"Why is that?"

"To accommodate *Mr.* and *Mrs.* McKellar, and *Mr.* and *Mrs.* Kade. I figure there's a good chance I'll be the only single, young man on the premises soon."

Ethan chuckled at his brother's comment, though he knew the words weren't far off the mark. Rory and Jessica's feelings for one another were obvious, and there was no doubt that he was deeply in love with Susannah. Since declaring their affection for one another that day at the ice cream parlor, Ethan and Susannah had spent as much time together as possible. The evening before he was to go back to the ranch, he'd summoned up the courage to kiss her. The memory of that kiss still lingered sweetly on his lips.

Ethan and Samuel continued their discussion about cattle ranching as they ate. When they were nearly finished with their sandwiches, Jessica burst into the kitchen, her gray eyes dancing. "Boys, come with me outside," she said, motioning to them. "You have to see this!"

The two brothers exchanged a questioning glance as they left the table and followed Jessica outdoors. From the porch, Ethan saw Rory rubbing the neck of a black horse, its coat as shiny and glistening as polished obsidian. "Dynamite!" Ethan exclaimed. "What's he doing here?"

"I purchased him from Brother Bartlett," Rory explained. "As a gift for Jessie."

Ethan's gaze slid to Jessica. She was standing beside the mustang, stroking the horse's nose. "Isn't it wonderful!" she crooned. "He's actually mine."

"Well, I'll be hog-tied and horse-whipped," Samuel uttered, striding over to the ebony stallion. "I knew you'd ridden him on the trail drive to Ogden, but I had no idea you had this up your sleeve," he said to Rory.

Dynamite pawed at the ground restlessly as he stood tethered to the hitching post in the yard. "He's still a little skittish, but I think Jessie can handle him," Rory responded.

"You bet I can. Dynamite and I are kindred spirits." Jessica smiled as she caressed the horse's neck.

The mustang tossed its head and whinnied.

"You see? Dynamite agrees," she said, laughing.

While Samuel and Jessica stood admiring the horse, Rory stepped to Ethan's side. Lowering his voice, he said, "Ethan, those men who attacked us, Peyton and Quaid, squealed on their employer. Just before I left with the herd for Ogden, Travers was arrested on rustling charges. He's in jail with the other two. I wanted you to know, in case you hadn't heard."

Ethan blew out his breath slowly. "That's good news, especially for Brother Bartlett. Now he can relax and concentrate on running his ranch. Thanks, Rory, for telling me."

"You bet. Let's hope the sheriff can make the charges stick so none of those men see daylight anytime soon."

Ethan unconsciously rubbed his shoulder where the bullet had struck him, feeling only a stiffness there now, instead of pain. He made a deliberate effort to block out the memories of the attack, and strode over to where Jessica stood with her fingers laced through the mustang's black mane. "He's a beauty," he said to her. "You have yourself a fine cow pony. With a few steers, you can partner with us in the cattle business," he said with a grin.

Rory joined her beside the mustang and slipped an arm around her waist. As Ethan turned to pat Dynamite's sleek back, from the corner of his eye he caught Rory giving his cousin a kiss.

# CHAPTER TWENTY-THREE

The sun was high overhead when Jessica and Rory dismounted from their horses near the shore of the lake. Jessica gazed out over the rippling surface. As far as her eye could reach, the waters gleamed like quicksilver under the summer sky. "What a spectacular sight," she said, taking in the scene.

"The lake's a lot bigger than I thought it would be," Rory responded as he stood beside her.

"You can't see the end of it," she marveled. "Look at those peaks to the north. Is that an island?"

"It must be Antelope Island, and further to the west is Stansbury Island."

Jessica nodded, admiring the distant turquoise peaks. Ever since Birgithe had first mentioned the Great Salt Lake to her, and related the story of the sea gulls and the crickets,

Jessica had wanted to see the lake for herself. When her Uncle James learned that she and Rory planned to ride out to the lake, he told them a little bit about its geography and history. Even though the lake was more than seventy-five miles in length, he'd explained, it was only a remnant of an ancient inland sea that had once filled the whole of the Great Basin. Several islands dotted the waters, the largest being Antelope Island, or as it was more commonly called, Church Island.

He'd told them that plans were being made to build a railroad line from Salt Lake City to the lake; but until the rails were laid, visitors to the lake had to get there by horseback or carriage. That arrangement suited Jessica. Since the day before yesterday, when Rory had presented her with the gift of the black mustang, she'd been eager to take the horse on a long ride. The seventeen mile trip out to the lake was the ideal destination. With Rory alongside on his pinto, she had galloped Dynamite over empty stretches of grassy plain with the wind on her face and the sun on her back. She had exulted in Dynamite's strength and speed; though trained to the saddle and bridle, the animal was still spirited and had gloried in the run across the flats as much as Jessica had.

Jessica's gaze moved from the island's peaks to the mammoth, black rock that jutted out of the water several yards off shore like the hump of some gigantic, prehistoric whale. Its gleaming, ebony planes and angles reflected the sunlight. The cry of dozens of sea gulls wheeling and swooping overhead echoed in her ears, the pungent smell of brine stung her nostrils, and the salty breeze brushed against her skin.

No one else was visiting this particular stretch of beach. Further up the shoreline on the eastern side of the lake was the new Lake Side resort, established by one of the sons of Church president Brigham Young. From its dock, a three-decked steamboat called the *City of Corinne* offered scenic excursions on the lake for twenty-five cents. Rory and Jessica were planning to visit the resort later in the week and take a ride on the excursion boat. Although she was eager to be out on the lake and explore its beauty, the name of the vessel conjured unpleasant memories for her. It carried a reminder of the difficult days she'd spent in the town of Corinne after the theft of her traveling bag.

The beach here at Black Rock, on the southeastern point of the lake, had been a favorite spot for bathing and picnicking during the early years when the pioneers first entered the valley. But after the resort was built on the eastern shore, the popularity of Black Rock beach declined. Jessica was glad that her uncle had suggested they visit Black Rock, rather than the busier, more distant resort at Lake Side. Here she and Rory could watch the waves wash ashore and view the bluish-green peaks of Antelope Island undisturbed by other sightseers.

"I understand there's a band of wild horses running free on Antelope Island," Rory remarked.

Jessica turned to look at him, and her heart quickened at the sight of his handsome profile etched in golden sunlight.

"The rights to the island were granted to Brigham Young in behalf of the Church to be used as a herding ground for the Church stock," he explained. "But a few years later, President Young directed the removal of the cattle from the island because of the rising lake waters, and they were taken to new herd grounds. The range horses were left on the island to shift for themselves."

Jessica's gaze followed his over the expanse of water.

"I heard about the horses when I first started work at Bartlett's ranch," Rory continued. "Those island horses have a reputation for being among the finest in the Territory because of their bloodlines and their sure-footedness. Brother Bartlett told me that there's more than a thousand head of horses on the island, nearly as wild as antelope. I'd sure like to get a look at them." He peered across the waters of the lake as if hoping to catch a glimpse of the horses galloping over rocks and wild grasses along the shoreline.

"Do you want to swim out there to see them?" Jessica joked, nudging him in the shoulder.

"Yeah, if you go with me." Without warning, he swooped her up in his arms and started toward the water's edge.

"Put me down!" she shrieked playfully. "You'll drown us both."

"Not a chance. We'll float like corks in this salty water," he said as he threatened to dump her into the brine.

"If you'll set me down, I'll go wading with you," she bargained.

"Is that a promise?" Grinning, Rory carried her back onto the dry sand and let her go. He pulled off his riding boots and stockings and rolled up the cuffs on his trousers. She did the same and they waded out into the briny water.

Jessica giggled as the cool water lapped against her ankles. They stood together, hand in hand, enjoying the sensation of the salt water rubbing against their legs and watching the scores of sea gulls crisscrossing the sky, calling out with their shrill cries.

After a time they splashed out of the water, laughing at their clumsiness in avoiding the sharp rocks underfoot and clumps of soggy seaweed clinging to their ankles. They sat down on a flat strip of sand to let their feet dry. Their horses, tied by the reins to patches of brush, nosed through the sparse grass.

Jessica studied the scene surrounding her. The landscape was raw and desolate, but there was an austere beauty to it. In the midst of the desert, the lake lay like a glittering, silver mirror, reflecting sun and sky. The gentle salt breeze barely stirred its placid surface. She wiggled her toes in the gritty sand. The water had dried, leaving behind a film of salt. "I'd like to bring my mother and sister out here to see the lake," she remarked.

"When do they arrive in Salt Lake?"

"In two weeks. Mother is finally willing to make the trip now that she can travel all the way by train."

"Are both of your sisters coming?" Rory asked as he dusted sand off his legs.

"No. Just Emmaline and her baby. Clarissa is staying home with my father. I'm a little surprised that Father is allowing my mother to come." Her face grew somber as she thought about her father. He hadn't forgiven her for her carelessness in losing the money or for disobeying his directive to return home.

"I'm sure your mother and sister would enjoy a visit to the lake, and there are plenty of other interesting sights you can show them while they're here," Rory said.

"Yes. I'm anxious for them to come and excited to see them. But I'm a little apprehensive, too," she replied, pulling her knees up to her chest and wrapping her arms around them.

Rory looked over at her. "Why is that?"

Jessica squinted up at the sky where a snowy gull sailed overhead. "I'm worried about how Mother and Uncle James will get along. The last time they saw one another, they parted with bad feelings between them. I'm afraid they'll get into a disagreement again." Jessica bit her lip, surprised at the depth of emotion she felt concerning the subject.

Rory reached for her hand. "Everything will go smoothly. Your Uncle James and Aunt Inger are the most gracious people I've ever met." He gave her a reassuring smile. "Your mother wouldn't be making the trip all the way out west if she still harbored ill feelings for her brother."

"I suppose you're right," Jessica conceded, encouraged by Rory's words and the feel of his hand in hers. "It's just that I know how difficult Mother can be."

"Don't worry, Jessie. Everyone will get along fine, and it will be a joyous reunion for your family."

"I hope so. I want so much to see a reconciliation heal the rift between our families."

Rory put an arm around her and pulled her close.

Jessica snuggled against his shoulder. "I sent Emmaline a Book of Mormon, and just received a letter back from her, saying she'd read it all," Jessica said softly. "I'm eager to talk with her about it when she gets here."

"Look at you. You're spreading the glad message of the gospel to your family already."

Jessica smiled at his remark, but she was serious about the importance of sharing the gospel with her loved ones. She knew that the gospel of Jesus Christ brought peace and harmony to families—that was what had attracted her to the Church. Living the principles of the gospel made the difference between the kind of family life she had known, and what she had observed and felt in the Kades' home.

"Spreading the gospel, and not even a member of the Church yet yourself," Rory added. "That's my girl."

"Only a few days more and I'll be baptized. I've just been waiting for you and my cousins to get here, so you can see for yourselves that I'm actually going through with it," she said with a laugh.

She and Rory sat side by side on the beach watching the silver water stretch into the horizon. "Do you think we can stay right here all afternoon?" Jessica asked with a contented sigh.

"We can stay here as long as you like," Rory answered. He drew her closer and smiled into her eyes.

"If you're no longer planning to become a school-mistress, what will I do with the textbook on arithmetic I bought from the Quill and Ink for you?" Ethan asked, smiling, as he and Jessica sat together on the porch in the cozy darkness of evening.

"You purchased a book for me to use in the school-room?" Jessica answered in surprise. "That was sweet of you." She'd joined Ethan on the porch before retiring for the night, and they'd been chatting and watching the moon rise. "Perhaps you can give it to Samuel instead. He's planning to enroll at the university in the fall."

Ethan chuckled. "How you talked him into doing that, I'll never understand."

"I didn't talk him into it. We'd had a few conversations about schoolkeeping and such, and he settled upon the idea himself. He thinks he might like to become a teacher."

"I can't imagine Samuel as a schoolmaster," Ethan said, shaking his head.

"I think he'll make a very good teacher. And at least one of us in the family will be joining the profession," she added with a grin.

"If you're going back out to the ranch with me, then you might as well have this." Ethan dug into his trousers pocket and withdrew a stub of wood carved into the shape of a steer, complete with long, sharp-tipped horns, sturdy legs as if in motion, and a rippling tail. He handed the piece to Jessica.

"Oh, Ethan, this is extraordinary work!" she declared, examining the carved piece of wood in the lantern's light.

"I was making it for you all along. But now, since you've decided to learn the cattle business, it seems even more appropriate."

"It's beautiful, Ethan. I love it." She flung an arm around his neck and gave him a hug. "Thank you very much."

Ethan leaned back in his chair and stretched out his legs. Jessica's thoughts dwelled on the decision she'd made to join him at the Running W where she planned to learn all she could about ranching. He and Rory were still going forward with their plans to start a cattle ranch, and Jessica hoped to be of some assistance to them.

Thinking abut Rory brought a smile to her face. She'd enjoyed their experience at the Great Salt Lake yesterday, and when they'd returned in the evening, they'd made plans to spend the following day with Ethan and Susannah.

"Did you and Susannah have a nice time today?" Jessica asked as she toyed with the carved steer in her hand.

"The day didn't last long enough to satisfy me," Ethan returned with a smile.

"I like Susannah so much. Not only is she pretty, but she's witty and very sweet."

"Sweet as the scent of lavender," Ethan agreed. "With eyes the shade of summer grass."

Jessica giggled. "You've been reading poetry again, haven't you?"

"I don't have to. Susannah is living poetry."

Jessica recalled the long, companionable hours she'd spent with Ethan, Susannah, and Rory. The four of them had eaten a picnic lunch in the canyon, then idled away the rest of the afternoon following a winding path through the trees and wading in the crystal mountain stream. Afterward, they'd come back to the Kades' home to visit and relax, and then in the evening the foursome attended a violin concert at the Social Hall. Jessica had hated to say goodnight to Rory when they'd reached her door. Under a canopy of starlight, he'd kissed her before she went inside. The memory of his kiss still lingered on her lips.

"I'm planning to see Susannah again tomorrow," Ethan said, interrupting her pleasurable thoughts.

Jessica heard him draw an unsteady breath.

"Do you suppose Susannah would give up her comfortable circumstances in town to live on a cattle ranch in some remote corner of the valley?" he questioned.

Jessica darted a look at him, but couldn't read his expression in the dark. "You'd have to ask her that."

Ethan folded his arms against his chest. "I'm going to ask her to marry me," he confided in a quiet voice. "I'm not sure if she'll consent, but I don't think I can live my life without her."

"Susannah would make a perfect wife for you, Ethan. I'm thrilled for you."

"She hasn't said yes yet," he replied, thrusting his hands into his trouser pockets.

"Is that why you're seeing Susannah tomorrow?"

"I'm planning to speak to her father tomorrow, yes."

Jessica heard him give a nervous gulp. She patted his knee. "Everything will go all right. Just have a little faith."

Ethan chuckled softly. "I'm going to need more than faith. Susannah told me she thought she was in love with her old beau because he was handsome, wealthy, and well-mannered."

"That description also fits you."

"All except the wealthy part."

"And you'll be that someday, too. A cattleman with a big spread and thousands of head of cattle." Jessica took the carved steer and galloped it through the air in front of Ethan's nose.

Ethan laughed.

They stayed outside talking together until Jessica's aunt called them for evening family prayer. She joined the family in the parlor, and as they knelt to pray, Jessica's eyes drifted to the mantle above the fireplace where the Kades' Book of Mormon rested. Her heart skipped a beat as she gazed at the book of scripture. The significance of that book in her own life and in the lives of her relatives was immeasurable. She thought about her Grandfather and Grandmother Kade and the sacrifices they had made for the gospel's sake—and the legacy of faith they had left her. She closed her eyes in grateful appreciation as her uncle began the prayer.

Afterward, she slipped upstairs to the bedroom she shared with Birgithe, opened the bottom drawer of the dresser where her few belongings were stored, and located the object she sought. Gazing at the framed portrait, she smiled to herself and then hurried downstairs to the parlor with it.

The family was still in the room. Jessica took a chair beside the couch where her uncle and aunt were seated. "I'd like to show this to you," she said, turning the portrait toward them. Moonlight coming through the lace curtains on the window cast a muted glow on the flowing lines of the drawing.

Birgithe leaned forward in her chair to stare at the sketch, and Ethan and Samuel came to the couch to get a look at it, too. Jessica handed the framed portrait to her uncle.

"What do you have here?" he asked, gazing at the drawing.

"When I left home to come out to California, Mother gave this to me. Her mother had given it to her."

"I remember this," James said, nodding. "It's a portrait of my mother, Lydia Kade."

"Yes. That's right," replied Jessica.

Her uncle's eyes roved over the sketch. "My father drew this portrait of her before they were married, while they were both living in Independence. I recall Mother showing it to me." His face glowed with a smile. "Look at this, Inger. Wasn't Mother lovely?"

Inger took the drawing from her husband's hand and studied it. "It's exactly as I remember her when I was a girl. She had the most lovely blue eyes."

"And the prettiest red hair," James added.

Ethan and Samuel bent over the sketch. The portrait showed a young woman with her hair loose about her shoulders and a slight smile parting her lips.

"She's so pretty," Birgithe said, turning to Jessica with a smile.

"She looks a lot like you, Jessie," Ethan remarked, studying the penciled lines of the drawing from over his father's shoulder.

"I think so, too," Samuel agreed.

James looked up from the portrait. "Yes, you have the same auburn hair and fair complexion as she did," he said to Jessica. "And the same shape of mouth. Though her eyes were not as gray as yours, you bear a strong resemblance to your grandmother."

"I wish I'd known her, Uncle James. I wish I could have met her and Grandfather Kade even just one time."

"Your grandparents were fine people," James said to her. "You can be proud of your heritage." He took the pencil drawing of his mother from Inger and stared at it, a smile resting on his face.

Inger put an arm around Jessica's shoulders, and Ethan and Samuel hovered close by. Birgithe slipped her hand into Jessica's. As Jessica gazed at each face surrounding her, she thought back to the moment she had stepped off the train at the depot in Salt Lake City, feeling alone and afraid, full of pride, and determined to rely upon her relatives' charity as briefly as possible. She smiled ruefully at that memory.

Had the whole chain of events been happenstance? she mused. A coincidence that led to her acquaintance with the

Kade branch of the family? Or was there a higher power at work, guiding and directing the circumstances of her life? She looked into the faces of those she had grown to love and knew the answer to that question.

# CHAPTER TWENTY-FOUR

Jessica's baptism took place the following Sunday in a clear, sparkling pond near the Kades' home. Ethan stood beside the water's edge as his father led Jessica into the rippling pool. He watched as his father said the few sacred words of the baptismal prayer, then gently lowered Jessica into the depths of the water and lifted her up again. Jessica came forth from the water beaming with happiness. As she stood with her hair hanging wet and dripping onto the simple white frock and the sheen of water on her cheeks, Ethan thought she looked prettier than he'd ever seen her.

She stepped from the pool to a round of hugs and kisses from Ethan's family and a few close friends who had gathered to witness her baptism. As he offered his congratulations with a warm embrace, he felt an immense joy in seeing his cousin come into The Church of Jesus Christ of Latter-day Saints.

"Isn't she amazing?" Rory crowed.

Ethan turned to his friend. Rory's smile, and the look of admiration and affection evident in his eyes as he gazed at Jessica, brought a chuckle to Ethan's lips. "She's something special, all right," he agreed.

Jessica started toward the house to change into dry clothing, with Rory and the others accompanying her. Ethan took Susannah Hamilton's hand as they walked behind them. "I don't think Rory is going to be able to wait until after the celebration to speak with my father about marrying Jessica," he said, grinning.

"I know someone else who was just as impatient," Susannah replied. "My father had barely learned your name before you asked his permission for my hand in marriage."

Ethan laughed. "I had to hurry and do it before I lost courage. Your father is as gruff as a billy goat." He leaned over and kissed Susannah's cheek.

She smiled up at him. "I believe you made a good impression on Papa."

"I'm glad about that. But the one I want to make a good impression on is you." Ethan kept tight hold of her hand as they continued toward the house.

"I said yes to your proposal of marriage, didn't I?"

"You did. But you haven't told me how you feel about being a cattle rancher's wife." Although Ethan's tone was light, his concern about the subject weighed on his mind.

Susannah hadn't yet disclosed her feelings about living on a secluded ranch miles away from town.

Susannah stopped in mid-stride and looked Ethan squarely in the eye. "Ethan Kade, I'd follow you to the ends of the earth if you asked me to."

Ethan was shaken by her reply. The tide of love he felt for her was nearly overpowering. He drew her into his arms and kissed her.

"Hey, cowboy, can't you wait until after the wedding for that?" Samuel's voice interrupted the sweet sensation of Susannah's kiss. When Ethan drew back, he saw his brother standing a few feet away, grinning at him.

"Go away, Samuel. I'm busy," he said, only partly in jest.

"It's going to have to wait. Jessica is ready for you to do the confirmation."

"I'll be right there," Ethan told his brother. "Just give me a minute."

Samuel nodded and started back to the house.

Ethan took Susannah's hands into his. "I'll make you happy. I promise you that, Susannah. Once we get the ranch established, we can go into town to visit as often as you like. And I'll build a house for you on the ranch you can be proud of."

"Will there be shade trees in the yard and a sunny brook running alongside it?" Her eyes were teasing, yet Ethan sensed this promise was important to her.

"Yes, with green grass at your door. And cattle dotting the hillsides." Ethan drew her closer to him, smiling into her shining eyes.

She gave a little laugh. "And when we're old, we'll sit on the porch together and eat lemon drops."

Ethan kissed her. "Exactly."

"Then I'll be by your side," she said softly. "For wherever you are, Ethan, that place will be home for me."

# The Kade Family Saga

### by Laurel Mouritsen

The popular *Kade Family Saga* series of historical novels is steeped in likeable, life-like characters in the fictional story of the Kade family and their adventures spanning from Missouri to the Great Salt Lake.

In Volume 1, *In Quest of Zion*, the saga begins with the romance between the much-travailed Lydia Dawson and the intriguing Christian Kade, who writes for *The Evening and the Morning Star*—controversial newspaper for the Mormons, who have recently arrived in Missouri.

In Volume 2, *A Place of Promise*, the Kade family is in Nauvoo. Young James tries to shield the prophet Joseph from an assassination plot. Meanwhile, his sister Elizabeth is abandoning the faith for a forbidden love. Brother and sister are set on a collision course that will shatter their family and have repercussions for generations of Kades to come.

Volume 3, *Between Two Shores*, continues the breathtaking drama as the Kade family moves west with the saints. James lives the ecstasy and agony of young love in an unyielding desert while sister Elizabeth welters in shattered dreams back in Nauvoo where she has chosen to remain.

In Volume 4, *Beside Still Waters*, Elizabeth's daughter Jessica Scott finds herself waylaid in 1870s Utah while on a railroad trip to California. When she seeks help from her Mormon relatives, her presence disrupts the carefully laid plans of her cousin, Ethan Kade. Sparks fly, but more than one flame is kindled as the two face the dangers awaiting them at the Running W Ranch.

Told with the skill of a masterful storyteller against a historically accurate backdrop, the Kade series is at once exciting, heart-wrenching, and very satisfying.

| | |
|---|---|
| Volume 1 (ISBN: 0-929753-07-0) | Hardcover, $19.95 |
| Volume 2 (ISBN: 0-929753-08-9) | Hardcover, $25.95 |
| Volume 3 (ISBN: 0-929753-10-0) | Hardcover, $25.95 |
| Volume 4 (ISBN: 0-929753-21-6) | Hardcover, $25.95 |

*Look for it in your favorite bookstore, or see Ordering Information.*

*Or order online at:*
**www.stratfordbooks.com**

# The Porter Rockwell Chronicles

by Richard Lloyd Dewey

This best-selling, historically accurate biographical novel series renders Porter's life in riveting story form, bringing it alive for adults and teens alike.

Volume 1 begins with his childhood years in New York where he becomes best friends with the future Mormon prophet Joseph Smith. The story continues through Porter's settlement with the Mormons in Missouri, where he fights against mobs and falls in love with and marries Luana Beebe.

Volume 2 covers the turbulent first four years in Nauvoo, where he continues to fight mobs and becomes Joseph Smith's bodyguard.

The Nauvoo period of his life draws to a close in Volume 3 as his best friend Joseph is murdered and his wife Luana leaves him and remarries, taking his beloved daughter Emily with her. Porter must bid a heartbroken farewell as he and the Mormons are driven from Nauvoo and flee west.

Volume 4 continues with his first ten years in Utah, where he is joyously reunited with his daughter Emily, takes on the U.S. Army in a guerilla war, and enters a new phase of adventures as U.S. Deputy Marshal.

| | |
|---|---|
| Volume 1 (ISBN: 0-929753-16-X) | Hardcover, $26.50 |
| Volume 2 (ISBN: 0-929753-17-8) | Hardcover, $26.50 |
| Volume 3 (ISBN: 0-9616024-8-1) | Hardcover, $23.88 |
| Volume 4 (ISBN: 0-9616024-9-X) | Hardcover, $24.88 |

*Look for them in your favorite bookstore,*
*or to obtain autographed copies, see Ordering Information.*

*Or order online at:*
**www.stratfordbooks.com**

## *Porter Rockwell: A Biography*

by Richard Lloyd Dewey

The epic biography that traces Porter Rockwell from turbulent Eastern beginnings to battles with Midwestern mobs to extraordinary gunfights on the American frontier. Quotes hundreds of journals, letters, and court records. Illustrated by western artist Clark Kelley Price. Includes a detailed bibliography and index.

Hardcover, $29.95                                  ISBN: 0-929753-23-2

*Look for it in your favorite bookstore,*
*or to obtain autographed copies, see Ordering Information.*

*Or order online at:*
**www.stratfordbooks.com**

## *Joseph Smith: A Biography*

### by Richard Lloyd Dewey

The author of the perennial best-seller *Porter Rockwell: A Biography* has brought his extensive research and irresistible writing style to bear on the history of Joseph Smith. This all-new biography is aimed at a general LDS market as well as investigators who are looking for a frank and objective exposition of the life and career of one of the most controversial figures in 19th-century America. Between the covers is crammed a wealth of inspiring and startling facts not readily found elsewhere.

Hardcover, $26.50                                 ISBN: 0-929753-15-1

*Look for it in your favorite bookstore,*
*or see Ordering Information.*

*Or order online at:*
**www.stratfordbooks.com**

## *History of Joseph Smith by His Mother*
### THE UNABRIDGED ORIGINAL VERSION
### by Lucy Mack Smith

Compiled by R. Vernon Ingleton
Foreword by Richard Lloyd Dewey

Three reasons why this is the best version by far: (1) It's the *complete original version*—for the first time ever. (2) It has *all the corrections* added later by Church historians. (3) It contains *all the facts from the rough draft* that have until now been missing from published versions. Compiler R. Vernon Ingleton has pulled all the elements together to allow Lucy at last to tell her story in its entirety in an easy-to-read format. The book is a masterpiece. This second edition also includes a detailed, exhaustive index.

Hardcover, $29.95                    ISBN: 0-929753-22-4

*Look for it in your favorite bookstore,*
*or see Ordering Information.*

*Or order online at:*
**www.stratfordbooks.com**

## Life of Joseph Smith the Prophet

by George Q. Cannon
Foreword by Richard Lloyd Dewey

This is the *only* biography about Joseph ever written from personal interviews with his friends! The author served as First Counselor to four prophets, all of whom knew Joseph. Having full access to Church archives, Cannon weaves the intricate tale of Joseph's intriguing biography in a mesmerizing manner. He stays focused, keeping the reader spell-bound as Joseph has to flee time and again for his life. The reason? Apostates and bigoted religious leaders seek his blood. Seen from an insider's view of what really took place in Nauvoo, Cannon shows how the conspirators worked, even recruiting the governors of two states to get Joseph taken down. But in the end it was Joseph who prevailed spiritually—proven in part by the success of the restored church and its thirteen million members today. This must-read biography gives insights, humorous stories and anecdotes with suspenseful plotting rarely seen in this long-out-of-print book that has been republished in clean, modern type for easy reading. Includes a detailed index.

Hardcover, $27.95                                    ISBN: 0-929753-09-7

*Look for it in your favorite bookstore,*
*or see Ordering Information.*

*Or order online at:*
**www.stratfordbooks.com**

# Hübener vs Hitler

*A Biography of Helmuth Hübener,*
*Mormon Teenage Resistance Leader*

REVISED, SECOND EDITION

by Richard Lloyd Dewey

Nobel Laureate author Günther Grass said Hübener's life should be held up as a role model to every teen in the world. Regional best-selling author Richard Lloyd Dewey (*Porter Rockwell: A Biography*) holds up Hübener's life as a light not only to all teens, but to adults as well.

As an active Latter-day Saint, young Hübener recruited his best friends from church and work and established a sophisticated resistance group that baffled the Gestapo, infuriated the Nazi leadership, frustrated the highest judges in the land, and convinced the SS hierarchy that hundreds of adults—not just a handful of determined teens—were involved!

While other books have told the story of the group of freedom fighters Hübener founded, this tells their complete story from numerous sources, *and* is the first biography of Hübener himself—the astounding young man who led and animated the group. The inspiring, spell-binding, true story of the youngest resistance leader in Nazi Germany.

Hardcover, $27.95                                    ISBN: 0-929753-13-5

*Look for it in your favorite bookstore,*
*or see Ordering Information.*

*Or order online at:*
**www.stratfordbooks.com**

## New Evidences of Christ in Ancient America

by Blaine M. Yorgason, Bruce W. Warren, and Harold Brown

When world-class scholar Bruce Warren led a research team into the jungles of South America, they found a *mountain* of evidence supporting Book of Mormon claims. Now the reader can follow their adventure as they unearth amazing archaeological discoveries and ancient writings, all of which shut the mouths of critics who say such evidences do not exist. In this volume, the newest archaeological evidences are also presented.

Endorsed by Hugh Nibley.

Hardcover, $24.95                                ISBN: 0-929753-01-1

*Look for it in your favorite bookstore,*
*or see Ordering Information.*

*Or order online at:*
**www.stratfordbooks.com**

## Autobiography of Parley P. Pratt
### The Complete Historical Classic

Foreword by Richard Lloyd Dewey

Parley P. Pratt's riveting autobiography has thrilled generations of Latter-day Saints. More than just a biography, it is also one of the richest sources of amazing facts from early church history and a treasure trove of classic passages frequently quoted to this day in lessons and over the pulpit. It deserves a place on the bookshelf of every Latter-day Saint and the attention of every student of Mormonism.

Elder Pratt's death was as colorful as the rest of his life. It is generally known that the apostle was assassinated in Arkansas while on a mission, but the fascinating details surrounding this crime are not widely known. In the foreword, bestselling author Richard Lloyd Dewey pulls together the long-obscure historical facts to tell the rest of the story.

In this new edition of Parley P. Pratt's renowned autobiography, a staff of editors spent months perfecting the work, correcting and modernizing spelling, grammar and punctuation so that Pratt's narrative is now easier than ever for readers to enjoy.

Softcover, $19.95                    ISBN: 0-929753-12-7

*Look for it in your favorite bookstore,*
*or see Ordering Information.*

*Or order online at:*
**www.stratfordbooks.com**

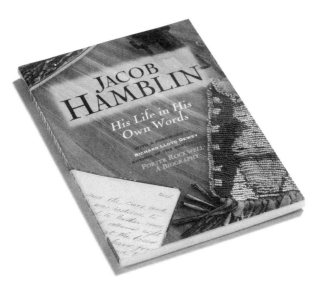

## *Jacob Hamblin:*
## *His Life in His Own Words*

### Foreword by Richard Lloyd Dewey

Far from the gun-toting reputation of super-lawman Porter Rockwell, Jacob Hamblin was known in early Western history as the supreme peacemaker.

No less exciting than Porter's account, Jacob's adventures encountered apparent Divine intervention at every turn, a reward seemingly bestowed to certain souls given to absolute faith. And in his faith, like Porter, Jacob Hamblin was one of those incredibly rare warriors who are absolutely fearless.

His migrations from Ohio to Utah with life-and-death adventures at every turn keep the reader spellbound in this unabridged, autobiographical account of the Old West's most unusual adventurer among Native Americans.

In his own words, Jacob Hamblin bares his soul with no pretense, unveiling an eye-witness journal of pioneer attempts to co-exist peacefully with Native brothers, among whom he traveled unarmed, showing his faith in God that he would not be harmed.

Easily considered the most successful—and bravest—diplomat to venture into hostile territory single-handedly, Hamblin takes the reader into hearts of darkness and hearts of light.

Softcover, $10.95                                   ISBN: 0-9616024-5-7

*Look for it in your favorite bookstore,*
*or see Ordering Information.*

*Or order online at:*
**www.stratfordbooks.com**

# 1830 Book of Mormon Replica

### AUTHENTIC, LEATHER-BOUND REPRODUCTION OF
### ORIGINAL 1830 EDITION

This special edition of the Book of Mormon is an authentic replica of the first edition printed by E. B. Grandin in Palmyra, New York. Like the original, it features thick covers and leather binding. The pages for this special edition have been photomechanically reproduced at actual size, preserving the appearance of the type and content of the book exactly.

As a unique visual aid, this intriguing conversation piece reveals to family and friends what few have seen—the beauty of the original Book of Mormon.

See for yourself how this sacred book appeared when early converts read it. It reads more like a novel, not yet having been divided into the now-familiar verses and chapters that break up the flow of reading in later editions. Gospel scholars will find this edition handy in tracking the minor changes that have been made in subsequent editions.

Hardcover, leather bound, $34.95          ISBN: 0-929753-20-8

*Look for it in your favorite bookstore,*
*or see Ordering Information.*

*Or order online at:*
**www.stratfordbooks.com**

## *Hand-bound leather Book of Mormon*

### UNIQUE POCKET EDITION
### BOUND IN GENUINE LEATHER

Perfect for students, missionaries, military personnel, Scouts, and backpackers, this pocket-sized standard edition of the Book of Mormon is hand bound in genuine top-grain cowhide. The leather binding is not merely a slip cover, but is permanently bound to the book. Compact in size (approx. 3.5" x 5.5") and extremely durable, the book can be stowed most anywhere, while the handy wrap-around leather strap keeps it closed tightly to protect the pages. Because it is hand-crafted in very limited quantities, this intriguing edition is one few people will own. A unique and practical gift!

Softcover, leather bound, $39.95        ISBN: 0-929753-24-0

*See Ordering Information, or order online at:*
**www.stratfordbooks.com**

## *Porter Rockwell Returns*
by Clark Kelley Price

This classic color print of the painting by renowned western artist Clark Kelley Price depicts Porter Rockwell coming home at night in a lightning storm through downtown Lehi, Utah.

In this vivid scene, Rockwell is returning from a hard day's work, with an outlaw draped over the horse he has in tow.

36"w x 24"h, $30.00                    ISBN: 0-929753-0-6

*Add $10.00 shipping and handling for first print
and $1.00 for each additional print sent to same address.
Utah residents, add 6.25% sales tax.*

### Send check or money order to:
Stratford Books, P.O. Box 1371, Provo, Utah 84603-1371

### Or order online at:
www.stratfordbooks.com

*Prices subject to change.*

## *Porter's Ranch at Point of the Mountain*
### by Clark Kelley Price

Limited-edition art prints of this oil painting, which is featured on the dust jacket of Volume 4 of *The Porter Rockwell Chronicles*, are available at $75 each. The edition consists of 880 11" × 14" prints on canvas, signed and numbered by the artist.

Mr. Price's work, found in private collections worldwide, sells in exclusive art galleries and has often been featured on covers of *The Ensign* magazine. A longtime friend of the author, Mr. Price was among the first to inspire Richard Lloyd Dewey about the life of Porter Rockwell. He did the illustrations and back cover painting for Dewey's *Porter Rockwell: A Biography*.

*Add $10.00 shipping and handling for first print*
*and $1.00 for each additional print sent to same address.*
*Utah residents, add 6.25% sales tax.*

### Send check or money order to:
Stratford Books, P.O. Box 1371, Provo, Utah 84603-1371

### Or order online at:
www.stratfordbooks.com

*Prices subject to change.*

### *Nauvoo, Illinois, mid-1840s*
by Dan Thornton

Art prints of *Nauvoo, Illinois, mid-1840s*, depicted on the dust jackets of Volume 2 of *The Porter Rockwell Chronicles* and of *The Kade Family Saga*, are available from the publisher.

- **Limited Edition** signed and numbered, large size (28.5"w × 19"h)
  $135.00 each, plus $15.00 shipping & handling (add $1.00 shipping & handling for each additional print sent to same address)

- **Artist's Proof** (same size)
  $200.00 each, plus $15.00 shipping & handling (add $1.00 shipping & handling for each additional print sent to same address)

- **Greeting Card Packs** unsigned, 10 cards and envelopes
  $25.00 per pack, plus $3.00 shipping & handling (add $1.00 for each additional pack sent to same address)

As the 860 Limited Edition art prints sell out, the collectors' value may substantially increase.

### Send check or money order to:
Stratford Books, P.O. Box 1371, Provo, Utah 84603-1371

### Or order online at:
www.stratfordbooks.com

*Utah residents, add 6.25% sales tax.*

## *Heber C. Kimball Home, Nauvoo*
### by Al Rounds

Full-color, 25" × 15" signed-and-numbered, limited-edition art prints of *Heber C. Kimball Home, Nauvoo*, depicted on the dust jacket of Volume 3 of *The Porter Rockwell Chronicles*, are available from the publisher at the price of $150.00 each plus shipping and handling.

Shipping and handling charges are $15.00 for the first print, plus $1.00 additional shipping and handling for each additional print ordered at the same time and shipped to the same address.

As the 700 limited-edition art prints sell out, the collectors' value may substantially increase.

### Send check or money order to:
Stratford Books, P.O. Box 1371, Provo, Utah 84603-1371

### Or order online at:
www.stratfordbooks.com

*Utah residents, add 6.25% sales tax.*

# ORDERING INFORMATION

**1830 Book of Mormon Replica** $34.95
Hardcover, leather-bound, 592 pp. ISBN: 0-929753-20-8

**Hand-bound leather pocket Book of Mormon** $39.95
Softcover, leather-bound, ISBN: 0-929753-24-0

**History of Joseph Smith by His Mother: The Unabridged Original Version** $29.95
by Lucy Mack Smith, compiled by R. Vernon Ingleton.
Hardcover, 548 pp. ISBN: 0-929753-22-4

**Life of Joseph Smith the Prophet** by George Q. Cannon $27.95
Hardcover, 615 pp. ISBN: 0-929753-09-7

**Joseph Smith: A Biography** by Richard Lloyd Dewey $26.50
Hardcover, 531 pp. ISBN: 0-929753-15-1

**Porter Rockwell: A Biography** by Richard Lloyd Dewey. $29.95
Hardcover, 612 pp. ISBN: 0-929753-23-2

**The Porter Rockwell Chronicles** by Richard Lloyd Dewey
    **Volume 1**   Hardcover, 486 pp. ISBN: 0-929753-16-X   $26.50
    **Volume 2**   Hardcover, 452 pp. ISBN: 0-929753-17-8   $26.50
    **Volume 3**   Hardcover, 527 pp. ISBN: 0-9616024-8-1   $23.88
    **Volume 4**   Hardcover, 570 pp. ISBN: 0-9616024-9-X   $24.88

**Autobiography of Parley P. Pratt** $19.95
Softcover, 426 pp. ISBN: 0-929753-12-7

**Jacob Hamblin: His Life in His Own Words** $10.95
Foreword by Richard Lloyd Dewey. Softcover, 128 pp. ISBN: 0-9616024-5-7

**The Kade Family Saga** by Laurel Mouritsen
    **Volume 1: In Quest of Zion**   $19.95
    Hardcover, 396 pp. ISBN: 0-929753-07-0
    **Volume 2: A Place of Promise** $25.95
    Hardcover, 389 pp. ISBN: 0-929753-08-9
    **Volume 3: Between Two Shores** $25.95
    Hardcover, 364 pp. ISBN: 0-929753-10-0
    **Volume 4: Beside Still Waters** $25.95
    Hardcover, 394 pp. ISBN: 0-929753-21-6

**Hübener vs Hitler** (revised, second edition) $27.95
A biography of Helmuth Hübener, Mormon teenage resistance leader,
by Richard Lloyd Dewey. Hardcover, 594 pp. ISBN: 0-929753-13-5

**New Evidences of Christ in Ancient America** $24.95
by Blaine M. Yorgason, Bruce W. Warren, and Harold Brown.
Hardcover, 430 pp. ISBN: 0-929753-01-1

FREE SHIPPING & HANDLING
*Utah residents, add 6.25% sales tax.*

*Send check or money order to:*
**Stratford Books, P.O. Box 1371, Provo, Utah 84603-1371**
*Or order online at:*
**www.stratfordbooks.com**

*Prices subject to change.*